Youth and Positive Uncertainty

Praise for this book

'Given the pervasive sense of uncertainty that has come to dominate everyone's lives over the past few years, a book that addresses the question of how young people confront and respond to the uncertainties in their lives is not just timely but absolutely necessary. This lively and fascinating text draws on the voices of a large number of highly marginalised youth living in particularly precarious settings to depict their struggles and strategies. The internationally collaborative and comparative approach draws out important commonalities and presents important lessons for policy and practice.'

Professor Nicola Ansell, Brunel University London

'Whether you are a practitioner, academic or student, this book provides invaluable and inspiring insights into the ways in which young people in Ethiopia and Nepal are navigating uncertainty—and making choices that balance their desire to meet adults' social expectations, with their need to build their own futures. Importantly, the authors recognise young people as critical, and creative thinkers, and centrally involve them in shaping their research.'

Tessa Lewin, Research Fellow, Participation, Inclusion and Social Change Cluster, Institute of Development Studies

'In this innovative and timely volume, marginalised youth in difficult environments in Ethiopia and Nepal tell us how they negotiate intergenerational relationships deeply embedded in traditional norms and expectations. Of relevance far beyond the study countries, the book highlights how youth expertly navigate uncertainty to forge innovative strategies towards new futures for themselves, their families and communities. I recommend it highly to anyone interested in learning about creative youth-centred methodologies, youth decision making, migration, and the power of partnerships in improving youth access to rights.'

Professor Jo Boyden, Oxford Department of International Development, University of Oxford

'A highly original take on uncertainty, precarity and poverty in the lives of youth. Grounded in extensive qualitative research with young people in Ethiopia and Nepal, it shows how young people approach the certainty of poverty by embracing uncertain journeys that could generate new futures for them and their families.'

Professor Karen Wells, Professor of Human Geography, Birkbeck, University of London

Youth and Positive Uncertainty
Negotiating Life in Post-conflict and Fragile Environments

Vicky Johnson and Andy West
with Andrew Church, Melese Getu, Sumon Kamal Tuladhar,
Milki Getachew, Shubhendra Man Shrestha, Amid Ahmed,
Sabitra Neupane, and Signe Gosmann

Practical Action Publishing Ltd
25 Albert Street, Rugby,
Warwickshire, CV21 2SD, UK
www.practicalactionpublishing.com

© Vicky Johnson and Andy West, 2022

The moral right of the authors to be identified as authors of the work and the contributors to be identified as contributors of this work have been asserted under sections 77 and 78 of the Copyright Design and Patents Act 1988.

All rights reserved. No part of this publication may be reprinted or reproduced or utilized in any form or by any electronic, mechanical, or other means, now known or hereafter invented, including photocopying and recording, or in any information storage or retrieval system, without the written permission of the publishers.

Product or corporate names may be trademarks or registered trademarks, and are used only for identification and explanation without intent to infringe.

A catalogue record for this book is available from the British Library.

A catalogue record for this book has been requested from the Library of Congress.

ISBN 978-1-78853-099-6 Paperback
ISBN 978-1-78853-100-9 Hardback
ISBN 978-1-78853-102-3 Electronic book

Citation: Johnson, V., and West, A., (2022) *Youth and Positive Uncertainty*, Rugby, UK: Practical Action Publishing, http://doi.org/10.3362/9781788531023.

Since 1974, Practical Action Publishing has published and disseminated books and information in support of international development work throughout the world. Practical Action Publishing is a trading name of Practical Action Publishing Ltd (Company Reg. No. 1159018), the wholly owned publishing company of Practical Action. Practical Action Publishing trades only in support of its parent charity objectives and any profits are covenanted back to Practical Action (Charity Reg. No. 247257, Group VAT Registration No. 880 9924 76).

The views and opinions in this publication are those of the author and do not represent those of Practical Action Publishing Ltd or its parent charity Practical Action.

Reasonable efforts have been made to publish reliable data and information, but the authors and publisher cannot assume responsibility for the validity of all materials or for the consequences of their use.

Cover photo credit: Vicky Johnson
Typeset by vPrompt eServices, India

Contents

Acknowledgements — vii
About the authors — ix
Foreword — xi

1. Introduction: Why uncertainty? Why listen to marginalized youth? — 1

Part 1
Research concepts and methods — 11

2. Key concepts — 13
3. Youth-centred research and uncertainty: Method and approach — 27

Part 2
Ethiopia — 41

4. Ethiopia: Context and themes — 43
5. Rural Fogera: Land shortages, adult status, and migration — 55
6. Urban Woreta: Migrating into street situations — 69
7. Drought-prone Hetosa: Status, success, and migration — 81
8. Addis Ketema: Identity and support in street situations — 95

Part 3
Nepal — 111

9. Nepal: Context and themes — 113
10. Rural Kapilvastu: Discrimination and uncertainty — 127
11. Urban Kapilvastu: Dealing with change and tradition — 143
12. Sindhupalchowk: Environmental fragility, youth responsibilities, and migration in rural Nepal — 153
13. Kathmandu: Environmental vulnerability, slums, and family support — 167
14. Genderfluidity: LGBTQI and third gender in Kathmandu — 183

Part 4
Policy themes   191

15. Policy themes and impact: Introduction   193
16. Youth and migration   201
17. Youth in street situations   213
18. Youth and disability   227

Part 5
Conclusion   239

19. Conclusion: Listening to marginalized youth on uncertainty   241

References   253
Index   265

Acknowledgements

The YOUR World Team would like to thank the young people across Ethiopia and Nepal who took their time to share their wisdom with us about uncertainty in their lives and how they are finding creative and imaginative strategies and new futures.

None of this would have been possible without our local civil society organizations, CHADET and ChildHope in Ethiopia and ActionAid Nepal. Thanks to the Directors of these charities, Anannia Admassu, Jill Healey, and Sujeeta Mathema. We are also very grateful to our academic partners, Addis Ababa University and the Research Centre for Educational Innovation and Development (CERID) at Tribhuvan University.

We would also like to say particular thanks to David Oswell at Goldsmiths, University of London, Bimal Phnuyal, previous Director of ActionAid Nepal, and Matiyas Assefa Chefa, Director-General for Youth Participation in the Ministry of Women, Children and Youth (MOWCY) in Ethiopia, for help at transition times during the research and in impact activities.

In Ethiopia we would like to thank the local facilitators from CHADET who made the fieldwork possible: In Addis Ketema, Ahmed Hassen; in Hetosa, Birukt Fikeru; and in Fogera and Woreta, Adem Desalegn and Aemero Tilahun. We are also very grateful to the Ethiopian National Reference Group for their advice during inception and analysis: Dr Abebaw Minaye, Dr Abeje Berhanu, Dr Alula Pankhurst, Dr Annabel Erulkar, Aynadis Yehuanes, and Dr Guday Emirie.

In Nepal we would like to thank the local partners who made the fieldwork and impact activities possible. In Kathmandu: Youth Advocacy Nepal, HomeNet Nepal, Nepal Mahila Ekata Samaj, CWIN Nepal, CWCN, Blue Diamond Society, SOBER Recovery. In Kapilvastu: Sahaj Nepal. In Sindhupalchowk: Community Self Reliance Centre. Thank you also to the reference group that included: Professor Kedar Bhakta Mathema, Professor Jiba Nath Dhital, Dr Kishore Shreshtha, Mahendra Paudyal, Tarak Dhital, Usha Hamal, and Narendra Khatiwada.

Thanks also to the international reference group who participated at inception and during impact activities: David Oswell, Dorte Thorsen, Etienne Wenger-Trayner, Gina Crivello, Juliet Millican, Mark Carew, Mark Erickson, Mark Johnson, Nora Groce, Rachel Hinton, Robert Chambers, and Suna Eryigit-Madzwamuse.

Funding

The team would like to thank the funders: ESRC/FCDO (formerly DFID) Joint Fund for Poverty Alleviation Research (ES/N014391/1 and ES/N014391/2).

The team would particularly like to thank Catheryn Flynn from ERSC, Tim Conway from FCDO, and the team led by James Georgalakis with communications led by Kelly Shephard at the ESRC's Impact Initiative.

About the authors

Dr Vicky Johnson, Professor of Childhood, Youth and Sustainability and Director, Centre for Living Sustainability, University of the Highlands and Islands. Vicky led Youth Uncertainty Rights (YOUR) World Research in Ethiopia and Nepal. Her key focus of research and publication is in the field of children and young people's participation. Monographs and books include: *Listening to Smaller Voices* (ActionAid, 1995); *Stepping Forward* (IT Publications, 1998); and with Andy West, *Children's Participation in Global Contexts: Beyond Voice* (Routledge, 2018). Vicky has led research and managed programmes and partnerships in Africa, Asia, and Latin America for international organizations and provided expert advice for a range of UN and government departments. She has also developed programmes of community research with local authorities, NHS, government regeneration programmes, and non-governmental organizations in the UK.

Dr Andy West, Independent Researcher/Writer and Community Fellow, University of Brighton. Andy worked on YOUR World Research in Ethiopia and Nepal throughout. He has worked with children and young people, practice and policies, for over 35 years, especially rights, participation, protection, mainly in Asia and the UK, but also in the Middle East, Africa, and the Pacific, for local, national, and international organizations, communities, universities, governments, and the UN. In addition to the 2018 book *Children's Participation in Global Contexts: Beyond Voice* with Vicky Johnson, his publications include books, articles, chapters, policy, and research reports mainly concerning children and young people, protection and participation, and on his other interests including colonial collections history and material culture.

Professor Andrew Church, Pro-Vice Chancellor (Research and Innovation), University of Bedfordshire. Andrew was previously Associate Pro-Vice-Chancellor at the University of Brighton, also Professor of Human Geography, focusing on human–nature relations and environmental change. He has over 25 years' experience of linking his research in geography to policy issues and the concerns of a wide range of public, private, and community sector stakeholders in many different countries.

Dr Melese Getu, School of Social Work, College of Social Sciences, Addis Ababa University. Melese works for the School of Social Work of Addis Ababa University where he also served as associate dean of the College of Social Sciences and associate dean and dean of the School of Social Work.

He also worked for the Organization for Social Science Research in Eastern and Southern Africa (OSSSREA).

Dr Sumon Kamal Tuladhar, British Council, Nepal. Sumon has worked as an Independent Equity Specialist for the British Council/ADB Nepal since August 2020. She spent 22 years in Tribhuvan University as a lecturer and a senior researcher. For 15 years she worked as an Education Specialist in UNICEF Nepal and worked with the government of Nepal on gender equality and social inclusion issues.

Milki Getachew, Goldsmiths and Department of Social Work, University of Addis Ababa. Milki is a PhD student at Goldsmiths, University of London. She has been seconded from her role as a lecturer in Social Work at Addis Ababa University. She is currently researching youth and intergenerational decision-making in migration in a fragile area of rural Ethiopia.

Shubhendra Man Shrestha, Goldsmiths and Independent. Shubhendra is a PhD student at Goldsmiths, University of London. He has worked for several international and local NGOS in Nepal on childhood and youth programmes. He worked for ActionAid Nepal, partner in this research and he is currently undertaking a programme of research on youth resilience in an earthquake-affected Himalayan region of Nepal.

Amid Ahmed, Department of Sociology, Debre Markos University and PhD Student at the Institute of African Studies, Addis Ababa University. Amid lectures in the Department of Sociology at Debre Markos University in Ethiopia. His research interests include youth studies with a particular emphasis on marginalized youth, migration, addiction, and crime.

Sabitra Neupane, HomeNet Nepal and Independent. Sabitra graduated with a Master's in Philosophy in Education from Tribhuvan University. She has worked for more than decade on non-profit organizations in Nepal specializing in children, youth, girls, and women in the informal sector. She is involved in a building resilient community programme in Canada.

Signe Gosmann, Independent and Justlife. Trained as an anthropologist, Signe has more than 15 years' experience in international development, research, and civil society advocacy; including for local civil society organizations in Africa and the UK, international NGOs, and multilateral organizations such as the Global Fund and the World Bank. She works on homelessness in England for Justlife and as an independent consultant.

Foreword

I am very pleased to be able to write a few words about this book, which is clearly more than a book in as much as it is more an expression of a set of programmes of engagement and change. I am pleased because I have the good fortune to know some of the team and to have met and conversed with those I didn't know over the course of this project. And I am pleased because the work of the team is so much more than this book.

The research is an active engagement in as much as it is driven by a deep-rooted focus on dialogue and translation. The project, split across teams homed in England and Scotland, in Ethiopia and in Nepal, traverses the difficulties of language and culture, practicalities and logistics, but also power and history with great sensitivity. At a rudimentary, but important, level, the degrees of resource available to different members of the team in their different geographic locales was readily apparent. For example, well stocked libraries, internet and communication connections, transport and other support systems were not evenly spread across the different sites. Not only did the project need to surmount the political, economic and military shifts over the course of the project, but toward the end of the work it has faced the problems and sufferings of the Covid pandemic. And flowing through all this are changing lives of the team (the big events that bring us joy and sorrow) and the changing lives of the young people and their relations and dynamics. The linguistic, cultural and other differences though are not purely obstacles to be overcome, rather they feed the research and the team as a series of creative tensions, pleasures and insight. The conceptual apparatus that provides some of the structure to the work is nourished through these creative differences, not all of which is simply apparent in the book itself. And, of course, any engagement with people is emotional and empathetic. Across the team that sense of connection is evident, but also in their relations with participants we see how their labour is cut through with a series of concerns, learnings, understandings, pathos, responsibility and ethical obligation. Far from falling for the fallacy of translation, some myth of simple transparent communication, the project evinced a sense of realism but also joy in the necessary noise of such a complex series of programmes of activity.

The project is rooted in a commitment to understanding young peoples' lives, their uncertainties and their 'rights' through understanding the experiences of the young people. Structure is certainly not ignored. It stands as a moving, uneasy, bedrock of law, force, habit, history, tradition, and environment. There are clearly inequalities. Resources and forms of capital are held and deployed in uneven ways. But structure does not guide the force of law in a simple set of commands. Nor are the 'rights' of the young people in Ethiopia and Nepal simply protected or denied in the codifications of the State. The team draw on the notion of 'living rights', namely rights that are always rooted in actual and particular practices and processes, embedded and embodied. As such, these young peoples' rights are not guaranteed (or dismissed) by laws instituted from the top down, but are centred through a series of intergenerationally inflected experiences and supported through various interdependencies. Rights, in this sense, are intrinsically dynamic, yet grounded in the lives of the young people themselves.

It is through this orientation to the young peoples' actual and particular experiences, and through the sensitivity of the team to the dynamics of circumstance and force, that the authors of this book provide an important and powerful intervention, not only with regard to deepening our understanding of young people and their various intergenerational struggles, but also with regard to how to approach and be supportive of young people. The book foregoes any patronising account of children as social agents and instead shows how, across distant lands, connections and dependencies can be forged as a powerful and deeply intermeshed co-creation oriented to reversing inequalities and marginalisation.

David Oswell, London, October 2021

CHAPTER 1

Introduction: Why uncertainty? Why listen to marginalized youth?

The introduction presents why we chose to address uncertainty, and how this has become increasingly important not only in the fragile and conflict-affected environments where the research took place, but also throughout all of our lives and every part of the globe. The introduction outlines who conducted the research, its locations, and the questions the teams sought to answer. The importance of listening to the most-marginalized youth in formulating and implementing policy and practice is emphasized, because they are not only experts in their own lives, but have the potential to contribute to policy solutions in the face of uncertainty. The chapters and parts of the book are summarized: Part One on key concepts and methodology; Part Two on Ethiopian findings; Part Three on Nepalese findings; Part Four on comparative themes of street-connection, disability, and migration; and Part Five, the conclusion.

Keywords: uncertainty, marginalization, youth, rights, partnership, comparative, qualitative research, change-scape

Introduction

Youth Uncertainty Rights (YOUR) World Research carried out detailed, large-scale qualitative and participatory research with over 1,000 youth, of whom case studies were carried out with 500 of the most-marginalized young people across eight fragile environments in Ethiopia and Nepal. The research shows that when youth are included in research processes, their views listened to and taken into account, a picture emerges of creativity and innovative ideas in the face of significant challenges and uncertainty in their lives and environments. The research began in 2016 and has generated new knowledge about how marginalized youth perceive, navigate, negotiate, and respond to uncertainty. By building on youth strategies, the research illuminates understandings of youth realities and rights, and how they can be supported to confront feelings of marginalization and find pathways out of poverty.

This book intertwines the theoretical and practical approaches taken to ensure that the research informed policy and practice, working with national partners in both Ethiopia and Nepal. Some key findings for each of the four urban and four rural fragile environments comprising the research sites provide insights into the perspectives of marginalized youth. Engaging local services and national policy-makers has also been an important part of the research, carried out with civil society and academic organizations in both countries. The book thus provides an indication of the impact created by the research together with youth at different levels of governance. This was only possible due to valuable research partnerships built with youth, organizations, and researchers from the Global South.

Gaining youth perspectives on uncertainty

The aim of the research was to generate new knowledge about how marginalized youth perceive, navigate, negotiate, and respond to uncertainty and how this may affect their rights and pathways out of poverty in fragile and conflict-affected communities also prone to environmental disasters. The relationship between poverty and uncertainty was examined on the ground in partnership with CHADET in Ethiopia and ActionAid Nepal, organizations that have demonstrable local expertise in working with the most-marginalized children and youth on poverty, rights, and participation.

Research analysis paid attention to how youth perceptions of uncertainty intersected with their feelings of exclusion and discrimination. These reflected structural inequalities such as income/wealth, gender, caste/ethnicity, and disability, and also generational power dynamics in communities where the research was conducted. The project helped deepen understandings of how young women and men in both countries, and genderfluid youth in Nepal, address uncertainty in their everyday lives and how these experiences are associated with causes and symptoms of violence. In understanding uncertainty, the research team recognized that youth can seek what we have termed 'positive uncertainty'. The understanding, across the project, of uncertainty being potentially positive and not necessarily negative was encouraged through the applications of Bauman's theories of insecurity and community (2001) and is further discussed in Chapter 2 on concepts and in the Conclusion. This is also aligned with ethnographic work across Africa which affirms that uncertainty can be helpful to navigate insecurity and find new futures (Cooper and Patten, 2015). The international longitudinal research of Young Lives has also stressed the importance of understanding young people's perceptions of risk and their creative strategies in the face of uncertainty. This international team examining children's lives across continents reminds us how young perspectives need to be analysed within contexts of changing power dynamics and structural disadvantage (Crivello and Boyden, 2011).

The YOUR World project worked early on to understand not only how youth conceptualized uncertainty in their lives but also how they responded to uncertainty. This co-construction approach to understanding uncertainty was encouraged and developed with Etienne Wenger-Trainer early in the project. Engaging in uncertainty and how participants can be 'driven to make a difference' can be facilitated by social learning spaces (Wenger-Trainer and Wenger-Trainer, 2020: 21) and this is reflected upon with reference to findings in the concluding Chapter. These authors add that uncertainty can be expressed verbally or through other mediums including emotions and the way people relate to each other, and is experienced differently and unevenly including consideration of power and poverty. Inspired by this encouragement and by youth-centred participatory practice and research (discussed below and in Part One), the team used creative, visual, and moving methods as well as spending time with young people, observing their lives and fragile environments, in order to explore uncertainty in the lives of the most-marginalized. Youth helped the team to stratify uncertainty into different domains that could then be understood further through in-depth case-study interviews. These domains are explained in Chapter 3, and include uncertainty in transitions growing up, in their feelings about themselves and their relationships with others, and in their fragile and fast changing political and environmental contexts. The team explored youth strategies in uncertain times and uncertain and fragile environments.

The research team explored how young people viewed autonomy, freedom, and relationships in order to understand their decision-making within intergenerational dynamics in households and communities and social norms across both countries. The project regarded child and youth as subjects, ensured analysis was contextualized, and examined historical, generational, and structural inequalities and power dynamics (following Wells, 2017). The research investigated the feelings of youth and the kind of support they received or wanted from peers, family members, and others in communities and services. Many youth interviewed individually and in small groups discussed how they negotiated traditional perspectives in communities, and social norms, alongside rapidly changing and fragile environments.

More parallels were found than had initially been imagined in comparing youth stories across the two countries. Ethiopia and Nepal were chosen as lower-income countries, both with mountainous and flatter landscapes and with fragile environments linked to disasters and post-conflict contexts. Strategies of youth in both countries have increasingly included migration in search of work and alternative futures, and included destinations in Middle Eastern countries, referred to in both as 'The Gulf'. The team explored how youth felt about migration decisions, their separation and their relationships with families when away and on return. Youth in street situations were also interviewed in urban sites and marginalization and uncertainty understood from their perspectives. Many of the most-marginalized are involved in the informal sector, becoming street-connected and sometimes lacking access to rights. Their stories on the streets were also explored. The research highlights the ongoing strategies of youth to survive and provide for their families, and their suggestions for local services and provincial and national youth policies.

Change-scape: listening to marginalized youth

The approach to power, listening to the most-marginalized, and including children in this research was also inspired by project advisers including Robert Chambers. Over past decades Chambers (2012) provoked transformation of power relations through participatory pedagogies, understanding and confronting inequalities and striving for gender equity, and including young people as active participants in development. The research project followed a change-scape youth-centred approach (see Chapters 2 and 3) that embodies such underpinning philosophies alongside cultural and socio-ecological theories, linking youth agency to cultural, political, and environmental context (Johnson, 2011, 2015). The project also followed a rights-based approach to research with children and young people (Beazley and Ennew, 2006) and an emancipatory approach that surfaces the perspective of the most-marginalized (Freire, 1970). The research process included mechanisms such as: co-construction and use of creative methods with youth; contextual analysis involving key stakeholders from early research stages; and building spaces for peer-to-peer communication and for dialogue between youth, adults in communities, service providers, and policy-makers. Building capacity of national teams of researchers and practitioners to take youth views seriously while following ethical protocols and procedures for the research were central elements of the project. This also involved selection of engaging methods and media, while ensuring that large-scale qualitative research was convincing to policy-makers and participants in the research.

For purposes of comparative research, the United Nations (UN) definition of youth was followed, and older age brackets discussed with appropriate ministries in the development of youth policy. The UN youth definition is those aged 15–25 years, overlapping with children under-18 years (as defined by UN Convention on the Rights of the Child). Since some young people at the beginning of the research were under-25 but would be older at the end of three years, the age range of case studies was extended to include 26–28 years at the time of write-up and in processes of feeding into policy and practice. In the research, highlighting and focusing on youth perceptions of 'tradition' and social norms and their own and adult expectations provided a basis for intergenerational analysis, alongside looking at young people's perspectives on generational differences in aspirations, uncertainty, and the strategies available.

At a time of constant change in fragile, earthquake-affected, and drought-prone areas, and with governments in both Ethiopia and Nepal going through substantial change, the research provided large-scale qualitative evidence about the reality of lives of most-marginalized youth. Their stories are not often sought or heard, but in this research the team members, partners, and governmental and non-governmental staff acknowledged changing the way their perspectives can be taken into account to make new and more hopeful futures within both Ethiopia and Nepal (Johnson et al., 2019b). It is striking how, in the research, many youth proved resilient and sensible in the face of difficulties, and embraced and navigated uncertainty in a positive way, demonstrating that we can all learn from them in uncertain or difficult times.

Research objectives

The research examined experiences of youth in Ethiopia and Nepal, their perceptions of uncertainty and alternative pathways out of poverty, and how these intersect with exclusion and discrimination. Youth presented strategies in the face of uncertainty and these, with their resilience in the face of risk and vulnerability, can help inform local support and, in turn, national/international policy on sustainable routes out of poverty, and how these might be replicated and scaled-up. The specific objectives for YOUR World Research were to:

- scrutinize conceptions of uncertainty and how uncertainty is perceived to affect pathways out of poverty from the perspectives of marginalized youth;
- examine marginalization and uncertainty in the lives of young men and women in impoverished areas, including understanding how youth feel about their developing identities and notions of autonomy and belonging;
- analyse youth agency in dealing with uncertainty and insecurity, their awareness of and access to their rights, and their migration behaviours and daily coping strategies;
- inform and change policy discourses and practices concerning youth rights and youth-focused community development using an improved understanding and re-conceptualization of child and youth rights and uncertainty.

Personnel and partners

International and national teams

Johnson, leading the research, worked across both countries with co-researcher West and adviser Church who acted as mentors. Each country had a national research lead, a researcher also undertaking a doctorate, and a research assistant. The Research Officer/Fellow, Gosmann, supported the project on coding, reporting to donors, and administrative tasks. In Ethiopia the Research Lead, Getu, and the doctoral Researcher, Getachew, were both from Addis Ababa University, the Research Assistant, Ahmed, from Debre Markos University. In Nepal the lead, Tuladhar, had been working with the Research Centre for Educational Innovation and Development (CERID) at Tribhuvan University and then UNICEF, the Doctoral Researcher, Shrestha, was from ActionAid Nepal, and the Research Assistant, Neupane, seconded from HomeNet in Kathmandu.

National teams were based at national partner non-governmental organizations. The UK, Ethiopian, and Nepalese teams met during inception, analysis, and writing-up to share ideas and approaches across countries. The international team provided ongoing opportunities for sharing learning, mentoring, and support across the teams in the two countries. The teams were all involved in co-construction throughout the process so that there was more ownership and national capacity built during the process.

National and local partners

National and local partner organizations in each country were involved from the inception, and provided support, advice, contact with communities, and liaison with government and policy-makers at different levels. These partners have in-depth knowledge of the research locations, communities, and relevant policies and programmes, and have built up long-standing relationships with local government, businesses/enterprise, and civil society. This gave the research the potential to lead to meaningful and measurable initiatives and impact, and partner organizations were involved in local and national youth seminars held near the end of the research to communicate findings and policy messages from young people to government and non-government organizations.

In Ethiopia, the main partners were CHADET, ChildHope, and Addis Ababa University. CHADET is a national non-governmental organization working with poor and migrating girls and young women across Ethiopia and has also set up a research department. They provided logistics and facilitated access to marginalized youth in the research sites through their local offices and staff facilitators. ChildHope UK have worked in partnership with them and the YOUR World lead researcher for a number of years. The national university also provided a strong academic base and key academics involved in the national reference group were from the departments of Anthropology, Sociology, Social Work, and Psychology.

In Nepal, the main partners were ActionAid Nepal and CERID. ActionAid Nepal is a national, rights-based, non-governmental organization familiar with participatory action research and strong monitoring and evaluation of its community-based programmes. They had previously been partners with the lead researcher. ActionAid has international links and strong relationships with a number of local NGOs across the country. Local partner organizations who facilitated access to communities included, in Kathmandu: Youth Advocacy Nepal, HomeNet Nepal, Nepal Mahila Ekata Samaj, CWIN Nepal, CWCN, Blue Diamond Society, and SOBER Recovery; in Kapilvastu: Sahaj Nepal; in Sindhupalchowk: Community Self-Reliance Centre.

Reference groups

International and National Reference Groups of decision-makers and academics were established to advise on methodology and inform impact, research uptake, and influence policy and practice. Attention was given to ensuring academics, practitioners, and policy-makers were also balanced in gender, discipline, and policy area. Groups provided input on national political and cultural contexts, including academic research and evaluations relating to youth insecurity, uncertainty, policy, and practice for youth and marginalized groups, and specifically on structural inequalities including gender, age, and a range of social drivers such as ethnicity/caste, religion, disability, socio-economic and educational status, and spatial factors. An international reference group met in the UK at the beginning and towards the end of the project.

Research locations

Four research locations in each country were selected with partners on the basis of having been affected by previous conflict and being environmentally fragile or prone to disasters. They were also chosen because they are particularly impoverished and show diversity in terms of, for example, religion and ethnic group. This allowed detailed qualitative research to explore how different vulnerabilities, processes of marginalization, and structural inequalities affect uncertainty in the lives of youth. Two locations were urban and two rural in each country to take account of differences in urbanization and increasing exposure to globalization on youth growing up.

The regions/districts selected for research were as follows. In Ethiopia: Addis Ketema sub-city in Addis Ababa and the drought-prone rural area of Hetosa in the surrounding Oromia District; Woreta Town in South Gondar Zone and the surrounding area in the District of Fogera in Amhara. In Nepal: a particularly impoverished urban area of central Kathmandu, and a rural area of Sindhupalchowk (Himalayan mid-high hills) which were heavily affected by earthquakes in April 2015; and an urban and rural area of Kapilvastu District in the plains of the Western Region (Terai and Chure Hills) that experienced riots, and in which traditional ethnicity/caste and gender-based discrimination are prevalent (including during the research). These communities, in both Ethiopia and Nepal, have been destabilized by poverty and post-conflict situations and throughout the research they experienced local religious and ethnic conflict. These locations are specified in the research as they have large enough populations so that youth case studies can remain anonymised. See Part Two on Ethiopia and Part Three on Nepal for further information on research sites.

The book

This book is testimony to the co-construction of all stages of YOUR World Research between the international and national teams in Ethiopia and Nepal.

Part One unpacks some of the concepts included in the book so that it is clear how researchers approached these different issues. Literature is referred to in Chapter 2 on marginalization, uncertainty, living rights, youth-centredness, and power relations. The methodology is covered in Chapter 3, including how youth-centred research was undertaken and the co-constructed approach with national teams of academics and practitioners and with marginalized youth. The chapter provides details on the way in which different domains of uncertainty were determined using creative and participatory methods and then systematically covered in case-study interviews with youth. Ethics and the way in which different stakeholders were engaged in the research and in gaining impact are also presented.

Although discussions with reference to literature are included at the beginning and end of the book, Part Two on Ethiopia and Part Three on Nepal are dedicated space for presentation of the voices of the most-marginalized across research sites of YOUR World Research. This focuses on presentation of empirical findings, adhering to ethical protocols and using pseudonyms. Quotes are translated by bilingual research team members who are co-authors of this book. The key themes that emerged from analysis at site level are presented in keeping with the approach which was to start with the perspectives of youth. The team had to put assumptions aside, and in these chapters, youth priorities are presented. Parts Two and Three include some literature references to provide the research context, but then allow the perspectives of participating youth to be at the forefront. Implications for policy and practice are discussed in Part Four, and broader theorization and conclusions at the end of the book.

Part Two introduces some key themes from Ethiopia starting with Chapter 4 as an introduction to the country and the sites chosen for study. The country has undergone rapid political change moving from a situation where rights were rarely discussed to a government willing to consult with marginalized youth to develop national policy. Findings from sites in the Amhara region of northern Ethiopia are presented in Chapters 5 and 6. In rural Fogera, marginal youth describe how they move out of the area due to landlessness or lack of access to resources and how the most-marginal do not see their futures through formal education. In the small town of Woreta, the evidence focuses on youth in street situations where they work to find employment in the informal sector, but many end up using substances such as *khat* to ease the difficulties they face. Chapter 7 describes the fragile environment of many drought-prone small settlements or *kebeles* during the research period, with social norms that youth feel they need to escape, such as early marriage, and adult expectations to provide for families that lie as heavy burdens, particularly on young men. The role models of many youth are migrants. The lives and shifting identities of street-connected youth is the focus for Chapter 8 on Addis Ababa. There was a shift in government and conflict associated with this during and after the research was conducted and this is reflected in some of the discussions in these Ethiopian chapters.

Part Three introduces the context of Nepal in Chapter 9, which has comparatively recently experienced conflict, governance change, and a devastating earthquake, and has many policies referring to rights, women's empowerment, and young people's education and employment, but which have fallen short of supporting the most-marginalized. Chapters 10 and 11 describe the Terai research site Kapilvastu, birthplace of the Buddha. The rural findings focus on discrimination due to language and gender with voices of the most-marginalized describing their experiences. The urban location is a site of in-migration from hill areas, out-migration to India, and local religious and ethnic conflict, and the chapter discusses changes in traditions. The fragile, earthquake-affected Himalayan site of Sindhupalchowk is presented in Chapter 12, highlighting migration to gain skills and employment, and how seriously youth take their responsibilities to their communities. Chapter 13 discusses youth vulnerability and family support in Kathmandu slums or informal settlements. Chapter 14 discusses genderfluidity in Nepal and the way that youth need to seek solace with peers and groups that can support them in developing and celebrating their identities.

Part Four addresses comparative cross-case analysis across three main themes with a short introduction in Chapter 15 about the mechanisms to impact throughout the research and how marginalized youth worked with national teams to influence policy and practice and gain impact. Chapter 16 provides youth perspectives on migration: even if uncertain and often unsafe, mobility and migrants as role models offer alternative futures to youth who cannot see their futures in formal education or employment. Chapter 17 focuses on youth who are connected to the streets and trying to make a living in the informal sector. In Chapter 18 youth living with disability describe how they feel marginalized, through the social barriers arising from mental and/or physical impairments or through caring for others disabled in their families and communities.

Part Five provides conclusions on 'Listening to marginalized youth on uncertainty' and completes the book. It restates the importance of listening to marginalized youth who can energize policy and practice with creativity in the face of uncertainty. It suggests that youth require support and that adults would do well to listen to the most-marginalized as experts on uncertainty in their lives.

PART 1
Research concepts and methods

CHAPTER 2
Key concepts

YOUR (Youth Uncertainty Rights) World Research explored uncertainty and vulnerability in everyday lives of marginalized youth in fragile disaster-prone and conflict-affected areas of Ethiopia and Nepal. A set of key concepts underpinned the research and methodology, including uncertainty, both negative and positive, marginalization, living rights, and youth-centredness, as well as notions of youth, power, and young people in street situations. The research started from the perceptions of marginalized and vulnerable young people to understand how they have become experts in navigating and negotiating uncertainty in realizing their rights and finding pathways out of poverty. The project used young people's perceptions of marginalization, insecurity, and uncertainty, and a reconceptualization of child rights in development to understand young people's 'living rights' that takes account of their complex lives, how rights are translated and realized in different contexts, and how addressing rights may be seen within broader strategies of achieving social justice.

Keywords: positive uncertainty, marginalization, living rights, youth-centred, street-connection, street situations

Introduction

YOUR (Youth Uncertainty Rights) World Research, 'Insecurity and uncertainty: marginalized young people's living rights in fragile and conflict-affected situations in Nepal and Ethiopia' was conducted across both countries between July 2016 and June 2019, funded by the Economic and Social Research Council (ESRC)/Foreign and Commonwealth Development Office (FCDO, formerly DFID) Joint Fund for Poverty Alleviation Research. As the title suggests, the research focused on a number of key concepts, which are outlined in this chapter: youth, marginalization, uncertainty, and living rights. Underlying and drawing together these concepts are issues of power, and the research itself and methodologies used aimed to be youth-centred, with young people involved in co-construction as well as their own perceptions and definitions being placed at the centre. This is clearly seen below in the section on defining marginalization, which made use of young people's ideas and definitions in practice in order to reach those considered to be the most-marginalized. It is also evident in the dimensions of uncertainty that were developed through co-construction and used as the basis for case studies with over 500 young people across Ethiopia and Nepal.

The concepts were initially developed from literature and discussion among researchers and partner organizations involved in producing a proposal. The research aimed to be academic, in making contributions to theory and understanding of children's, young people's, and community lives, but also have impact in terms of being of use to policy-makers, government departments, and non-government organizations as well as beneficial to youth and their communities. Concepts were therefore co-constructed and then refined with youth so that the research had relevance to their lives and could also be clearly communicated and understood.

Youth

The term 'youth' is here used along with and meaning the same as 'young people'. It is an age-based concept, frequently seen as a period of transition, and a stage bridging childhood and adulthood. This period has been conceived as one where individuals move from dependence to independence, shifting domicile and relationships, predominantly into marriage (for example Wallace and Cross, 1990). But this is problematic (see Christiansen et al., 2006), for example because the notion and meaning of dependence and independence has cultural and linguistic variations, and issues such as early marriage involve periods of life defined as childhood, as do other forms of transition, in particular work and migration (Van Blerk, 2008).

The term 'youth' is widely used in national and international policy as well as academic and other literature. It is usually defined by particular ages, and often characterized by being a period where legislation provides increasing individual autonomy, power or permissions, such as to consent to sexual activity, sign contracts, drive vehicles, get married, and own land and other goods. It is, in practice, the operation of power that underlies the concept, with most young people having significantly less power than those defined as adults. Whatever power youth have is structurally affected not only by age but by other diverse social categories such as gender, sexuality, dis/ability, ethnicity, forms of status and inheritance as well as wealth and income, which also affect children (Johnson and West, 2018).

Childhood is internationally defined as the period of life up to 18 years (that is, 17 and below) by the United Nations (UN) Convention on the Rights of the Child. Youth is not the subject of similar international instruments, and there is some variation even within UN agencies on the age range, for example, some suggesting young people as aged 10–24 years and others as 15–24 years (see Johnson and West, 2018: Chapter 3). It is a period up to 25 years, the age range of 15–24 years that is most commonly used by the UN and others to define youth and which has been used in this research. National policies also vary, including those of Ethiopia and Nepal. In Ethiopia youth is defined as extending up to 29 years and in Nepal the youth policy includes those aged up to 40 years. As some youth who started to interact with this research at 24 years were 26–28 years by the end, the initial upper limit of 25 years was later extended to allow their ongoing participation.

This research focused on marginalized youth (see below) and included street-connected youth as well as those who feel socially excluded and discriminated against. The research recognizes the disproportionate impact that violence associated with social hierarchy has on youth of different gender and ethnicity/caste, and how this affects youth involvement in acts of resistance. The research in different locations (see Parts Two and Three) looked at the importance of understanding youth subjectivities and structural violence (Wells, 2014) and experiences of violence in different contexts (Thomas de Benitez, 2011a).

Marginalization

The marginalization of some people has been of particular concern since the 1980s and there has been a marked growth in inequality. Marginalization is 'that complex and disputatious process by means of which certain people and ideas are privileged over others at any given time' (Tucker, 1990: 7). Marginalization is about power, and is often seen as the ability of those who are implicitly at the centre where power is located to define others as being at the margins. But this centre is elusive. 'When we say marginal, we must always ask, marginal to what? But this question is difficult to answer' (Ferguson, 1990: 9). As found in this research, marginalized people should not be seen as those living on the geographical periphery since they are also within the bounds of the centre. The 'phantom centre, elusive as it is, exerts a real, undeniable power over the whole social framework of our culture, and over the ways that we think about it' (Ferguson, 1990: 9). Much depends on how marginalization is defined in a particular culture, but also how it operates and is experienced in practice.

Manchala (quoted by Walters and Jepson, 2019) suggested the term firstly:

> seems to hold the marginalized people as objects, as a category, often referring to them as 'the poor'. But their faces and names are many – discriminated, despised, exploited, and kept disempowered so that the centres of power and privilege remain intact in the hands of a few. Secondly, this categorisation hides the many causes of their marginalization. Thirdly 'margins' is a fluid concept. Some experiences of marginalization are not the same as those who experience multiple or intense forms of marginalization (Manchala, 2017: 202).

This fluidity reflects findings about marginalization in the research. There are various factors contributing to marginalization, such as age, gender, sexuality, dis/ability, religion, ethnicity/caste, income, and wealth, and other factors dependent on local forms of status, in addition to geographic location and status as domestic or international migrant or refugee. The experience of marginalization may have an influence on individual and group identities, and how these shift in relationship to others. This was evident in the research as those youth identified as marginalized by organizations would often say they were not and point to others who they saw as being marginalized. The experience is relational, temporal, and dependent on place, and status may change by location as well as over time and in regard to other people who are around. In some respects this may also be seen as degrees of marginalization or what Walters and Jepson (2019), citing Smith and Pitts (2007) and Kwong (2011), refer to as the intensity of being marginalized.

Young people's own experiences and perceptions of marginalization lie at the core of the research.

Rather than only following external or government definitions, the research aimed to hear from youth about their understanding of marginalization. For example, legal and policy definitions of marginalization in Nepal (see Chapter 9) particularly refer to ethnicity/caste membership, which is inherited, and which, especially in the past, has been not only a primary marker of identity but also gave status as part of a complex and rigid social structure. Changing definitions of marginalization in Nepal reflect shifts in politics and government. But these definitions are not how young people only see marginalization. They perceive it to be not limited by the peripheries of a country or to certain genders, ethnicities/castes, but having a variety of other dimensions such as disability. The research found marginalization to be central to young lives throughout Ethiopia and Nepal.

Youth definitions of marginalization

Young people's definitions of what is marginalization and who is marginalized include their experience of abuse in families, linking to ongoing uncertainty in family relationships. These youth definitions of marginalization were developed through the snowballing approach to sampling and the co-construction of concepts including marginalization with youth (see Chapter 3 on methodology). Many of the young people interviewed felt that workloads, and expectations of them to support their families, are heavy burdens. Expectations to follow some traditional paths, such as to marry early, are also reasons youth gave for moving away from families and communities. Migration is historical in many sites even if accentuated during times of local conflict, environmental fragility, or disaster (see Parts Two and Three). However, returnee migrants who have not been successful, especially in Ethiopia, do not feel they are welcomed back into communities and are sometimes rejected by families.

As youth age and develop multiple and shifting identities, they may experience discrimination on a variety of grounds. For example, discrimination due to their gender, sexuality, ethnicity/caste, religion, disability, or their family and living situation, level of education attainment, landlessness, or whether they have migrated into a community. Also their experiences of personal crisis due to illness or debt in their families, conflict in communities, and life in fragile environments. Some also feel marginalized simply because they are not consulted or listened to about decisions made that affect them. See Chapter 3 for the rationale for involving the most-marginalized youth in the research and the processes for their selection and participation.

Translation of concepts and terms

Along with concepts such as marginalization, there was a need to agree on translations of other terms among research teams and with young people, particularly in locations where several languages are involved. Teams discussed how to translate key words into local languages and the range of words that could be used for different terms into English. The discussion extended to how to use these translations and words in the way the project is introduced and in key questions. A range of key concepts were involved, particularly uncertainty and insecurity, and key terms used in discussions relating to marginalization such as aspirations, rights, and living and working in street situations. Such translations back and forth were important from the outset in clarifying concepts and understanding, and showed the importance of recognizing fluidity and change, and the particular context of use. Other key words included youth, children, violence, vulnerability, risk, resilience, transitions, intergenerational, and power dynamics. Uncertainty and the idea of positive uncertainty, living rights, and youth-centredness are explored below as central concepts.

The teams spent time discussing how to translate the concept of uncertainty into Amharic or Nepalese so that there was not necessarily a negative or positive association with the wording or phrases used. After much discussion during co-construction with national teams and youth, it was decided that the translation of not knowing what will happen next in a sequence of time was closest to youth understandings of uncertainty. *Anischitata* was used in Nepali and *Ergetegna alemehon* in Amharic.

Insecurity was also identified as important, in providing a key element of the environmental and political context in both Ethiopia and Nepal. The project took a human development view of insecurity that it includes aspects of personal insecurity as well as insecurity in context (following UNDP, 1999). It was found to be crucial that insecurity is separated from uncertainty as a concept because insecurity may almost always be seen as negative and more aligned with risk, whereas uncertainty may be seen as positive. The concepts needed to be separated in investigation of young people's perspectives, and the main focus was on uncertainty.

Uncertainty

Since the research project was conceptualized, uncertainty has become a trope for the times, initially from the Western bank crises of 2008 and subsequently the punitive austerity policies particularly affecting the poorest and disabled, through Brexit and youth protests against climate change. Before this, since the end of the 20th century, connected to the consequences of globalization including ethnic violence in different parts of the world, there has been recognition of a growing sense of radical social uncertainty (Appadurai, 1998). Increasing levels of uncertainty and its impact on the lives and perceptions of young people were key elements informing the development of this research with marginalized youth in Ethiopia and Nepal prior to 2016.

Prior to the burgeoning use of 'uncertainty' in popular discourse, particularly associated with politics in Europe and climate change, academic work looked at various dimensions of uncertainty. These included connections with risk, objective and subjective perceptions, management of uncertainty, political uses, globalization, and cross-cultural differences as well as discussions on the use of the term technically, and meanings for scientists such as imprecision in outcomes of a modelling exercise. (For example, Wright and Phillips, 1979; Appadurai, 1998; Boholm, 2003; Taddei, 2012; Barnes, 2016.) Recent increasing use and perceptions of uncertainty, to the extent that 'uncertainty defines our times' (Scoones, 2019: iv), have included disaggregation into different perspectives (societal, political, cultural, practice, individual) and domains (finance, infrastructure, disease, climate) as part of thinking about why uncertainty is important and how it is constructed (Scoones, 2019).

The research teams in Ethiopia and Nepal sought to understand how uncertainty affected the lives of youth, and how this fitted their feelings about marginalization, aspirations, and social expectations placed on them. Although there was a general trend to move away from resource-based traditional livelihoods in fragile rural environments (as found in rural Asia by Punch and Sugden, 2013), the findings set out later in this book show that youth were creative in the face of environmental disaster, such as the earthquake in Nepal, and formed youth movements to support the reconstruction in rural areas (such as Youth Advocacy Nepal). In both countries youth strongly identify with their rural places of origin as their homes, and wanted to belong back in their families and communities in the future. Youth subjectivities relating to uncertainty were the basis of analysis in this research, including their experiences of marginalization (also noted as important in research in Ethiopia by Di Nunzio, 2019) and of changing contexts, including changes in political economy, education, and the way in which these link to the labour market (as noted in Ethiopia by Mains, 2013 and in Nepal and Asia by Johnson and West, 2018).

Many marginalized youth in this research lacked access to school, dropped out or were not successful in national exams. The research aimed to analyse young people's understandings of uncertainty linked to power dynamics in relationships with peers, adults in families, and communities of origin and destination, in both their decisions relating to migration to find new futures in cities, and their experiences of working in the informal sector, where they might sometimes then be pushed into exploitative and illegal work. The research therefore sought to explore how uncertainty interacted with the way in which youth may break with family and social bonds in communities (following Bauman, 2001), but then also want to maintain links with their families and preserve their pride, despite authorities and adults labelling and criminalizing them in their lives connected to the streets (for example, Di Nunzio, 2019). Also relevant for understanding uncertainty in this research is the importance of understanding youth subjectivities towards violence and abuse (Wells, 2014), and the often highly gendered social norms that youth experience, for example the high prevalence of early marriage in the rural sites for this research (Getu et al., 2018).

Positive uncertainty and creativity

A key part of the research focus lies in the concept of positive uncertainty, drawn from Bauman's work, and recognizing uncertainty as not necessarily negative (see Johnson et al., 2019b; Johnson and West, 2021a). Uncertainty may be associated with moments of creativity. The research applied Bauman's (2001, 2004, 2007, 2011) theories of community and insecurity to understand how identities and notions of autonomy and belonging are developed in response to insecurity and uncertainty, including whether youth reject traditional norms, form new social norms, and seek support and leadership in alternative groupings and forms of peer support.

The constantly changing context of uncertainty and insecurity facing marginalized youth in both countries align with Bauman's ideas about liquid modernity and the world being like a minefield full of uncertainty. At inception, the project was informed by Bauman's theories of community (for example, 2001), in that uncertainty may not necessarily be negative. In the face of uncertainty, young people may find creative solutions and develop innovative strategies towards new and more hopeful futures in attempts to support their families.

When co-constructing ideas of uncertainty at the beginning of the research, the team suggested that many people deliberately place themselves in situations of uncertainty, for example by initiating change such as migration, different employment, new sources of income, that they hope will be beneficial but do not know will be. They are uncertain of outcome, and there may be risks depending on circumstances and how well their decision-making has been prepared. In discussing how to ask questions about uncertainty, it was suggested in co-construction with youth and teams that uncertainty is about not knowing what may happen next: that is potentially positive or exciting and/or negative or fearful for young people.

When adults do not know what is going to happen in their lives, they are often apprehensive or fearful. This research sought to co-construct initial ideas about the concept of uncertainty with young people who are experts in uncertainty in their lives in their transitions as they grow up, and as they interact with rapidly changing and fragile environments. This had already been clearly demonstrated by the emergence of youth movements in the aftermath of the 2015 earthquake in Nepal. Youth expertise was further confirmed and is discussed in later chapters, presenting findings including resilience and creativity of youth living in adverse conditions and processes of marginalization, as they offer innovative strategies and pathways out of poverty in both Ethiopia and Nepal (see Part Two onwards).

Young people co-constructed stratification of uncertainty that included places and spaces they inhabit, transitions as they grow up and their changing relationships with peers, families, and communities (see Chapter 3). The research explores how identities and notions of autonomy and belonging are developed in response to uncertainty, including whether young people reject existing 'traditional' norms, create new social norms, or seek support and leadership in alternative groupings and forms of peer support.

Findings discussed at the end of the book suggest a shift away from a simple path from formal education into employment. For many marginalized youth, certainty means persistent poverty and insecurity. Many of the young participants seek hope in uncertainty and have been embarking on risky journeys migrating nationally and internationally (for example see Chapter 16).

Uncertainty may also be regarded as positive by young women if their certainty in rural communities in Ethiopia and Nepal is usually early marriage and highly gendered discrimination. Young people of all genders may take risky pathways or choose illegal migration if their certainty is continued poverty, marginalization, and discrimination (also see Johnson et al., 2021 and Johnson and West, 2021a).

Living rights

The research explored how marginalized youth react to uncertainty in their complex lives and what role uncertainty plays in shaping their *living rights* (as formulated by Hanson and Nieuwenhuys, 2013). This re-conceptualization of child rights acknowledges that universal rights can be seen as 'living rights' as they are translated into legislation and the complex realities of local service provision and young people's lives. It highlights the importance of taking account of context (see also Johnson and West, 2018) and that young people's agency is embedded in family and communities (Abebe, 2013). This reconceptualization helped national teams place notions of child and human rights into different cultural and political environments.

The research recognized and took account of the constantly changing political contexts, and that rights are contested to varied extents in Ethiopia and Nepal, and differently in local, national, and regional discourses. Ethnic, caste, class, dis/ability, sexual, and gendered inequalities and politics have saturated notions of rights for different actors in development, and researchers worked to analyse and take account of how the cultural and political context can constrain or support youth agency. Youth agency is seen as relational in the research and dependent on the power dynamics and relationships that exist between young people and their families, adults in communities, and peers (following Oswell, 2013).

Young people's right to participate, for those aged up to 18 years, is expressed in the UN Convention on the Rights of the Child in Article 12, and their freedom to association, in Article 15. It was interpreted differently in the varied communities where the research took place. Notions of social justice are also recognized to vary nationally and locally across sites and communities. Stammers (2013) discussed the importance of social movements in achieving routes to social justice and the importance of this in children's rights. This project also sought to make the participation of youth in the research meaningful, so that their evidence can inform tangible social inclusion outcomes for the most-marginalized (following Tisdall et al., 2006).

This re-conceptualization of rights has been useful by taking into account its three pillars: living rights that appreciate the complexities and relational agency in young lives; translation from universal rights into legislation and cultural realities; and the aim of moving towards social justice. An issue raised through the research is that attention must be paid within this framework to take into account young people's agency and their identities as different individuals within changing intergenerational power dynamics. The transmission of cultural ideas and poverty needs to take account of how youth, as agents of change in their own right, can contribute to new and innovative solutions towards their wellbeing and to social justice, even if alone and not embedded in family or community. The 500 young people in each country who were interviewed for in-depth and detailed case studies desperately wanted to provide for their families and to be respected. But they also want to challenge and break from some traditional values and be supported in their creativity outside their family and community contexts. See Parts Two and Three for detailed evidence from the research sites in Ethiopia and Nepal.

Youth-centredness

The research placed youth at the centre. It aimed to listen to young people and make their input meaningful through interaction with policy-makers and practitioners. It took youth agency as a focus for examining uncertainty and recognized how this is relational: that young people interact with confidence and creativity as well as being restricted by social norms and cultural and religious beliefs and practices.

The change-scape framework (Figure 2.1) recognizes that different places and spaces for youth can feel safe or insecure and may or may not facilitate participation and living rights. Young people also experience transitions as they grow up, developing shifting and multiple identities and strategies for inclusion. The research incorporated attention to change over time, so that both changing contexts and transitions as youth grow up are taken into account in analysis. The research aimed to start from youth perspectives that reveal the nature of uncertainty in their lives.

22 YOUTH AND POSITIVE UNCERTAINTY

Cross-cutting issues of structural inequalities, and the effect of generational power dynamics on marginalized and street-connected youth (aged 15–24 years), were examined in their local cultural, political, urban, and rural contexts. The research recognized the disproportionate impact that violence associated with social hierarchy has on the lives of youth of different gender and ethnicity/caste and, with them, looked at which measures can help youth deal with their experience of violence in different contexts.

The research began with examining perceptions of young people on marginalization and their understanding, views, aspirations, and experiences that revealed the nature of uncertainty in their lives. The change-scape (for example, Johnson, 2010, 2011, 2017) helps to place youth experiences at the centre and provides a framework in which to analyse political, economic, cultural, and environmental contexts that shape uncertainty, insecurity, marginalization, and living rights.

The diagrammatic change-scape representation in Figure 2.1 was developed by the research lead (Vicky Johnson) and co-researcher (Andy West) from Johnson's change-scape (2011) and Bauman's theories of liquid modernity, community, and autonomy (2001). This diagram shows how the project follows change-scape theory in that the methodology was rights-based and youth-centred. The change-scape methodology seeks to understand how young people are affected by their physical, cultural, and political context, and in turn recognize how they can also change their lives, communities,

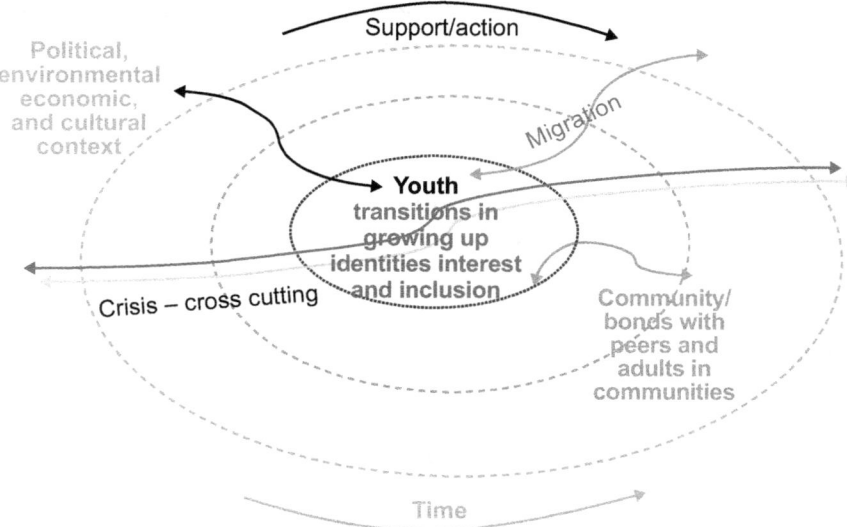

Figure 2.1 YOUR World change-scape
Source: Diagram constructed by Johnson and West, modified from the change-scape (Johnson, 2011) and including Bauman's (2001) theories

and broader social and political environments. It starts from the perceptions of young people on marginalization, vulnerability, and uncertainty in their insecure lives and contexts. The research examines peer and intergenerational relationships and power dynamics in communities as youth grow up in ever-changing cultural, political, and environmental contexts.

The change-scape incorporates analysis of time in terms of changing contexts and transitions as youth grow up. It also considers issues of crisis or fragility as cross-cutting, including experience and perceptions of crisis both in social and political context and in young people's individual lives. Crisis or fragility in context may include different aspects of insecurity, including conflict in both countries, drought in Ethiopia, and earthquake in Nepal.

The project also applied Bauman's (2001) concepts of community and social bonds to the research with young people. Bauman discusses insecurity in contexts that are fluid or liquid, constantly changing. He also presents a tension between the security or certainty that 'community' may offer and young people seeking autonomy as they grow up, which may include breaking traditional bonds with family and community and forming new social bonds, for example in peer groups. The approach taken in this research was to understand young people's agency and rights in the context of inter-generational relationships and social norms and to recognize interventions, especially in adversity, as being developmentally and culturally sensitive (Louw et al., 2000).

Youth aspirations

The way in which aspiration was approached in this research aligns with Appadurai's (2004) understanding. Rather than attempting more trajectories between formal education and formal employment, the most-marginalized, many of whom have dropped out of or failed at formal schooling, may simply hope for better futures. Many of the most-marginalized children and young people living in poor families have to balance work and education with survival needs, often making it hard for many young women but also young men to pursue any educational aspirations. This has historically been found in both Nepal and Ethiopia where young people combine work and education where possible (Johnson et al., 1995; Pankhurst, 2015). Their aspirations are shaped by structural inequalities and social norms and dynamics that determine many of the adult expectations in families and communities. Youth transitions as they grow up may be understood as experienced individually but also strongly associated with cultural understandings and practices in families, at work, and in young people's communities (Pankhurst, 2017). This research addressed youth experiences and the strategies and support they may require as dependent on social and cultural hierarchies, inequalities, and how they feel differently included or marginalized.

The 'Migrating out of Poverty Consortium' (funded by FCDO) suggested that youth experiences of vulnerability due to extreme poverty in rural areas, early marriage, violence, and sexual abuse led to youth decisions to migrate. Here and in other low-income contexts, youth migrate into seemingly uncertain situations where they are subjected to poor working conditions and low wages. Despite insecure employment, many view their living conditions after migration to be better and feel a greater sense of autonomy (Atnafu et al., 2014). Youth in Nepal have to face a lack of economic and educational opportunities and resources. As a result, many young people have to start working at an early age. It was striking at the early planning of this research how many of the marginalized youth in both countries saw new futures in migration rather than in formal education (this is discussed further in Chapter 19) and although youth across the research migrated, their aspirations and reception back into communities was found to be different in Ethiopia and Nepal.

Literature on youth in conflict-affected contexts suggests that young people are participants in a society affected by political insecurity, unequal access to resources, and social injustices (Daiute, 2010). Thus, in this research, the overall social, political, and economic contexts of youth informed initial understandings of youth agency and vulnerability in conflict-affected Nepal and Ethiopia. As the project progressed there were also situations of current conflict such as across Ethiopia with three periods where a 'State of Emergency' was enforced, and a change of government, and in Nepal more local conflict over resources in the Terai research sites (see Parts Two and Three on context for the research in Ethiopia and Nepal).

Street-connections and situations

The term 'street-connected youth' refers to young people living and/or working on the street and who may be alone in this situation or be connected to their families. In this concept and understanding of what it means to be a street-connected youth, the research followed the work of the Consortium for Street Children and the United Nations Committee on the Rights of the Child General Comment 21 on the Rights of Children in Street Situations (OHCHR, 2017).

The most commonly used to term to describe this group is 'street children', but this term has often led to stereotypes of children and young people as living alone, as either a danger to others or as helpless, which can lead to and has led to oversimplified and inappropriate policies and attempts at finding what is seen as a solution (see also Ennew 1994, 1995). As defined in the General Comment, the term children in street situations comprises:

> (a) children who depend on the streets to live and/or work, whether alone, with peers or with family; and (b) a wider population of children who have formed strong connections with public spaces and for whom the street plays a vital role in their everyday lives and identities. This wider population includes children who periodically, but not

always, live and/or work on the streets and children who do not live or work on the streets but who regularly accompany their peers, siblings or family in the streets (OHCHR, 2017: paragraph 4).

This research uses this concept, replacing 'children' with the higher age bracket of 'youth' up to 25 years and the terminology of street-connection as well as in street situations. The research aimed to understand the complexities in the lives of young men, women, and youth of the third gender, living and working on the streets in varying familial and group situations, and individual circumstances.

Conclusion

The nature of the research was co-construction with youth and national research partners and building capacity across the national teams. The UK team therefore embarked on the project with these concepts, but with the view to translating them in the research across global contexts. Time and space was planned in the process to ensure ownership, understanding, and development of these concepts that were meaningful to practitioner and academic researchers and to youth, including time spent on literal translation into different national and local languages.

Following an approach that is open, flexible, and participatory was important to respond to changing contexts and to work in a youth-centred way, but equally the team wanted to ensure the large-scale qualitative research was rigorous and acceptable as evidence to decision-makers at all levels nationally and internationally. Placing rights in the context of the everyday lives of youth was accompanied by impact activities that intended to inform inclusive policy and practice with evidence from the most-marginalized in a move towards social justice. This applied nature of the research was embedded in the values of the international team and was particularly important to local and national research partners who facilitated access to the most-marginalized and spaces for dialogue at all levels of governance.

CHAPTER 3
Youth-centred research and uncertainty: Method and approach

Key method components included co-construction, dimensions of uncertainty, creative methods, and marginalized youth participants, as well as research locations, personnel, and partners. This was a predominantly interpretative, large-scale, comparative qualitative research project, working with over 1,000 youth (500 participating in case-study groups and interviews), 400 adults, and 100 service-providers and policy-makers in Ethiopia and Nepal. The research followed a participatory approach particularly in early co-construction and later case-study phases. Starting from the perspectives of marginalized youth, it feeds into new academic knowledge, policy, and practice. In each country national teams identified marginalized youth for 150 in-depth and 100 additional case studies. In-depth case studies looked across domains of uncertainty in young lives that were identified in youth workshops, including uncertainty in transitions, relationships, and fragile and changing contexts. After analysis of case studies, focused discussions explored gaps or emerging themes in small groups, followed by local and national youth verification and policy development seminars.

Keywords: co-construction, participation, creative methods, domains of uncertainty, qualitative, marginalization, youth rights

Introduction

This chapter explores the main components of qualitative and participatory elements of methodology and approaches used in YOUR World Research: 'Insecurity and uncertainty: marginalized young people's living rights in fragile and conflict-affected situations in Nepal and Ethiopia', conducted across both countries during 2016–2019. The research was predominantly qualitative in order to understand and analyse the complex realities of marginalized youth and how these are influenced by structural inequalities. Creative and engaging participatory and visual methods were used to enable in-depth investigation of how uncertainty affects the lives and context of youth, and how in turn youth seek strategies to shape their rights and change their contexts.

The research was conducted in phases, following a preliminary period of setting up partnerships, negotiating, and agreeing the proposal. Key starting points included developing a relationship with potential national research team members and partner organizations prior to completion of the proposal, and agreement on an outline of work over three years. Team members and partner organizations agreed with core approaches to the research (outlined in Chapter 2), particularly its youth-centredness, but also that it would be both academic and aim to have impact, for use by policy-makers in government, non-government, and other organizations. This theme and practice of co-construction was core and ran throughout the research, from inception to launch.

The conceptual approach (see Chapter 2), and the limitations of existing research in youth, uncertainty, and rights led to the key research questions for the project:

1. How do marginalized and street-connected youth across communities in fragile and conflict-affected situations understand and respond to uncertainty as they shape and influence their rights?
2. How do perceptions of uncertainty change, depending on intersecting aspects of poverty and wellbeing, inclusion and identity, age, gender, and other structural inequalities?

The international teams worked together at an inception meeting in Nepal (2017) and at an analysis meeting in Ethiopia (2018) to further develop sub-questions relating to experiences of violence, peer and inter-generational relationships and dynamics, and youth strategies to find pathways out of poverty.

This chapter looks at the core approach of co-construction which underpinned the research and fed into the participatory elements used. It also looks at key components of location and partnerships, and outlines dimensions of uncertainty used in the research, and processes of working with marginalized young people, identifying the most-marginalized and the use of creative methods to explore uncertainty, circumstances, experiences, and aspirations. The case-study approach used to provide details from over 500 marginalized young people is outlined along with group and individual processes with local adults and stakeholders to amplify intergenerational perspectives.

A Methodology Guide was produced for the research and became an ongoing processual document, providing details of methods and approaches, facilitation tips, analysis forms, information, consent, and other basic materials. This is not reproduced here because of lack of space, except for some information on ethics, consent, and safeguarding.

Countries and locations

Nepal and Ethiopia were selected for the research as both countries remain among the poorest low-income countries in the world: 157 and 173, respectively, out of 187 countries in the Human Development Index (UNDP, 2013). They have key differences but some similarities in terms of historical conflict and specific locations of current conflict due to clashes between different ethnicities and/or religions. They have mountainous regions, and have both suffered recent environmental fragility and disaster including drought in Ethiopia and earthquake in Nepal.

Research locations in each country were selected in discussion with partners on the basis of having been affected by previous conflict and being environmentally fragile or prone to disasters. They were also chosen as particularly impoverished and show diversity in terms of religion and ethnic group, to explore how different processes of marginalization and varying vulnerabilities of young people affect uncertainty. The capital city was selected as an urban location in each country, with another place relatively close as a rural location, and from which there is migration into the capital. A third location was selected further from the capital, on the basis of ensuring the research is nationally relevant to policy-makers and practitioners. In this location, youth in both urban and rural situations were selected. See overview of locations in Chapters 4 (Ethiopia) and 9 (Nepal).

The overall approach

The research was predominantly qualitative and interpretive in nature, in starting from the perspectives of marginalized youth living in poverty in Ethiopia and Nepal (see Langevang, 2008). Qualitative research can also help us to understand local constructions of and definitions of 'youth' within the context of their social relations and position in society, and how these are problematized in society (Mizen, 2004). This project also took the approach that research with youth is different from research with adults, and researchers need to understand local constructions of childhood and youth (Punch, 2002). The research team took time to listen to youth, overcome assumptions about what they say, and value their evidence alongside often differing perspective of adults (following Johnson, 2015).

The approach of comparative case-study research was taken (Stake, 1995). Research teams needed to understand differences between individual youth as case studies, but also compare their stories and interviews within and across research sites and, to some extent, across different country contexts. The approach included contextual analysis and attention to power dynamics, which can lead to positive engagement with youth, adults, NGO, and government staff and policy-makers. It can result in lasting and transformational institutional and societal/policy change (Beazley and Ennew, 2006). While treating children and young people as active participants and agents of change (Boyden and Ennew, 1997; Johnson et al., 1998), the research also acknowledged the limitations of rights-based approaches (Tisdall et al., 2009) and the vulnerabilities and stresses facing young people (Mizen and Ofosu-kusi, 2013).

Uncertainty dimensions and stratification

A core concept throughout the research was uncertainty, although the range of meaning in English is not easy to translate into local languages. It is a difficult, ambiguous, and contested term and that is why the team had to plan how to introduce it and research it. For example, for young people uncertainty may be associated with the many mixed feelings associated with not knowing. These feelings are what the research wanted to explore further, such as excitement and creativity, as well as apprehension and even fear. Research teams needed to explore dimensions of uncertainty in the fieldwork: the stratification that emerged was based on concepts discussed in Chapter 2 and co-construction with youth.

Uncertainty was stratified into the following dimensions based on youth perceptions through piloting as well as the co-construction and theoretical framework:

- places and spaces
- mobility and migration
- transitions and growing up
- self/others, autonomy, and relationships
- conflict and environmental crisis, e.g. drought/earthquake

In addition, two cross-cutting themes were used: strategies and interventions – what helps and doesn't help in times of uncertainty; and time, including how contexts, lives, and relationships change as young people grow up (see Figure 3.1).

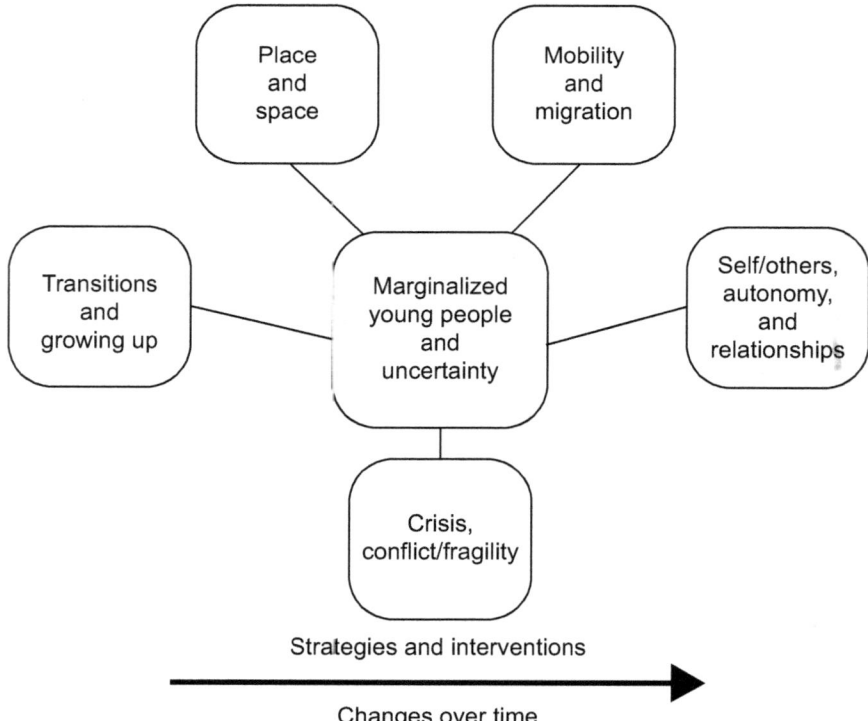

Figure 3.1 Dimensions of uncertainty

Key research approaches

Co-construction

The practice of co-construction was central to all research phases, from inception through to launch and compilation of reports, articles, and this book. The initial co-construction and planning of methodology with partners in Ethiopia and Nepal was led by Johnson while writing the funding proposal. This process included reaching agreement on core research approaches, that it would be youth-centred, aim to involve the most-marginalized, and follow conceptual themes outlined in Chapter 2.

Co-construction continued during inception phases of the project in the development of methods, local piloting, and establishing categories of social hierarchies/groupings for the participant coding system. Creative visual methods co-constructed with partners and used in inception workshops included: physical and drawn mapping to explore safety, security, belonging, communications, and connections; support network diagrams to gauge what does (or does not) help youth in realizing their rights and achieving their aspirations; timelines and drama to understand changing contexts and youth reactions to events/shocks.

The inception stage consisted of a workshop with marginalized youth in each research site which served to help teams co-construct the research with young people. This included increasing shared understanding of who is marginalized in different research locations and how to address uncertainty and insecurity in the research. It also included initial translations and understandings of key terms such as insecurity, uncertainty, and marginalization, and how to address them in the research. The translations and agreements on the most appropriate methods to use in later phases were piloted and further co-constructed with marginalized young people.

The evidence produced through case studies was subsequently checked with young people and their communities, and finally relayed to policy-makers in government and non-government organizations through joint national and local seminars. At these meetings young people produced their own statements and declarations, which have been used in-country by youth and adults, and examples are provided in this book (see Chapter 15). The aim of co-construction was to develop a methodology which would provide data that is sensitive to context, rigorous in its analysis across location, and relevant to local, national, and international policy development.

Youth-centredness in the research, and young people's participation at appropriate junctures were crucial to this approach, following practices established in child and youth focused disciplines and organizations. As discussed in Chapter 2, the youth-centred approaches and pathways to gaining impact are based on the change-scape approach to ensure more meaningful participation of young people. This youth-centred approach is reflected across different child and youth rights approaches to research and interventions (Beazley and Ennew, 2006; Johnson et al., 2020a).

Individual case studies with young people

The dimensions of uncertainty (described above) were used in 300 individual detailed case studies for young people that went into more depth on what uncertainty means to them in their insecure lives and contexts. Case studies were conducted with 4–6 young people using creative methods in a small group and more sensitive issues covered in individual interviews. Analysis completed on individual case study and small group sheets drew out common issues emerging among the youth group. A further 200 case studies across both countries were collected using participatory methods during co-construction, and follow-up on particular emerging themes after the individual interview phase.

Intergenerational and stakeholder analysis

As previously suggested (Chapter 2), the way in which youth interact with peers and intergenerationally and with their contexts is part of the socio-cultural-ecological change-scape approach to youth-centredness. This follows many others who have suggested the importance of understanding power dynamics in research with youth and in understanding differences and dynamics between young people and adults and how they navigate and negotiate social norms and power dynamics (see Punch et al., 2018; Johnson and West, 2021b).

Creative methods

The project developed and piloted creative and participatory methods with research teams and young people which were then used to collect information about particular dimensions of uncertainty, in addition to overall experiences, relationships, and aspirations. Tips for facilitation were shared and listed as part of the Methodology Guide, along with checklists for probing and guidance for small group discussions and case studies. This Guide was added to throughout and acted as a tool in the process to ensure consistency and quality through sharing experiences.

The main methods used to explore different dimensions of uncertainty, experience, and aspirations included roads and rivers of life, network diagrams, mobility maps, seasonal lines and changes (all of which might be done on paper or using local materials), in addition to youth-led walks, photographs of places, and the possibilities of performance or role play. The key to the use of these methods is not technique, instructions, and recording, but the initial development of a relationship between researcher and participants, facilitation skills, and the creation of an enabling environment. (See, for examples of methods and research, and background to participation and research: Boyden and Ennew, 1997; Johnson et al., 1998, 2014; Percy-Smith and Thomas, 2010; Roelen et al., 2020; Johnson and West, 2021b).

The 'roads and rivers of life', for example, provided a useful basis for young people to illustrate their transitions, challenges, uncertainties, and support gained at different times of their life, as well as where they saw themselves heading and their hopes. Researchers were able to discuss and probe further. Network diagrams illustrated the quality and extent of relationships and could be used as a basis to explore perceptions of what were seen as traditional norms and customs. Mobility maps and youth-led walks built on these to look at perceptions of the potential and reality of migration, significant places in localities, and aspirations. These also looked at conditions in the community and environment, and the effect of these on hopes and aspirations, and uncertainty.

Ethics, consent, and safeguarding

An ethical and safety framework was developed during inception, including consideration of team safety, child protection, and respect for participants of all ages. Protocols of informed consent for young people and adults were developed locally, following ethical requirements and clearance nationally (for example in Ethiopia by the School of Social Work of Addis Ababa University as per the National Research Ethics Review Guidelines) as well as by Research and Ethics Committees at the University of Brighton and Goldsmiths, University of London, UK. Considerations of disclosure from a legal and institutional perspective and support for youth if required during the process of research were considered and put in place.

A set of five protocols were agreed by the full team involving: safeguarding researchers; respecting participation of the most-marginalized and vulnerable; providing proper information and ensuring consent of young people; ensuring the safety and wellbeing of participants; with the fifth concerning processes of verification and dissemination.

- Safeguarding researchers included supporting researchers to anticipate any issues that might arise which they might find upsetting, to reflect on difficult issues that come up, providing support as necessary, ensuring team members did not work alone with young people, adhering to emergency protocols, and liaising with partner organizations.
- Respecting the participation of the most-marginalized and vulnerable included training and practice on not being judgemental, recognizing diversity, and finding appropriate spaces and group sizes.
- Providing proper information and ensuring consent of young people included ensuring marked and where possible signed informed consent was obtained for all aspects, such as photographs, recordings, general involvement, and checking throughout the research, exploring confidentiality, being clear about data use, and ensuring information provided was clear and understood.
- Ensuring the safety and wellbeing of participants included piloting and reviewing methods for appropriateness and care throughout, recognizing

dignity and respect, providing opt-outs and spaces for conversation, following procedures in cases of disclosure or suspicion of, for example, abuse or harm, and not continuing if inappropriate.
- Protocols for processes of verification and dissemination included not putting young people at risk, maintaining anonymity, managing data, checking consent, ensuring reasons and debates over disagreements on information between participants are recorded. Ethical approaches were informed by previous experiences of working with children and youth (for example, Johnson et al., 1998; Mayall, 2002; Alderson, 2005). In addition, safeguarding was taken into account across the project (UKCDR, 2021).

Youth participants: marginalization and young people

Over 1,000 young women and men, and in Nepal 10 genderfluid young people, participated in the research. Of these, 500 youth participated in group and individual sessions and interviews to collect more detailed case studies. The terms youth and young people are used interchangeably, using the UN age of 15–25 years, despite national definitions extending to higher age ranges (see Chapter 2).

The participant sample and criteria of marginalization and vulnerability were developed through the inception and piloting phases of the project. Snowballing was used to reach the most-marginalized, as defined during co-construction and then throughout the research by other youth in impoverished or environmentally fragile and conflict-affected areas. Participants were selected to maintain a balance of gender, ethnicity/caste (depending on locality) and to be inclusive of youth with disability, youth who had experienced abuse, those in different family and working situations or other circumstances of exclusion, poverty, and vulnerability.

Official notions of marginalization were not the only way in which the project determined which young people are most excluded from society. This research embraced a wider conception of marginalization that took account of how youth may challenge and go against social norms of sexuality, traditional, and religious local belief systems and other forms of behaviour expected by adults in communities. The construction of marginalization in this research was informed by how youth saw their exclusion and inclusion, their vulnerability, and processes of marginalization in their society and local communities. Criteria for sampling were put together from the piloting. Purposive sampling was intended to reach the most-marginalized young people but a snowballing approach was added.

Sampling criteria: marginalized and vulnerable young people

The following criteria for purposive sampling of marginalized and vulnerable young people were agreed from team analysis, work with local partners, and initial workshops with young people about their perceptions of marginalization in the research locations.

Street-connected children/young people were a main criterion but also intersecting with other groups: prostitutes/sex workers (terminology depending on context); migrants – internal and international; asylum seekers/refugees and internally displaced people; young people with disability; former gang members; youth who have suffered family abuse; young people out of school/ illiterate; young people who have HIV; child/youth hard labourers, agricultural labourers; young people using/misusing substances such as alcohol and drugs; child brides/early married; orphans; youth single parents; youth in extreme poverty; stigmatized youth linked to identity such as third gender, sex workers; domestic workers; landless young people.

In Nepal specific groups included Dalit and other particular ethnic/ caste groups depending on the research site. In Ethiopia specifically young people who follow ancestor worship/traditional religions. The coding system (see below) was checked to monitor and report on the diversity of young people in the case study sample.

Coding for individuals

A youth profile was developed to provide detailed monitoring and reporting on diversity of young people in the detailed case studies in each country. This also enabled analysis of findings with reference to these intersecting issues of difference, and coding was designed to enable the team to do this in themed team analysis and using NVivo.

A participant coding system (after Johnson and Nurick, 2003) was designed during inception that maintains confidentiality of participants while facilitating analysis across genders, generations/age, and structural inequalities. At the start of research with youth or adults the team explained the project fully using an information sheet and gained informed consent before continuing. Each participant was assigned a number and the coding grid completed through a short interview. Coding maintained anonymity in research findings and outputs as well as facilitating analysis.

Case studies with young people

Creative methods used during co-construction with youth at the outset established relationships with participants and snowballing to reach the most-marginalized. This phase established the stratification of uncertainty used in interviews and set up key themes for further exploration in detailed case studies. Preliminary work was less detailed and used more participatory approaches to establish youth understandings of marginalization and uncertainty in co-construction; follow-up worked on emergent themes after analysis of the detailed interviews.

The detailed individual case studies across both countries followed a semi-structured format so that each section was aligned to the different domains of uncertainty in young people's lives. The researchers began by adding the youth profile that included aspects of identity and situation: age, gender, disability, ethnicity, religion, family and living situation, household and family size and structure, employment or work responsibilities, education status and experience, and personal or family migration including destination.

The in-depth case studies started with very open questions about uncertainty in young people's lives. A river or road of life was drawn that indicated the way in which uncertainty featured in the transitions of youth, with bumps in the road or rapids indicating problems and traffic signals or bridges as solutions or positives. The team had a set of open prompts to use with youth. The next section of the interview discussed relationships and how youth felt about themselves in relationship to others and the ideas of autonomy and freedom. The interview went on to discuss migration and the discussion depended on whether the young person or their family had experiences of migration although sometimes youth wanted to talk about migration as an aspiration because others had migrated or because they saw migrants as role models.

The next section of the interview was about the spaces and places that youth inhabited, moved around, and connected to in their lives. This could include a youth-led walk as a moving interview, but it was up to the preference of the young person as to how they wanted to show or talk about their environments and mobilities. The final section focused on the young person's understandings about marginalization. This also helped the team to snowball to identify other marginalized youth to interview.

Interviews with adults

In order to gain understanding on intergenerational perceptions on lives, circumstances, and uncertainties of youth, interviews were held with two groups of adults from their communities, one of mainly parents and guardians and the other of local stakeholders, people with influence. These interviews were also used as both verification of information given by youth and highlighting differences in perceptions, especially on uncertainty and changes over time.

Piloting with adults

Through piloting in Ethiopia and Nepal it was found preferable to carry out group interviews rather than participatory visual activities. Groups worked better when split by gender, and groups of stakeholders who held similar status or positions in the community worked best. During pilots in both countries, issues about youth were discussed, and research teams asked about experiences when adult participants were young and compared this to the lives and contexts for young people today. Perceptions of marginalization, vulnerability, violence, changing values, and uncertainty were discussed. What did they think about the future of their children and how does this compare to their generation? They were also asked about how they could support young people.

Small group interviews with adults

Partner organizations selected adults with the help of youth. They included parents, guardians, and other adults who are significant to young people in the sample. They aimed for an equal number of women and men, parents of the age group of the youth in the sample (15–24 years), so the age range of adults was 30 years plus.

Small group discussions involved 8 to 10 adults. Topics ranged from uncertainty in place and space to changes in growing up, relationships, and (adult) expectations of young people, changes in migration, education, employment, and differences in experiences between the period of youth of adults and today. Also changing perceptions of marginalization, vulnerability, violence, values, and uncertainty.

Key stakeholders

Interviews with stakeholders were conducted in groups or, as appropriate, with individuals. These primarily focused on regional and local policy and practice, and services. These were held with people who have power and influence in the community. For example, village and political leaders/elders/chiefs, religious leaders, government and non-governmental decision-makers and service providers, public sector services, social and youth movement leaders, women's group leaders, local journalists and media, head teachers and teachers, business leaders and employers.

Piloting with stakeholders

The Nepal team tested individual interviews and group interviews. The Ethiopian team conducted individual interviews to map local stakeholders. Rather than using visuals or participants writing, in both countries interviews were conducted, and learning from this process fed into planning key stakeholder engagement and youth seminars.

A 'stakeholder mapping' carried out in each research site with advice from partner organizations and reference group members identified key stakeholders to interview. This extended beyond government officials and services, key non-governmental/civil society organizations and services to include teachers, religious leaders, elders/chiefs, and community leaders.

Interviews with key stakeholders

Topics covered in interviews included policies, programmes, and interventions relating to youth, uncertainties and changing contexts, who are marginalized young people and their problems, mechanisms of participation for youth, resources and services available for young people and their accountability processes, changes in social norms and perceptions of traditions.

Analysis

The team conducted thematic team analysis, building on the six steps suggested by Braun and Clarke (2006) and ensuring a full, rigorous, and agreed process across national and international teams. This was embedded in the methodology guide and built upon at full team meetings.

In the analysis the team used a combination of detailed field diaries in which they recorded ethnographic information about their observations and their reflections on interactions and interviews. They had recordings of all interviews to replay and to double-check quotes and passages from the interviews. Although selected interviews were transcribed, there was also an analysis sheet for every interview and focus group discussion with youth, adults or stakeholders. These sheets enabled an ongoing process of pulling out relevant themes and quotes for every interview immediately after fieldwork had been carried out and also a systematic way to co-construct analysis in the field and for use in the online database. This helped to build thematic analysis from the bottom up, identify key issues and gendered analysis by site, across national contexts, and then also for the cross-country analysis.

All of the analysis sheets for 300 individual in-depth interviews were imported into an NVivo database and then agreed nodes from this themed analysis coded across all detailed youth case studies. These 300 interviews and the 200 additional case studies were also analysed using team-themed analysis as described above. Using qualitative computer analysis such as NVivo was not seen as an alternative to team-themed analysis but a way to systematically verify, triangulate, and add depth to the overall findings.

Building mechanisms to gain impact

The change-scape approach applied in this research specifically incorporates mechanisms that help research to gain impact (Johnson, 2015). These include creating participatory spaces at different levels to ensure that there is more interaction between youth themselves to share experiences and build confidence, and between youth and service providers and policy-makers so that they can have more interactive discourses to share innovative ideas. The teams of researchers planned these local, national, and international spaces and processes in cross-team interactions, in Nepal for inception and planning co-construction, in Ethiopia for analysis and planning impact, and in the UK for dissemination and further impact activities.

At national level, the methodology included not only individual interviews but spaces where youth worked together with the team to co-construct ideas about marginalization and uncertainty. There were focus groups as well as in-depth interviews so that youth could also build confidence and feel comfortable to express their opinions. At local level youth met groups of service providers and policy-makers at site level to verify information and discuss local support in Ethiopia, and to influence provincial government and community leaders in provincial youth seminars in Nepal. National Youth Seminars in both countries engaged marginalized youth with academics, service providers, and non-governmental and government officials, including from ministries, in both countries. This led to national level impact in terms of youth engaging with provincial and national policy formulation (Johnson et al., 2020b).

The strong long-term partnerships the research lead had built over many years with research partners in both countries were invaluable for both carrying out the research, especially in terms of access to the most-marginalized, and gaining impact (Johnson et al., 2019a). The national reference groups (see Acknowledgements) and tireless efforts of national team members and partners in feeding evidence from marginalized youth into practice and policy processes demonstrated strong commitments across the whole team to ensuring voices of marginalized youth are heard.

PART 2
Ethiopia

CHAPTER 4
Ethiopia: Context and themes

Ethiopia is well-known for its long independence, and its place in religious and human history, including a site of some of the earliest hominins found. The diverse population, with multiple ethnicities and languages, has also seen problems of drought and famine, sometimes associated with political change. Conflict and change in the late 20th into the early 21st century brought political change. In this chapter, the diverse population and its distribution in research locations is outlined along with a short background to the present social and political situation. A national youth policy implemented since 2004 is now subject to change. Youth perceptions of marginalization are outlined. The locations of four YOUR World research sites in Ethiopia and their characteristics are briefly described, followed by an outline of key themes in the research running across all findings in the Ethiopian research sites.

Keywords: Ethiopia context, population diversity, youth policy, political change

Introduction

Ethiopia is known for its geography, history of independence, and the site of some of the earliest hominins found. As the heart of the horn of Africa region, the country has a varied environment, with high mountains, low flatlands, and with a rich human past, including a long religious history highlighted by spectacular rock-hewn churches. The highlands were major centres of plant domestication and crop diversity, including the cereal *teff*, oil seed *nug*, narcotic *chat* (or *khat*), perhaps finger millet, and arguably coffee (Pankhurst, 1998: 7). Long before this domestication, the region was the site of early passages of humans out of Africa to the Middle East, with fossil remains of *Australopithecus afarensis* known in Ethiopia as *Denkenesh* (and in Northern countries best known as 'Lucy'). These are 3.2 million years old, found in the Awash valley: *Denkenesh* means 'you are marvellous' in Amharic.

The environment has very varied temperatures (icy cold high mountains, temperate highlands, torrid lowlands) and huge differences in rainfall (torrential highlands, parched, almost waterless lowlands). This variety led to different human economic activities, with agriculture (plant domestication in the highlands) and pastoralism (in the lowlands) as well as hunting and handicrafts (Pankhurst, 1998: 6–7). The ravines, rivers, and flash-torrents, especially in the rainy season, hindered communication in the past and 'resulted in the perpetuation of many different ethnic, linguistic and religious groups, which, although often significantly interacting, were over the millennia never fully assimilated' (Pankhurst, 1998: 7). Two principal language groups are Semitic, in the north and centre of the state, and Cushitic in the south, with some Omotic languages in the south-west, and Nilo-Saharan to the west. These groups include a number of languages, which indicates aspects of a population diversity including over 80 ethnic groups in the 2007 census, although Oromo and Amhara ethnicities account for over 60 per cent of the total population. The three main monotheistic religions are represented in Ethiopia.

Ethiopia is the oldest independent country in Africa, and second largest in population. It has a history of problems with drought and some famine, which was also associated with the onset of civil conflict in the late part of the 20th century.

Changes in government occurred during the research period. Protests led to a State of Emergency being declared in October 2016, which affected communication and travel in-country. In February 2018 the Prime Minister resigned, and his replacement, installed in April, lifted the State of Emergency, released political prisoners, and embarked on a programme of reform. This process will potentially affect the lives of young people in particular. This chapter provides a brief background to the diversity and categories of people, languages, conflict, and governance, and situates the research sites, issues, and findings.

People

The population of Ethiopia in 2020 was estimated at 115 million and, with nearly 40 per cent aged under-15 years, is mainly young (UNFPA, 2020). This is an increase of some 41 million people since the 2007 census recorded nearly 74 million people (73,918,505) with just over 50 per cent male (37,296,657) and just under half female (36,621,848). The 2007 census found an increase of some 20 million people since the previous 1994 census, which had in turn recorded an increase of 13 million people in the previous 10 years, from nearly 40 million people (FDRE-PCC, 2008). The population has nearly trebled over the past 36 years.

At that time, 'eighty percent of the population of the country was found in the three biggest regional states, namely: Oromia, Amhara, and Southern Nations, Nationalities, and People's Region (SNNPR) both in 1994 and 2007' (FDRE-PCC, 2008: 10). Amhara had 17.2 million people (23.3 per cent), Oromia 27.1 million people (36.7 per cent), and SNNPR 15 million people (20.4 per cent). The names of these states indicate some of the ethnic and linguistic diversity of Ethiopia. Although there are over 80 ethnicities identified in Ethiopia, 10 groups form the bulk of the population, and four account for some three-quarters of the total. Figures from 2007 indicate proportions. The largest group, Oromo, over 25 million people (34.5 per cent); second largest Amhara, nearly 20 million (26.9 per cent); and then Somali (4.5 million) and Tigrie (4.4 million) at 6.2 and 6.1 per cent, respectively

(FDRE-PCC, 2008: 16). In 2007 the Sidama numbered 2.9 million (4 per cent), and a further five groups had populations between 1 and 2 million: Guragie, Welaita, Hadiya, Afar, and Gamo, each accounting for 1.5–2.5 per cent (FDRE-PCC, 2008: 16).

The principal locations of the largest ethnicities are indicated in the names of regions, Oromia and Somali in the south and west, Amhara and Tigray and also Afar in the north. There are also linguistic differences, although both largest groups are part of the same language family, Oromifa being a Cushitic (also Sidamo and Hadiya) and Amharic (also Tigrie and Guragie) a Semitic language. Although the Cushitic speakers are principally in the south and Semitic in the north, pockets of each are found in other places (Pankhurst, 1998: 8).

The vast majority of the population are Christian and Muslim, proportions indicated by the 2007 census. Orthodox Christians (32.1 million, 43.5 per cent) form the largest religious group, also with Protestant (13.7 million, 18.6 per cent) and Catholic (0.5 million, 0.7 per cent) denominations. Muslims make up a third of the population (25 million, 33.9 per cent). Traditional religions, mainly practised in rural areas, accounted for nearly 2 million people (2.6 per cent) with less than half a million (471,000, 0.6 per cent) other religions (FDRE-PCC, 2008: 18). This last category includes Falashas, a small Judaic group (also known as Beta Esra'el) scattered in the north and north-west, generally following occupations held in low repute regardless of the practitioners' religious affiliation (Pankhurst, 1998: 8–9). Although the main religions are widespread, there are some concentrations, for example, Muslims forming the greater majority in Somali and Afar regions. There has been peaceful coexistence between followers of the two main religions in the country over many years. Ethnicity, rather than religion, has been associated with some civil conflict in the country, for example, through secessionist movements and anti-government protests. The rivalry has tended to be between elite and political leaders rather than between the communities in Ethiopia.

Background

A new Prime Minister was installed in April 2018, adopting new policies and so marking a shift in government. This also signalled an end to a round of anti-government protests, several months of which had led government to declare a State of Emergency in October 2016. Protests had continued, despite internet shut-downs, and in February 2018 the then Prime Minister Hailemariam Desalegn resigned. The new Prime Minister, Abiy Ahmed, grew up in the Oromo community, with a mother from Amhara and father from Oromo. He gained popular support among the Amhara and Oromo when he came into power although some tensions have flared up due to perceptions of Oromo nationalism which date back to the 1970s when a number of Liberation Fronts were formed in opposition to the military-led government.

Agreements made with neighbouring colonized countries around the start of the 20th century framed the country borders, following Ethiopia's defeat of invading Italian forces at Adwa in 1896, while processes of modernization also began in these last decades of Emperor Menelik II, who died in 1913 (Pankhurst, 1998: 194–5). The Italians again invaded in the reign of Ras Tafari Makonnen, who became Emperor Haile Selassie I in 1930. The occupation was defeated and Haile Selassie restored in 1941. A military coup overthrew and imprisoned the Emperor in 1974, following a famine in which hundreds of thousands died. Thousands of citizens seen as opponents to the regime were subsequently tortured and killed in the late 1970s.

The end of the highly centralized government 'led to the emergence of a number of ethnically based regional liberation parties, or movements. The most important spoke in the name of the Tegray, Afar, Oromo, and Somali peoples' (Pankhurst, 1998: 275). These were held off by the armies of Colonel Mengistu Hailemariam. Although a coup against Mengistu failed in 1989, in 1991 the Ethiopian People's Revolutionary Democratic Front captured Addis Ababa, and he secretly left the country by plane on 21 May. He was convicted of genocide in 2006 (absent from the country).

In 1994 a new constitution divided the country into ethnically based regions and a decade later a resettlement programme started to move some 2 million people away from parched highlands. The Prime Minister since 1995, Meles Zenawi, died in 2012 and was succeeded by Hailemariam Desalegn. He remained in post until February 2018, facing increasing anti-government protests, and declaring the State of Emergency in 2016. Abiy Ahmed became leader of the ruling Ethiopian People's Revolutionary Democratic Front, and Prime Minister.

The new government of February 2018 lifted the State of Emergency and released political prisoners in May–June. Also during that year some other long-standing conflicts ceased: the war with Eritrea declared over, and a peace deal made with the separatist Ogaden National Liberation Front. However, other conflicts have arisen or reappeared, particularly with the Tigray Region in 2020. In June 2019 an attempted coup was put down.

The government of Abiy Ahmed began a reform programme, which aimed to include proposals for changed youth policy, as explained by government representatives at the National Youth Seminar run by YOUR World Research with the Ministry of Women, Children and Youth and research partners CHADET in March 2019.

Youth policy and marginalization

YOUR World Research works with young people whose age ranges from 15 to 24, but youth policy age ranges differ in Ethiopia (and Nepal). The 2004 National Youth Policy in Ethiopia defines youth as the age category of 15–29 (MYSC, 2004). According to the 2007 census the proportion aged 14 to 29 accounts for 42.41 per cent of the population of the country, of which the majority (26.04 per cent) are aged 14 to 19 years, locally generally seen as the period of transition from childhood to early adulthood.

Youth were said to have been neglected for two decades after 1991, and at the forefront of public unrest that led to government change in early 2018. One source of discontent was youth unemployment, at a rate of around one-fifth. It increased from 16.90 per cent in 2016 to 19.10 per cent in 2018 and was still rising according to the Central Statistical Agency of Ethiopia. In launching a reform agenda, the State Minister of the Ministry of Finance specifically mentioned youth.

> Ethiopia's economy was driven by a massive investment outlay from the side of the government in the past decade and half, resulting in a fast and continuous economic growth over the indicated period. But, the economy encountered various structural and sectoral hindrances that made it difficult to sustain the pace with which it was growing. Therefore, the government is embarking upon a new economic reform which aims to capitalize on the potential of the youth and the private sector in Ethiopia, both said to be curtailed from playing a major role in the economy in the past two decades (Abdu, 2019).

The 2004 National Youth Policy was the first youth development framework in Ethiopia. Its stated objective is to empower youth to contribute to build a democratic system and good governance through active participation, but noting problems of social exclusion. A policy implementation manual was published in 2005. The then Ministry of Youth and Sports also prepared a series of guidelines to govern translation of the policy into practice, an administrative manual for basic and small-range skills trainings for youth, separate development packages for urban and rural youth , a national framework of life-skills training for youth, a training manual to accompany the national life-skills framework, and standards for youth voluntary services (MYS, 2005, 2006a, b, c, 2008, 2010, 2011). In recent years, 2,850 youth centres were established across the country to a set of standards (MYS, 2006d/2008), of which 1,545 were reported to be functional. Youth centres include library, café, healthcare, hall, in-door and out-door games, ICT, bathroom, art, trainings, guidance and counselling services, gym, voluntary services, mini media, creativity and lab centre, and shopping services.

Youth marginalization

Traditionally marginalization in Ethiopia has been thought of as being located on the country peripheries but YOUR World Research found young people experiencing marginalization at the centre of communities. In the research, working with some main ethnic groups including Oromo and Amhara, young people helped reconceptualize understandings of their everyday lives. They showed that marginalization for them includes experiences such as having to drop out of school, take up exploitative or uncertain employment, and face a necessity to migrate internally and internationally – sometimes without success. Some of these experiences are the consequences of abuse and discrimination in their own families or in communities they come from or travel to, including being affected by HIV. Young people find marginalization is further exacerbated because of their age and other status (such as gender and disability), which means that through social conventions they are generally not listened to and their concerns are overlooked or ignored, so their problems are not addressed.

Research locations

Research was conducted in two urban and two rural locations, selected through discussion with partners (national government officers, academics, non-government organization staff). These locations were chosen as having been affected by past conflict and environmentally fragile. These areas include different ethnicities and religions, to explore how different processes of marginalization and varying vulnerabilities affect uncertainty among young people.

The research locations in Ethiopia are in the regions of Oromia and Amhara, and the capital city Addis Ababa. As noted above, these two regions combined have around 60 per cent of the total population. In Oromia region, the location was the rural area of Hetosa, predominantly Muslim and affected by drought and with high out-migration to the capital and increasingly internationally. In Amhara region, the location was Fogera District, comprising the rural area of Fogera and urban Woreta, which are conflict-affected, predominantly Christian, and with high levels of seasonal and international migration. The sub-city of Addis Ketema in Addis Ababa is multi-ethnic, and its large market and bus station make it a national economic and transit hub.

Rural Fogera and urban Woreta

Fogera Woreda is a District (*Woreda*, also *Wereda*) in South Gondar Zone, and Woreta is the administrative centre of this District, which now has separate status. The research focused on rural parts of Fogera District (referred to here as Fogera) and the growing urban area of Woreta.

Fogera and Woreta are situated in Amhara Region, a large region which lies north of Addis Ababa, in the north of Ethiopia and extending to the Sudan border in the west. The Region is divided into zones. Fogera and Woreta are located in South Gondar Zone, which to its west borders Lake Tana, the largest lake in the country and the source of the Blue Nile.

Amhara Region, in 2007, had a population of 17.2 million, with 2.1 million in urban places and the majority, 15.1 million, living in rural areas. Most of the population are Orthodox Christians (14.2 million in 2007) with 2.9 million Muslims and several thousand following other Christian denominations, traditional religions, and other faiths (PCC, 2008).

South Gondar Zone, in 2007, had a population of 2 million, with 1.8 million living in rural areas. Although the total population showed some 30,000 fewer females than males, the urban population showed the female population to be larger than males by 4,000, with a corresponding depletion in the rural population (PCC, 2008).

Fogera Woreda or District in 2007 had a total population of 226,595, but the figures showed a similar disparity to South Gondar Zone with nearly 5,000 fewer females than males. The total urban population of the District at that time, 25,184 people, again has more females (500 more) than males, and also with a corresponding reduction in the rural population. Most of the population of the District are Orthodox Christian and of the Amhara group.

Woreta was established as a town in 1947. It was the capital of the District of Fogera until 2006 when it gained semi-autonomous status for self-governance. The town is 65 km to the north of the city of Bahir Dar, the capital of Amhara Region, close to Lake Tana. The altitude of the town and surrounds is 1,500–2,500 metres above sea level.

Woreta town lies on the main highway through South Gondar to the North. The processes of urbanization are evident in the census record indicating shifts of women to move away from rural areas and seek work in town. Woreta is a transit town, and has attraction to many children and young people who are on the move as migrant casual workers, daily labourers, domestic workers, and café and restaurant workers.

The key problem for young people in rural Fogera derives from their landlessness, related to scarcity of land, but also to allocation of land by elders. This and the lack of alternative employment leads to out-migration, and the town of Woreta is the closest destination which, through rapid urbanization, offers work in the informal sector, albeit often exploitative. The movements of young people, and the position of Woreta as a transit town, indicates how these two sites are closely interconnected, yet their rural and urban characteristics ensure distinct and different social and cultural lives.

Hetosa

Hetosa Woreda is situated in Oromia Region, which is the largest region in Ethiopia, extending both south (to the Kenyan border) and west (to the Sudan border) from Addis Ababa. Hetosa is located in Arsi Zone, in the centre of the Region.

Oromia Region, in 2007, had a population of 27.1 million, with 3.3 million in urban places and the majority, 23.7 million, living in rural areas. In terms of religion, in 2007, the population was divided between Christian (13.2 million) and Muslim (12.8 million) with several hundred thousand following traditional and other practices. The majority of Christians were Orthodox (8.2 million) with large Protestant (4.8 million) and smaller Catholic (0.1 million) communities (PCC, 2008). Across the region, agriculture is the dominant sector of the economy which provides foodstuffs, industrial raw materials, generates employment, and accounts for the largest share of the export items from the region. Oromia has fertile and irrigable arable land, and climatic conditions suitable for growth of different agricultural products (Oromia BOFED, 2014). Although the region has good agricultural potential, soil erosion due to exploitative activities such as deforestation, over-cultivation, and bad farming practices is a threat. Information on the situation of drought is scarce, but it is reported that the region is affected by drought almost every 10 years (Oromia BOFED, 2013).

Arsi Zone, in 2007, had a population of 2.6 million, with 2.3 million living in rural areas. The total population showed nearly 9,000 fewer females than males, with this gap predominantly in rural areas (PCC, 2008). Arsi Zone is considered as a food self-sufficient zone, although there are households with problems of food insecurity, the severity of which varies from year to year depending on rainfall. It also varies from district to district, because all districts are not equally vulnerable to drought (Oromia BOFED, 2011). The major economic problems of this zone include low productivity of agricultural sectors, high unemployment, vulnerability to drought, and family lack of experience in non-farm income generation. Major environmental problems are high soil erosion due to high deforestation, over-grazing, over-cultivation, and misuse of land resources; the main cause of environmental degradation is population pressure. Other social problems derive from inequalities, lack of training, low coverage of clean water, and lack of health services (Oromia BOFED, 2011).

Hetosa Woreda in 2007 had a population of 124,179, with only some 700 more males than females. The urban population was 18,478, and here there were nearly 400 more females than males. Correspondingly in the rural population, of 105,701, there were over 1,000 more males than females. Hetosa District has mountain ranges, highland plateau, and low plain areas in the rift valley with altitudes varying between 4,079 m and 1,736 m.

In the District, grazing land, natural forest, and fallow lands are decreasing while cultivated, human-made forest, and residential lands are increasing. Major annual crops in the district are cereals (mainly barley, teff, wheat, maize), pulses, and oil seeds. Cash crops (tomato, onion, carrot, sugar cane) may be grown. But agricultural activities are seasonal and many households seek alternative living strategies. Even during the main season, some farmers do not fully engage in agricultural work due to socio-cultural ceremonies. Cropping is characterized by one short, single season per year. But the consequence of engaging in rain-fed agriculture in a drought-prone environment is that households face substantial risk. Youth out-migration is not uncommon in Hetosa. Migration in Hetosa District is part of diversification strategies used by households to deal with risks such as shrinking land sizes, insufficient agricultural income, or job insecurity in the local non-farm sector. In addition, migration and remittances seem to be more easily accessible than other non-farm activities (Asnakech, 2014).

Addis Ketema

Addis Ketema is one of 11 sub-cities (one added in 2020) that make up the Ethiopian capital Addis Ababa, which is a chartered city and so considered to be both city and state, equivalent to a region. It is one of the largest cities in the world located in a landlocked country. Addis Ababa is situated in the centre of the country, and surrounded by Oromia region. The city lies on a plateau at an altitude of 2,440 metres, surrounded by hills and mountains. The total population, in 2007, was 2.7 million, with considerably more female (1.4 million) than male (1.3 million) residents. Projections of the Addis Ababa population in 2015, based on the 2007 census, estimated 3,384,569 people. In recent years the city has seen a robust annual population growth rate, and consequently in 2017, the projected population was estimated to have grown closer to 4 million persons. Even this figure is highly contested and some estimate far higher numbers.

The population of Addis Ketema sub-city in 2007 was 255,092, with some 6,000 more female (130,351) than male (124,741) residents. This will have grown accordingly, in line with projections that estimate the sub-city population in 2015 to have been 297,793 (144,954 males and 152,839 females), showing an increase of 2,000 female over male residents.

Addis Ketema is one of four smaller sub-cities located in the centre of Addis Ababa. Addis Ketema covers an area of 8.64 kilometres and is itself divided into 10 Woredas. The research was mainly conducted with young people in Woredas seven and nine. These districts cover a highly peopled slum area, where the population density is 37,488 persons per square kilometre.

The majority of residents in Addis Ketema work as daily labourers, civil servants, or businesspeople. Commercial sex work is also common partly due to the influx of increasing numbers of people from different parts of the country, arriving there for various reasons, including trade and transit. It has the biggest bus station in the country which in itself makes it a destination point as well as a place for easy transit. But Addis Ketema is a destination for many people because it is seen as a commercial core of the country, in which 'Merkato', the largest open-air market in the continent, is located.

The sub-city is home to many youth who work and live around the city bus station and the market. The key focus of the research in Addis Ketema was young people who are street-connected or living in street situations (see Chapter 17). Many of them were migrants from different parts of the country who had moved to escape from difficult situations, such as exploitative relationships in urban settings, after migration or death of parents and seeking freedom. Family breakdown and economic problems are the main reasons pushing many young people to live in the streets. Street-connected youth survive through begging, food scavenging, commercial sex work, collecting garbage, and other informal activities. They mostly sleep on the surrounds of the train station, garbage dump sites, verandas, doorways, and roundabouts in the surrounding areas.

The research findings revealed a tense relationship between police and street-connected young people. Labelling, which relates street-connected young people with theft, commercial sex work, and often addiction, is common. Street-connected young people contest local government's perception of them as passive recipients and/or beneficiaries of outcomes of development interventions. The research generally shows the impressive resourcefulness of street-connected young people in their resilience and adoption strategy. They can contribute and play a leading role in the preparation of interventions and projects concerning their life.

Themes in the research

Some main themes run through the research. Formal education is failing the most-marginalized; there is a need to support and protect them in work in the informal sector. Migration out of fragile areas is intensifying, including internationally. There is a need to address street-connections and situations for youth including issues of conflict with the law and substance use. Disability was raised by youth across the research in Ethiopia as being a reason for marginalization, whether young people themselves were living with disabilities or caring for others. In each of these main thematic areas young people creatively navigate uncertainty and offer innovative solutions and suggestions for support.

Relevant education, employment, and the informal sector

Across all four sites, formal education was found to have failed many marginalized youth because of its lack of relevance for their lives and circumstances, costs and pressures of combining domestic work and school. Many had dropped out of school or failed national exams (at 8th and 10th grade, a turning point for vocational and further education). Instead of seeing formal education as a solution to finding a job, being able to meet expectations of adults, and support their families, young people see successful international migrants as role models. These issues are discussed throughout Part Two, and in Chapter 19. Dropping out or failing at school was noted by youth as being an important issue both during co-construction and in subsequent snowballing to find the most-marginalized (see Chapter 3).

Young people continue to migrate seasonally and internally in search of work but increasingly seek alternative and creative employment in the informal sector or through international migration. Sometimes their attempts to find creative ways to make money end in exploitative or even unlawful work which they feel ashamed about and try to hide from families. Youth desperately want support to develop their skills and for setting up informal enterprises so that they can find alternative ways to support their families by staying in the country. Even when they have tried setting up enterprises with peer groups, when they have reached urban destinations through internal migration, they often find difficulties and feel they are working against the odds. For example, they meet barriers from authorities to working on the streets or face problems from adults who discriminate against them if they are street-connected.

Internal and international migration

Seasonal and internal migration is often a main feature of the lives of marginalized youth and families across Ethiopia. In Hetosa (Chapter 7), a fragile environment combined with threats of early marriage and abduction of young women have increased youth migration as an escape out of the area. Young people are also increasingly migrating from Fogera (Chapter 5) in the northern Amhara district in search of employment in plantations in the north of the country. Small towns like Woreta become transit 'corridor towns' with increasing numbers of youth seeking alternative futures so that they can provide for their families. But the services in these towns cannot support the numbers of youth seeking work, and many become street-connected and then turn to substance abuse when their endeavours in the informal sector are not successful.

The lure of international migration has been increasing because of limited opportunities and lack of support in the informal sector for the most-marginalized young people in urban centres. This may now change with increasing space given to listen to youth and developments in youth policy in the country after recent political changes (see Adugna, 2018; Tadele and Ayalew, 2018; also Chapter 16 for analysis on migration across YOUR World Research).

Street-connection and substance use

Youth who migrate to urban sites of Woreta (Chapter 6) and Addis Ketema (Chapter 8) do so with the best of intentions and aspirations to find different ways to meet adult expectations and to support their families. Far from breaking family and traditional community bonds, they want to feel proud of what they can contribute. (See Chapter 17 for further discussion on youth living in street situations across YOUR World Research.)

Many urban marginalized youth have grown up in towns or cities or migrated to them in search of better futures. They told their life-stories and how they ended up connected to the streets. For some this involved escape from abuse and discrimination within their families and communities. Others felt heavy expectations to provide for families in the face of high unemployment, landlessness, fragility in the environment, or simply that they sought to emulate role models who are successful migrants. On the street young men and women can feel insecure, out of control of their lives, and uncertain how to earn a living or just survive day-to-day. Some youth living and working on the street find it hard to survive on low incomes and turn to exploitative work, for example commercial sex work and/or the use of substances to relieve their difficulties.

Youth living with disability

The issues that youth raised about living with disability emerged from the research as a key aspect of marginalization across the Ethiopian research sites. In the inception phase, the research team were not necessarily expecting to work on how youth confronted their disabilities or their caring responsibilities. The team had decided to include disability within coding and questions asked when introducing the research and gaining informed consent, but this became an emergent theme from discussions about the most-marginalized in the snowballing approach to sampling in research sites (see Chapter 3). The Ethiopian team later used the youth profiles coding to follow up young people living with disability. Several videos were made to show their lived experiences and how youth felt about processes of marginalization they associated with disability. This coincided with international funder and national government priorities around inclusivity in policy formulation and became a theme of the final National Youth Seminar held by the Ethiopian team with the Ministry of Women, Children and Youth (see Johnson et al., 2020b; also Chapter 15 for examples of the youth declaration on living with disability, and Chapter 18 on living with disability across the research).

CHAPTER 5
Rural Fogera: Land shortages, adult status, and migration

Marginalized young people in the rural areas of Fogera Woreda, in northern Ethiopia, face land shortages and landlessness, involvement in domestic and farm work from childhood, school drop-out and examination failure, and work in the informal sector that is often exploitative. The expected transition to adult status as they grow up falters since attributes of adult status, such as marriage and supporting a family, are affected by landlessness and work availability. Their suspended social transition causes some youth to abuse alcohol and other substances. Consequently, these uncertainties are met by many young people seeking employment and funds through migration internally, and often internationally, although they often find the next stage of movement is not as positive as was expected. They find that return from migration, even with funds, may be disappointing, and still face rejection, leading to suggestions for local development in terms of education and alternatives to agricultural livelihoods.

Keywords: Fogera, Ethiopia, land shortages, landlessness, early marriage, adult status, migration, return uncertainty

Introduction

Fogera Woreda is a principally rural District (*Woreda*), located in northern Ethiopia, in the South Gondar Zone of Amhara Region. This chapter focuses on the experiences, circumstances, lives, and aspirations of marginalized young people living in rural parts of the District. While agriculture remains the major means of local livelihood, environmental problems, landlessness, and various other intertwined factors create situations and pressures on marginalized youth to migrate away from rural living to nearby urban areas and beyond. In rural areas marginalized young people experience problems in education, including attending school, in the work that is available and through varied social expectations depending on their age, gender, and (dis)ability. If they do migrate, in the urban areas where they arrive, although their circumstances have changed they often still face various issues and problems. These problems of migrants may also be based on perceptions and expectations of their abilities, for example concerning availability of work, discrimination, gender, and often lead to further difficulties (as described in later chapters on Woreta and Addis Ketema). The administrative, urban centre of Fogera Woreda, to which many marginalized young people migrate, is the town of Woreta and is the focus of Chapter 6.

Fogera Woreda, the whole District, has 33 *Kebeles*, the smallest administrative units in Ethiopia, which usually consist of around 500 families, comprising several thousand individuals. The majority of these Kebeles are rural (28) with only five urban Kebeles in Fogera Woreda. The population of the Woreda was 226,595 in 2007 (see Chapter 4) of which 51 per cent were male and 49 per cent female. The Woreda is largely inhabited by the Amhara ethnic group. Most of the people are Orthodox Christian.

In rural Fogera researchers worked with over 65 youth, producing detailed case studies with 30 of the most-marginalized young people aged 15–24 years. Participants in the research from Fogera were predominantly from a single ethnicity, Amhara, and religion (Orthodox Christian) as is representative for the area. In addition to the views of young people, the perspectives of local adults and stakeholders on the situation of youth were collected. The participant sample and criteria of marginalization and vulnerability were developed through the inception and piloting phase of the project (see Chapter 3 on Method and Chapter 4 on the Fogera and Ethiopian context).

This chapter looks at the living situation of marginalized young people, and strategies to deal with uncertainties generated through land shortages, early marriage, expectations of family, problems in making transitions to adult status, and consequent migration and return.

Living situation of marginalized youth in rural Fogera

Agriculture is the basis for rural life in much of Fogera Woreda, and a central concern affecting the lives of marginalized young people and their families is access to land. There are two major issues arising from this: first, for those with access to land, that of labour to work it; and second, the problem of landlessness, alongside which runs the problem of unemployment.

The problems of access to land use, land shortages and landlessness, and particularly unemployment have further consequences for the ways in which children and young people make a transition to the varied elements that comprise adult status, including work, the ability to support family, decision-making, and the option of marriage and availability of spouses. The question of adult status, particularly through income, work, and employment, is further affected by education levels which are in turn dependent on attendance at school. Non-attendance and dropping out of school is a problem for many marginalized young people, as is failure in national examinations for those who do stay on.

The outcome of how these factors interplay, and the particular living situation of marginalized young people, especially in terms of family circumstances and expectations, often results in out-migration from rural areas to local urban locations. Although seen as a solution by many left-behind marginalized youth and their families, life in urban areas may not provide employment or the income wanted, and other problems are often faced (see Chapter 6). Many young people subsequently attempt or accomplish international migration in order to find work and gain status. Yet social conventions restrict mobility for many young women, even in their neighbourhood.

> I couldn't freely move in this area as I am female. The society has limited freedom of movement for females. I faced rejection and negative comments by the society. Females are supposed to work at home and if they are found going around they would be commented to stay at home based on the culture. I have received negative comments while moving around which made me to limit my daily mobility. (Mastewal, female, 25)

A further dimension is the marginalization of children and young people with disabilities. They experience marginalization through inaccessibility of places, including school, but also peer bullying and lack of support, and discrimination. They may also want to migrate, but find additional barriers. Furthermore, if they do migrate, they experience isolation through lack of social contact, and difficulties accessing services (see Chapters 16 and 17). The experiences and paths of marginalized children and young people in rural Fogera vary depending not only on family circumstances, but also age, gender, and disability. This chapter focuses on the major underlying patterns, concerning land, work, education, and migration, which have differences by gender but further ramifications for boys and girls, young men and young women with disabilities.

> One of my regrets about my physical disability is I can't move and live in another place. I sometimes get frustrated as most of my friends moved to big cities like Bahir Dar and Addis Ababa or moved out of Ethiopia. Here I have the support of my mother and the community as a whole. If I moved to other places I would have been a beggar. (Yeneneh, male, 28)

Agriculture and the land

Agriculture is a primary means of livelihood in rural Fogera, although much is essentially subsistence farming. The most-marginalized young people and their families are those with land shortages and landlessness. Access to land is at the root of many of the circumstances that underpin and characterize the lives of marginalized youth and their families. Shortage of land affects family abilities to produce and sustain livelihoods, but also impacts young people gaining status through their ability to inherit or be allocated land. Land shortages and landlessness initiates marginalization, affects the whole family, and increases dependency on employment, even for those with some land access. Children may be taken out of school to work family land so others can be employed elsewhere, or taken out for employment outside their family. Missing education through work affects their options and opportunities for future employment. Land shortages and landlessness and the question of inheritance also impact status and marriage for young people moving into adulthood.

> The soil in our area is fertile. We produce twice a year. However, the problem is that there is acute shortage of land in our kebele. There are some youth who formed a collective group and were given part of the community grazing land in the kebele. I didn't get that chance which means that the only means of obtaining land for me is from my parents. But it's difficult for my parents to redistribute land for their seven children. Now my two elder brothers are on their way to get married. My parents have the responsibility of providing each of their children with a plot of land. So it's better for me to work as a daily labourer and support myself. (Yosef, male, 20)

Children's and young people's rural informal sector work

Many marginalized young people have been employed informally from their childhood onwards. Shortage of land, and also because it is largely subsistence farming means that families with small plots of land use their children's labour to diversify their income. They may negotiate the employment of their young children to better-off households to herd cattle, engage in farming or in domestic work.

Girls and young women are mostly employed as domestic workers in their community, while boys and young men are employed to herd cattle. Those young people with an experience of such informal sector work, including domestic and farm work, reported many problems. These include abuse and violence from employers, being restricted from going to school including denial of primary education, and exploitation through a heavy workload with minimal pay.

> As my parents didn't have land they made me get employment formally from the age of 10. I worked for 10 years in 10 different households. My parents were the ones who negotiate on my behalf with landlords. I didn't get an opportunity to go to school. I rather work day and night for my employers with minimal payment. Besides, if the owners plant onion, it would be a very difficult task for me. I would be working day and night till harvesting. I would be resting once in a while in holy days. (Maru, male, 20)

Education and school

Many marginalized young people in rural Fogera Woreda have missed primary and secondary education, having not attended or dropped out of school for various reasons. Many reported their parents' reluctance to send children to school because of the need for their labour, in working family land or employment by other families. Some were enrolled late, which affected their performance alongside peers. Many who did attend school subsequently had to drop out because of cost, access to materials, need for them to work, or pressure to marry young. Marginalized children and families found formal education unaffordable or restricted and impractical because of limited access to a library and availability of books. These problems reinforce practices of children working and earning, including attempts to use children's earnings to pay for education. They may also reinforce decisions on early marriage, which mostly affects girls and young women.

> My parents have 11 children. I am the second child. My mother was sick critically. Hence, I was responsible as an elder daughter to handle all the domestic chores. I used to fetch water, clean the house and cook, herd cattle and help my father in agricultural work. I dropped out in grade two in order to handle these domestic chores. (Lisan, female, 20)

Children who have completed primary education and who want to move on to secondary school may face additional difficulties. Secondary schools are located in towns, so youth from poor rural family backgrounds engage in informal work to cover costs of living. Combining work and school is a challenge, and gives limited study time outside school.

> I struggle to continue until grade 8. When I am enrolled to grade 9 there comes the biggest decision. The high school is far from our village and I have to go there, rent house, stay there for the week days while returning back on the weekends. I have to choose between my family and my school. (Mekibib, male, 22)

Some migration for school is unsuccessful and then youth are reluctant to return. They, and others who fail in secondary education (as also do many of those who failed after migrating in an attempt to find work), feel that parents may reject them for having left and failed.

> My parents decided that I should get married at the age of 13. With a lot of struggle, I was able to complete grade 8. Then I moved to Woreta Town for grade 9 and 10. The struggles in Woreta were too many ... I came back to my parents. (Haimanot, female, 19)

Children and young people who do manage to combine work with schooling, may still fail to score a pass mark in the National Examination in grade 10. This perceived failure in education, despite the investment of time and earnings, not only affects young people's potential opportunities, but further reinforces notions that school and education are irrelevant to the lives of marginalized children and young people, especially with other pressures on how their days can be used and worked. Thus, this National Examination is a source of considerable uncertainty and reported as a barrier in young people's school journey, but formal education is also seen as irrelevant. School lessons are thought to lack appropriate content or applicability to young people's daily activities.

> As I couldn't prepare myself for the national school leaving exam well, I scored a grade point average of 2.14 which was not good enough for me to join the preparatory school. Only 12 students out of a total of 42 passed the exam. I came back to my parents. There is no training or other alternatives for those of us who failed in 10th grade school leaving national exams. (Martha, female, 19)

Although young people whose national exam results are too low to join public higher learning institutions often seek alternatives to attend private colleges by paying tuition fees, this is not possible for marginalized youth. Many young people in Fogera Woreda have farmer parents who cannot afford to pay private college fees, so instead they look to migration to urban places for work as a key strategy.

> I managed to sit for the 10th grade national exam, but I couldn't score a passing mark. I failed to join a preparatory school. I had no money for a private college. Hence I was forced to stay at home. I do not know what to do to get out of this situation. I am perplexed. I am thinking of migrating to the Middle East. (Martha, female, 22)

Transitions to adult status

Land shortages, landlessness, and limited alternative work opportunities cause problems for the conventions of young people's social transitions to adulthood, including work, income, and marriage, and which have further impact on divorce and migration.

Social conventions require obedience to elders and this, along with economic dependency on parents, is mentioned as a reason for lack of autonomy and freedom to make decisions, which has an impact on marriage and future life of young people.

> Youth who are disobedient for their parents are seen as deviants who don't abide by the community norms and rules. (Nardos, female, 19)

> As it was a marriage arranged by parents the newly married couple met at the marriage ceremony. Land is the main source of livelihood of the people in the community. However, average household land holdings are less than half a hectare. The newlyweds didn't have any agricultural land of their own. In the old days they ought to have received land from their respective parents. The marriage lasted only for a year and came to an end because of lack of agricultural land or any other alternative means of making a living for the couple. (Demeke, male, 25)

While some older children and young people, particularly female, face pressures from parents for early marriage when an opportunity arises, and may seek to resist this, others want to marry for different reasons, apparently including an aim to escape domestic work burdens, but don't necessarily find their situation has improved after marriage. Yet, as with perceptions of failed migration, subsequent divorce from early marriage may also lead to family and community rejection, as will refusal to obey parents' wishes to get married young.

> My parents started to pressurize me to marry young. I refused to accept their proposal. However, I am considered as a deviant for making the decision by myself. I don't have enough money to marry now. (Markos, male, 24)

The certainty of poverty in Fogera, exacerbated by landlessness and the absence of off-farming livelihood opportunities, has created a barrier for many young people to attain the social attributes of adulthood. Adult status is locally attributed by getting married, having capacity to support their family economically and start an independent life. Since land is an essential resource that young people are assumed to inherit upon marriage, many marginalized youth reported having feelings and perceptions of uncertainty about their future because of shortage of land and poor family background. Shortages of land and alternative employment present a particular problem in rural Kebeles of Fogera where land is regarded as an essential asset for marriage. This has resulted in a range of problems, including divorce among young married couples, and also led to migration.

> My parents didn't have land and it was very difficult for them to raise six children. My elder siblings started working in their childhood to make money. I grew up helping my parents in domestic chores. I used to herd cattle too. I got married at the age of 15 without my consent. My husband didn't have land. I decided to divorce him as I didn't want to have another child in that situation. I have a 9 years old daughter. I faced rejection for divorcing my husband. I rather insisted on ending that relationship. I am now a single mother and make money by selling local alcoholic drinks. (Mastewal, female, 24)

The issue of land means that young people whose parents are landless are unlikely to get married, which creates uncertainty about their status and future.

> It became mandatory to have land to get married. My sister got divorced as she was given a small plot of land from my parents. My parents remained landless. No one is going to marry me. I wish I could move out from this place where land isn't a requirement for marriage. (Mare, female, 20)

Such uncertainties over status, combined with unemployment, along with lack of recreational space and peer influence, led many marginalized young men to start using drug-related substances such as *khat* and alcohol. While this is a strategy to cope with feelings of uncertainty due to a suspended social transition, it also acts to further disrupt that transition through its effect on young men's time and capacities. Alcohol use is common among young men, while many women produce and sell local alcoholic drinks as their livelihood. Young people say that the most-marginalized people in rural kebeles of Fogera are alcoholic. They also point to family conflict and stressed relationships because of alcohol consumption.

> My husband was contributing to the household income for the first three years. Then he became alcoholic over time. He also suspected me of having extra-marital relationships with my customers. I stopped selling drinks for some time to deal with this problem. He nags me and comes back home drunk. He beat me up every now and then. I decided to get separated from him. He moved to Bahir Dar for good. I began to sell local liquor again. (Zeritu, female, 26)

Migration

The problems experienced by marginalized young people in finding appropriate work and status locally means that many frequently turn to migration. This includes both local and distant internal migration as well as international migration. Young people say that uncertainties in finding local work, in gaining attributes of adult status, provide a 'push' factor in considering migration; uncertainties in what can be found at the destination provide a 'pull' factor, despite or because many families of those who do migrate already have migration experience. Furthermore, the initial part of the movement may be to a destination already known from family visits; the uncertainty concerns exactly what opportunity can be taken up there.

> I migrated to Bahir Dar town and worked as a domestic worker for three months. I had heavy workload and used to get sick too. I was paid 400 ETB a month for working day and night. I think it is worth migrating to Middle East as you would be paid better. The workload is the same. I need to migrate and make money to help my family. I know there are brokers who facilitate your migration on loan. I heard people saying that I should be 23 years old to be legally eligible for migration. I am now 20. I will migrate after some time. However, I didn't gather enough information about the process and life in the Middle East yet. I saw return youth migrants from Middle East. They have a different character. They easily get angry. I might also face difficult circumstances in the Middle East too. But I believe in holy water, I could get healed if I faced problems that affect the state of my mental health. (Litifwork, female, 20)

The process of migration includes reasons to leave, family and other networks, experience of increasing internal movement, decision-making on factors involved in legal and illegal international migration, and the reception on return. Reported reasons to leave include lack of education, avoidance of early marriage, family size requiring additional support, marriage problems, unemployment, and lack of work. It also includes some expectations that the move will be beneficial. For example, Ayalqibet, aged 25 at the time of interview, was forced to drop out of school because of the death of his parents due to HIV/AIDS, one after the other in a space of six months. Instead of looking after livestock in a rural village, he decided to migrate to Bahir Dar where he lived on the streets and worked for others by carrying goods for pay.

Most young women and men who migrate internationally have experience of making internal visits or prior short-term domestic migration. Some internal migration was initiated by visiting relatives and most undertaken through use of networks to facilitate the move. Much of the employment gained through internal migration reported by marginalized young people from rural Fogera replicated the work they had done locally when younger. For example, young women becoming domestic workers, and young men undertaking farm work in other places.

Many young people reported experience of international migration, particularly to countries in the Middle East such as Saudi Arabia and Yemen, often from Djibouti bordering Ethiopia, as a transition and starting point for the journey. Most who have attempted this have used an illegal or irregular route, they say at first because 'payment for illegals is better in the destination'. But if a migrant worker is found who entered illegally, they are deported and their fingerprints taken, which means they cannot then try a legal route. The journeys are reported to be often dangerous, while at their destination, some experienced abuse and exploitative working conditions, as well as the problems of deportation.

> I didn't know what is going to happen to us. Our migration was facilitated by a number of chain brokers based in various places from Alember, Bahir Dar, Addis Ababa to Kuwait. On our way from Bahir Dar to Dejen we escaped attempted rape. And after two months stay in Addis Ababa we flew to Kuwait. Upon arrival in Kuwait we were taken and kept in a locked room where there was no food, access to bath room. We thought we are going for work and we never thought we are going to lose our freedom. We were oppressed. We had to meet challenges with or without the support of a fellow Ethiopian. (Achamyelesh, female, 23)

Yet the step process of migration followed by many marginalized young people means that there always seems to be a better option by going further.

> The next field always looks greener. When I reached Djibouti I aspire for moving to Saudi Arabia and when I reached there I understood that the previous place was better than here. I was dreaming of returning back to my home country which was a dream came true at last. (youth workshop participant)

But although international migration is seen as an important strategy for marginalized young people to overcome problems of landlessness and land shortages, and lack of employment, it is also difficult for them for those same reasons. Apart from social networks, international migration requires initial funds to pay for costs of travel and other necessities especially if following a legal route and getting visas and other documentation. But many most-marginalized youth are poor, and without appropriate social connections so that getting access to start-off funding for migration is difficult. Even internal migration may become a long-term strategy for some marginalized youth, made harder because of the need to support family through whatever earnings they can make.

> I wish to migrate to town or internationally. I have heard people make better money migrating internationally. However, I need to have money to cover the cost of migration. I try my best to save money but I couldn't as I have to support my poor family. (Maru, male, 20)

These economic constraints mean that some youth strategies and hopes are aspirations they are very uncertain will come into effect.

> I am currently living with my parents. We are leading a difficult life as we have not enough land. Some of my brothers and sisters have got married. What we are producing is not enough for the family. I aspire to migrate to the Middle East to help my family. Whenever I think of migration negative things comes into my mind. However, I have not any other option. I should try my fate, I might succeed or fail. My parents are very poor. They have a small plot of land. I want to migrate and help my poor family. However, I don't have money to cover migration related expenses. I asked my parents for it but they could do nothing as they were very poor. (Martha, female, 22)

Return

Many marginalized young people who migrated internationally returned, as evidenced in the numbers of returnees participating in research workshops and case studies in rural Fogera. Yet migrants reported being accompanied by feelings of uncertainty on their return, often finding it was not as they expected, that reintegration was difficult, and for example having to deal with, as one workshop participant put it, 'False rumours about why she return back from the brokers to the community' (youth workshop participant).

They reported that the reception of returnees 'depends on the amount of money you bring to your family' (youth workshop participant), which also meant particular difficulties for those deported and for those finding difficulties on their way home, such as a young woman who reported the theft of all the money she had on her return journey in Addis Ababa.

Young people return from their migration for various reasons including expiration of working contracts, but also problems experienced such as heavy workload, denial of salary, mistreatment, and illness. Migrants who return without the will or agreement of their family members who supported their trip and sent them, and who come back empty-handed face rejection.

For example, Lisan, a young woman aged 20 years, returned. She had decided to migrate to the Middle East and with support from her uncle and parents went to Saudi Arabia. But she returned after just a year away because of a heavy workload and physical abuse from her employers. She faced rejection by her family members following this unexpected return. Her family also then pushed her to marry someone she didn't know. She married, and had a child. But then decided to divorce her husband because he used to physically abuse her.

Even those who came back with funds found that the way they were treated changed over time. Returned migrants pointed to the shift from their initial reception, particularly experiences of a gradual change in attitudes towards the returnee 'as the money she brought declines over time' (youth workshop participant).

> At first I was thinking everybody is happy with my return rather than the money that I brought. I was also excited and happy to return back. When their attention for me began changing and when I see the warm reception for the new returnees I began to understand the mentality of the community toward the returnees. (youth workshop participant)

Young people also pointed to disappointment on not being supported or permitted to invest their funds on their return to develop land and business.

> While returning from Saudi Arabia to Yemen youth did not get a plot of land to establish their own small businesses; they didn't get support from the local kebele administration; even my father was not willing to rent me a plot of land for running a small shop; the returnees came back home with some amount of money which could have been used to start their own business. (youth workshop participant)

> Now we don't have seed money to start up our businesses; climate change – there is decline in the amount of precipitation our area receives; there is land degradation and soil erosion. (youth workshop participant)

For some marginalized young people, particularly returnees, these difficulties indicate the importance of and need for change and development at home, in rural Fogera, rather than attention to and reliance on out-migration.

Conclusion: landless uncertainties

The lives of marginalized children and young people from rural Fogera are characterized by uncertainty as they grow up and follow various paths, attempting to find income and work to fulfil the attributes of adult status through marriage, independence, and supporting family. Their circumstances of land shortages or landlessness, and initial experiences of education and work may indicate to them a future of a certainty of poverty unless they take steps to mitigate and change their situation.

Many marginalized young people in rural villages of Fogera Woreda mentioned school drop-out and failure as key experiences in their lives. Reasons included late school enrolment, unaffordability of formal secondary education, community expectations and pressure to marry young, heavy household workload and lack of study time, and absence of nearby secondary schools as well as failure in national examinations. Many also described problems in combining work (both household and informal work) with schooling. Furthermore, the formal education system and examinations are found to be failing marginalized young people.

The outcome of these experiences at school and work, together with family income needs and/or the need for alternative work in order to achieve marriage and adult status in conditions of landlessness, mean that many marginalized youth turn to migration. This process begins with land shortages and ultimately moves from local to more distant migration and often beyond, internationally. Yet, the experiences of return migrants, even those who have brought back money, suggests that they are not able to easily invest and maintain themselves without repeat migrations. This has led to suggestions for investment, change, and development in rural localities, so that marginalized young women and men have the opportunity of a place locally that enables fulfilment of status and future.

Young people say such changes would involve agricultural livelihoods as well as education and school, and recognize shifts in intergenerational relationships. This would include finding alternatives to current agricultural work through creation of sustainable off-farming livelihood opportunities for marginalized youth in rural contexts; agriculture is still a primary means of livelihood in rural Fogera despite land shortages and landlessness among marginalized young people and their families. Since they depend on subsistence farming, there is a significant and urgent need for alternative off-farming livelihood opportunities among youth and their families.

Marginalized young people also recommend more attention to and monitoring of the conditions of exploitative labour. They say that children and youth need education and protection from abuse and violence in the home and in workplaces, especially in domestic work. They also say they need advice about family relationships.

In terms of education development, changes would involve both schools and systems, including the curriculum and format of what is to be taught and learnt. Young people suggest that secondary schools need to be built in rural villages because moving to town is unaffordable. Strategies are needed to help marginalized young people to cope with failure in national examinations. This also means that education systems need to take into consideration marginalized youth living contexts, in addition to the access to and quality of education provided in rural areas. For example, vocational education and training needs to be developed along with academic guidance as part of the formal education system.

Marginalized young people find uncertainties in their future status because of land shortages, landlessness, the need to work from childhood, dropping out of school, and failing examinations, meaning that conventional attributes of adult status, such as abilities to support family and marriage, are difficult to take up. Seeking employment through internal migration has become an alternative route to gain funds, yet the exploitative experiences of young men and women reinforce perspectives that moving on again may bring better opportunities in terms of the nature of work and income. This ultimately leads to international migration, often illegal, requiring dangerous journeys, and which may also prove difficult and exploitative. Yet, despite their experiences, returnees often make repeat migrations, including illegal journeys abroad. This arises out of disappointments on their return, even with funds. Those without funds, seen as unsuccessful, feel rejected. Those with funds, as their money depletes, also feel a sense of rejection. This leads to repeat migrations in hope of better opportunities and feelings that it is preferable to their current situation. They report difficulties in investing and using funds in a developmental way. Their experiences suggest that changes are needed in the local situation, to take account of the circumstances of marginalized children and young people, in terms of alternatives to agriculture, work, and vocational education, and so provide different opportunities.

CHAPTER 6
Urban Woreta: Migrating into street situations

Many marginalized young people migrate into the small town of Woreta, which is a transit point for many migrants and seasonal workers. Many come from poor rural, landless or land scarce households, needing to find alternative livelihoods, but without education and skills, seeking employment in the urban informal sector. In-migrants find high rates of unemployment and out-migration, along with discrimination, abuse, exploitation, and lack of protection, particularly for casual workers. In the town, the most-marginalized youth are those who become street-connected, and there is much substance abuse, partly as a consequence of problems such as unemployment, discrimination, and exploitation, but also of the violence experienced from the authorities. Woreta is known for a high prevalence of khat *chewing, and this is especially used by street-connected young people in an attempt to mitigate their circumstances. Young people point to the lack of appropriate services to support their circumstances and prevent problems worsening.*

Keywords: street-connection, substance use, education, work, migration, uncertainty, Woreta, Ethiopia

Introduction

Woreta is a small town in South Gondar Zone, Amhara Regional State. It is a transit point for many migrants and home to many seasonal workers. In Woreta, the research assessed how most-marginalized young people, in particular street-connected youth in the town, perceive and respond to uncertainties shaped by the context of their lives. Youth perceptions change and differ depending on intersecting aspects of poverty, wellbeing, inclusion, age, identity, gender, and other structural inequalities. Marginalization and uncertainty among youth in Woreta involves a diversity of young people in a context of high rates of unemployment and migration, along with discrimination, abuse, exploitation, and lack of protection, particularly for casual workers, and partly in consequence of this, a prevalence of substance abuse. This chapter focuses on marginalized young people who are street-connected, problems emerging from their living situation and perspectives on marginalization, experiences of migration, issues of finding and maintaining employment and work in the informal sector, and links with substance use and abuse. Most of this community of marginalized young people have migrated in, many from rural areas of the district as have other workers in the informal sector.

Woreta is a town situated within Fogera District (see Chapter 5) in northern Ethiopia. The town was established in 1947 and until it gained semi-autonomous self-governing status in 2006, was the capital of Fogera District. Woreta town has an estimated population size of 44,978 in its four *kebele* administrative units. Woreta is a transit point for migrants travelling to and from big cities and small towns such as Bahir Dar, Gondar, Debretabor, Addis Zemen, and Hamusit. It is a home and destination for many seasonal migrants, many of whom become domestic, cafe, and restaurant staff, security guards, daily labourers or other informal and casual workers including street vending, shoe-shining, and unloading transport. In addition, Woreta is believed to have one of the highest rates of *khat* consumption in the country (Birhanu et al., 2014).

Researchers worked with a total of 125 marginalized young people in Woreta, with a gender balance in the sampling, including 40 who took part in extended case studies. Most had migration experience (26 internal and 3 international) and almost all (38 of 40) were out of school youth. The participant sample and criteria of marginalization and vulnerability were developed through the inception and piloting phase of the project, and snowballing was used to reach the most marginalized (see Chapter 3).

Most were street-connected. The terms 'street situations' and `street-connected youth' are used here (see Chapter 17). These terms aim to recognize the multiple dimensions, characteristics, backgrounds, and lives of young people for whom the street is in some ways a focal point of their daily life or their means of survival or making a living.

Marginalized young people and street situations in Woreta

Young people interviewed in Woreta who felt able to identify the most-marginalized included some who spoke about their own lived experiences. Although groups identified varied by locality, overall the most-marginalized groups were seen as people living with and at risk of HIV and AIDS, commercial sex workers, youth who live in street situations, people with disabilities, people with leprosy, people with addictions, people without relatives in a position of power, people who believe in witchcraft, and followers of minority religions. They also noted young people without parents, without skills, and young women who were pregnant and married early.

> The most marginalized group of people are street-connected children followed by persons with disabilities and followers of minority religions, that is other than Orthodox Christians and Muslims. (Zeleke, male, 19)

Many of these groups are interlinked and overlap. The predominant issues concern lack of employment and only having access to informal sector work that is often risky, exploitative, and sporadic. People without parents and skills, those with disabilities and leprosy, and those without a relative in a position of power are seen as having difficulties finding employment, as are those with addictions and living in street situations, although addictions and living in street situations are also outcomes of dependency on informal sector work.

> Marginalized people are those people who have no relatives in key positions of power. It is essential to have someone to get employed. Young people who have no relatives in key positions of power in offices are marginalized from the [formal] employment sector though they fulfil all the qualifications required. (Meheret, female, 20)

There is stigma associated with most of these groups and much informal sector work as well as having disabilities, leprosy, and HIV and AIDS. Working as a commercial sex worker is particularly stigmatizing as well as raising risks of HIV and AIDs.

> People's attitude toward HIV didn't change. Commercial Sex Workers are also taken as deviant and no one lets us involve in social activities. There is only one person in the neighbourhood who comes to my house in addition to other CSW. Especially if they know that I am HIV positive then I think I have to change my place of residence. They think that I am going to infect them with the virus and they might try to caution their children to be far from my home. (Senait, female, 24)

> Those who have HIV/AIDS and those who have disability are the most marginalized in our area though there is some change in marginalising HIV positives recently. (Tilahun, male, 20)

Living in street situations is seen as stigmatizing, and leading to discrimination from authorities, in addition to members of the local community.

> Street children are mostly neglected. When the administration provided the youth with working space there is no one who suggest that we should be included. They don't care about us and they can take the working space where we are working any time. The police also give cover and protection for others but perceive us as the evil ones. (Sewent, male, 15)

These youth are not supported by formal social protection programmes meant for poor and vulnerable individuals affiliated with households: street-connected children and youth with no permanent address and devoid of household membership are not covered by the Productive Safety Net Programme.[1] In addition, most street-connected youth do not have *Kebele* (local administration unit) IDs, which makes accessing public services difficult.

In-migration and the background to becoming street-connected

The reason for many young people being street-connected is a background of school drop-out, family break-up, poverty, and migration. Most (38 of 40) had dropped out of school, and just over half had experienced family break up through death, divorce, separation of parents or difficulties and stigma from being born outside marriage. Youth migrate in from rural areas, such as the surrounding district of Fogera (see Chapter 5), for many reasons. Young people are generally keen to meet expectations to help support their families but have to go into towns due to landlessness, unemployment, abusive family relationships or to escape from early marriage.

Absence of parental support may lead to street-connected life.

> I had a very difficult time in my guardians' house. I had no one except my peers and my teacher at school. I used to hear my friends saying that life on the street is better than living in a place where there is no freedom. I just run away from home and join them on the street. They gave me a place to stay on the street. They fed me for some days. The fact that I had friends on the street has made me to consider street as a strategy to lead my life. (Kalayush, female, 19)

Some moved on to street-connected lives from situations of exploitation in informal sector or domestic work.

> My mother sent me to another house for the second time. My employer was an old man who lost his wife. He gave me money to sleep with him. However, I refused to accept the offer and run away on the following day. I informed my uncle's wife about the incident. She didn't keep my secret. My uncle thought I slept with that man. Then everybody became suspicious of me. I then decided to run away from that area because of their wrong perception. (Bertukan, female, 26)

Although some of the children and young people living in street situations are from Woreta, many have migrated in from Fogera District (see Chapter 5), for reasons of landlessness, land and work shortages, school drop-out and failure, or exploitation at work. Among research participants, some three-quarters had migration experience (29 of 40), most (26) only locally, and just three had undertaken international migration. Some of those who had migrated locally aspired to move on internally, for example to Addis Ababa.

> As I grew up, I started asking my parents to send me to the capital city. I have had information about life in the city from my relatives. I was seeking my freedom from my parents' control. Besides, the high school in Gaynit was far from my home. It took four hours from my home to school. It was tiresome to walk for long distances every day. I wanted to be free from all of these challenges. I was also dreaming a city life. I called my relatives in Addis Ababa to help me out migrate. Later on, my parents allowed me to move to Woreta with my aunt. They convinced me that they will gradually send me to Addis Ababa once I adapted to life in Woreta. I agreed with their decision and moved to Woreta. I have completed high school in Woreta. My aunt was very good for me. I had faced no problem living with her. (Kuku, female, 21)

Others hoped for international migration, but the realities of street-connected life in Woreta, combined with stories of experiences abroad, acted as a deterrent for some.

> I used to aspire to migrate to the Middle East. Now I have abandoned that dream of mine as a result of hearing the stories of my nieces and girlfriend. (Amele, female, 22)

Education, work, and life in street situations

Education

Marginalized young people migrating in from the surrounding rural areas and elsewhere may seek to continue their education in Woreta, may have gained some qualifications but not have the certificates, or may have dropped out or failed national examinations. In these cases they are most likely to end up engaged in the informal sector, if they are able to find any employment at all, and are at risk of living in street situations. Certificates might help gain employment, but some reported problems in obtaining school certificates once they have left places of origin, first because going back entails transportation costs, and second because young people are not often allowed to receive school certificates in the absence of a parent or a guardian.

> They request you to produce original certificates to prove that you have completed 8th grade. I couldn't get my original school certificate as my uncle was not happy with me and he was not willing to help me to obtain that as a guardian. Only parents and guardians can obtain such a certificate from schools. (Aregash, female, 18)

Some attempted to maintain education despite having moved into street situations.

> I wish I could continue my education living on the street. I struggled for a year and got promoted to Grade six. I run away from home at the age of 12, completing grade 5. I needed to have nine exercise books for grade six. I could continue with the help of some volunteers who gave me five exercise books. I also got the remaining four exercise books from the people I worked for. However, later on, my friend refused to work for people who used to give us leftover food and exercise books. Thus, I couldn't register for grade seven. (Kassahun, male, 14)

But in general, most felt that formal education is pointless and does not provide skills to get a job or to flourish in the informal sector.

> I aspire to set up my own small business and do business in the future. I don't want to move out of Woreta. I do not want to continue my

> education too because there is no one in our community who has changed his/her life with formal education. I do not want to spend my time on nothing. I wish there is job opportunity for youth than expanding mere educational opportunities. (Kuku, female, 21)

> I joined school at the age of 6. When I joined grade 9 most of my friends drop-out of school to learn how to drive and obtain driving licences rather than pursuing their further education. I want to be like my friend and lost my appetite for education. Especially there are many unemployed youths who graduated from the university in our area while my friends who dropped-out of school already have work and earn income. This by itself pushed me to stop learning and search for some other life paths. (Zeleke, male, 19)

Many young people had dropped out or not attended school because of working at home or being sent out as domestic workers for others. A young woman who migrated into Woreta had spent her rural childhood as a domestic worker for her own and other families:

> I was born in a rural area of South Gondar. I grew up with my grandmother because she was alone and no one was there to look after her cattle and fetch water. I grew up assisting my grandmother. At the age of 10, my grandmother passed away and I was left alone. My uncle didn't want to let me join my family. As he did not have a grown up child to look after his cattle, he made me stay with him. I stayed for a year working for him and his wife. After a year I run away from his home and went to my mother. Then she made me work for a rich household in the neighbourhood and in return she received seven quintal of cereals per year. It was my mother who took the grain and sometimes bought me clothes ... My elder sister and I have started working for other people in our early thirteen's. (Meron, female, 22)

Meron subsequently experienced sexual violence from her employer, ran away, attempted to combine education with employment but moved on again, illustrating the complexities, mobilities, insecurities, and dealing with uncertainty necessary for most-marginalized young women seeking a safe livelihood.

> One of my employers tried to rape me and I run away from his home. I migrated to the city after this. Being a domestic worker in Bahir Dar, life wasn't easy too. It didn't help me to change my life. My employer in Bahir Dar has allowed me to go to school in the evening. However, it wasn't easy for me to attend classes while working the whole day ... I used to aspire to live in Woreta when I saw the city on my way from my birth place to Bahir Dar. I finally decided and moved to Woreta. (Meron, female, 22)

Work

Young people report high rates of unemployment among marginalized youth in Woreta. They say that because of corrupt practices, unemployed and marginalized young people, who are from poor households and without relatives in positions of power, are not able to secure the jobs made available by local government organizations. Also that many unemployed young people are engaged in casual labour with no access to social services and no protection if or when their rights are violated.

Marginalized young people, including migrants from rural backgrounds, may find work in the informal sector, even when living in street situations, becoming street vendors, seasonal migrant workers, labourers, domestic workers, scrap metal and used plastic collectors, and *khat* or local alcohol delivery workers or sellers. Work in the informal sector in Woreta can be insecure and exploitative, and in some situations, dangerous. Many casual workers in Woreta were found to be experiencing abuse and exploitation. These include many seasonal migrants, daily labourers, and waitresses who work in the widespread small restaurants and drinking places. Also, the work done by domestic workers and security guards is less valued, and they are often exposed to different forms of abuse and labour exploitation. The risks faced not only involve the workplace, but travelling to and from there and the processes of getting work. For example, a young woman domestic worker reported:

> The safest place for me is when I am at home ... While working I take many health risks. When I work late in the evening and walk back home and I fear the Duriyes/truants/... I try to minimise the risk by not working late in the evening. My partner also accompanies me on my way to home if I work late in the evening. (Beletu, female, 18)

Street-connected young men who do casual labour explained the processes and problems of engagement, as Bezuayehu explained in two examples:

> We stand on a spot where daily labourer and their employers meet. If we know the potential employer we don't enter into agreement. However, if we don't know the potential employer we would like to have agreement before we work for that person. Yet that is usually very difficult to achieve. Even the people's militia and police in town don't give us any protection. There are some investors who denied paying us after we worked for them. (Bezuayehu, male,20)

> One day I was with two other daily labourers in Gumara town. Three of us agreed with a man to dig an irrigation ditch for him. As per the oral contractual agreement our responsibility was to dig the irrigation ditch for a sum total of 2800ETB. We worked for six days and completed the work. However, the man complained about the quality of the work and refused to pay us. He scared us with a gun and injured some of us and we

got treated at a clinic. All we got was the advance payment but we lost most of it. (Bezuayehu, male, 20)

Shelter and support

Some working spaces are considered safe:

> I feel safe and good when I do petty trade by moving from block to block within Woreta Town. During major holidays like Easter I buy and sell chicken for profit. (Menen, female, 25).

But for the few street-connected youth who do have a permanent shelter, 'The safest place for me is when I am at home' (Beletu, female, 18).

Most-marginalized street-connected youth do not have a regular source of income to support themselves, and so they do not have a permanent shelter and access to food regularly. There is no temporary shelter or housing services for street-connected children and youth in Woreta. They often sleep in verandas or on the streets and get beaten up by policemen, people's militia, and disturbed by drunkards. 'If you sleep in the street after 9:00pm the militia will come and beat you up' (youth workshop participant).

> Life on the street is very tough. Though I could feed myself, I couldn't support my family. I could only make money for my daily subsistence. I am forced to spend the night on the street as I couldn't afford to pay for a bedroom. I usually sleep alone as I didn't know others. I only stayed two months here. The security guards beat me up if they caught me sleeping on the streets at night. They assume all street youth are thieves. That is why I frequently move to places where the security guards are not available. The community isn't supportive as well. Most street youth abuse drug to forget these challenges. I do not use any drug. (Kaleb, male, 15)

> We live on the street. We stay somewhere we believe is safe to stay in. We work for the owner of the veranda in return for spending the night there. They pay us nothing except for letting us to eat their leftover ... As we are children, everybody tries to take advantage of us. The guards beat us, our seniors took our money. People came drunk and wake us in the middle of the night and sleep in our place. The community wants us to work for them with minimal payment or sometimes refuse to pay us. Our payment is based on the good will of the person who made us to work. If they refuse to pay us, we couldn't negotiate. (Kassahun, male, 14)

A main problem reported by street-connected youth is lack of support from authorities and services. For example, Defaru is a young boy, 15, who lives in the streets. He works as a part-time shoe-shiner. He works for other shoe-shiners and gets paid for his labour. He sleeps at night in other people's verandas as he doesn't have a permanent shelter. The challenges of sleeping in the open and facing militias who do the policing at night are many. He talked about the decline in support given by school clubs, local kebele administration, and individuals partly because of an increase in the number of street-connected children and youth in Woreta.

> Life on the street was full of challenges. We were beaten up by guards who thought that all street-connected children are thieves. (Kalayush, female, 19)

A frequently cited theme is that street-connected youth support each other.

> I was new to the place and many young men from my village supported me. Especially those friends who moved to Woreta earlier helped me a lot. Actually I didn't have the courage to decide on my move to Woreta if my friends were not in the town. Adapting to the city life was not difficult. As there were many people who come from natal rural village I have to hide to sustain the dignity of my parents in the rural area. My parents also gave me a hard time – they oppose my effort to settle down and live here. (Yafet, male, 23)

Some street-connected youth support each other as if they belong to the same 'household'. They live together, share, and support each other. For example, Defaru and his friend support each other. When one goes to school, the other works and buys/or collects leftover food for both of them. They keep their clothes together in one household, they sleep together and they consider each other as a member of one 'household'. However, when it comes to finding work Defaru said: 'I have no one to trust. There is envy. There is competition for paid work' (Defaru, male, 15).

Street-connected youth generally have to support each other because of the precarious nature of work they do to make a living:

> When you are engaged in informal work you may not make money every day. My friends cover my maintenance costs, when I didn't work, and I also cover theirs when they don't have money. We work and live together. Most of our activities are performed in groups. When I felt worried about something or when I am happy they are always there for me. Living on the street without a friend is almost impossible. (youth workshop participant)

Substance use

As elsewhere in Ethiopia, *khat* leaves (*Catha edulis*) are widely used among young people. *Khat* chewing is more common among young men than women, and is also associated with smoking cigarettes, heavy consumption of alcohol, addiction, and exposure to sexually transmitted illnesses. Marginalized and street-connected young people are among those using *khat* in Woreta, where there is said to be a high and increasing rate of use and abuse.

> We don't have a permanent place that we spent our time in the town. As we are daily labourers we mostly move from place to place – places where there are building construction work and contract employment opportunity. In the afternoon and on our rest days we chew *khat* and drink alcohol. There are many local liquor houses in the neighbourhoods and it's easy to access them. In the centre of the town there are also *khat* houses which we go to when we need chew *khat*. (Yafet, male, 23)

Addiction to *khat*, and associated consequences are commonly discussed issues among youth and older people in Woreta. The attitudes and perception of people are said to be changing.

> I think that addiction is becoming a common trait among the youth. My friends and other young men in the neighbourhood think as if addiction is a sign of modernity. When we were children I didn't see such kind of perception about addiction from our elders. Now the youth are living in the world of addiction. If you are not strong enough you will be forced to be one of them. (Belay, male, 18)

Elders who participated in adult male and female stakeholder meetings reported that both in and out of school students, and even many civil servants, chew *khat* and consume alcohol. There has been a public outcry about the problem of substance use, abuse, and addiction and its consequences in Woreta. Groups popularly perceived as particularly using *khat* include high school students in Woreta with poor academic performance, unemployed young men, and those who work for people who chew *khat*, young men who work in and around the bus station, truants and school drop-outs, daily labourers and street-connected young men who commonly use *khat* and consume alcohol. Peer influence is said to be significant:

> My elder brother has not completed his high school education. I didn't have good friends. Most of my friends encouraged me to drink alcohol [local drinks, Tella and Araqi]. Some of them tried to inspire me to flee the country … 'Life is a school. I look back and look forward'. I would like to lead a better life. (Tadele, male, 19)

Conclusion: uncertainties from migration to street

Many young people, already marginalized, who migrate into Woreta from surrounding rural areas and elsewhere get work in the informal sector, are further marginalized, and often become street-connected. Marginalization in urban Woreta stems from stigma and discrimination, powerlessness, lacking access to services and particularly to labour and other social protection. The high rate of incoming rural-urban migrants into Woreta in search of jobs and a better life increases pressures on the numbers of unemployed young people seeking casual work in town, making services for labour protection and their implementation an urgent need, along with increased provisions for rural employment.

Young rural migrants have generally experienced various uncertainties along with their marginalization. They may know they are likely to experience poverty in their rural home, but are uncertain whether they can find work locally and what sort of work. Given the probability of difficulties at school and passing examinations, decisions are made as to preferability of uncertain options: essentially the form and degree of uncertainty. Not migrating offers limited opportunities within certainties of poverty; migrating offers chances of broader opportunities, greater income, and more positive uncertainties. Yet the opportunities available in urban Woreta for marginalized young migrants are also restricted to the informal sector, coupled with the problems faced without local documentation and, without a permanent address, entitlements to services.

Thus, many marginalized in-migrants ultimately become restricted within street situations even when they have regular work in the informal sector. Their lives are characterized by a different set of uncertainties, for example where shelter is temporary or transient, where informal work is on a daily basis, and especially when work available is risky, dangerous, and exploitative and payments may not be forthcoming. The remedy for some will be to migrate on to other places. Others suggest solutions that concern providing a degree of protection through services in the town, or provision in rural areas as alternatives to migration. Such urban and rural provisions would essentially offer some securities in their lives.

For example, marginalized young people in Woreta suggested that more help with rural employment would curb migration, because they often migrate due to lack of work opportunities. They suggested agro-processing as a sector they might find employment in if given appropriate training, which would also have an impact on the type of education provided. They also suggested that once in towns, youth need to be supported in the informal sector in casual work so that they are not exploited and their rights violated. This would need to be monitored to address corruption and to ensure that youth have access to social services.

Entitlement and access to services in towns is essential if issues such as the increasing use and abuse of *khat* are to be addressed. In circumstances of high rates of unemployment and migration, along with discrimination, abuse, exploitation and lack of protection, particularly for casual workers, many young people turn to substance use to cope with their daily realities. It was suggested that substance use, for example *khat* and alcohol, needs to be addressed through community-based interventions where youth are involved and listened to. Young people suggested that *Iddirs* (funeral associations) and also *Kebele* (local government) officials could work with school clubs and adults in the community to help young people with preventing and regulating substance use and establish rehabilitation services that includes counselling. But for that to be possible, marginalized and especially street-connected children and young people would need to be actively included and able to use such clubs and services, which they say is not the case at present.

Although respondents reported that services in small towns such as Woreta frequently cannot cope with the ever-increasing numbers of youth, the lack of provision appears to escalate problems by exacerbating uncertainties. Already, from reports of marginalized, street-connected young people, their certainties seem to concern behaviour and responses of authorities, which do not offer protection, so their situation becomes more precarious, more vulnerable to exploitation, more uncertain.

Note

1. PSNP (Productive Safety Net Programme) is a programme supporting very poor households while the Child Care and Support Coalition is a community-based child support mechanism, but limited in scope and not in a position to meet the needs of orphans and vulnerable children.

CHAPTER 7
Drought-prone Hetosa: Status, success, and migration

In drought-prone Hetosa in central Ethiopia, where agriculture is the dominant rural occupation, marginalized young people face environmental degradation, land shortages and fragmentation, and lack of alternative livelihoods. They work to support family from childhood, initially herding cattle and household chores and later in informal sector work in towns and for the better-off. Partly for reasons of cost and need to support family, many drop out of school or fail national examinations. Formal education is not seen as providing a viable path to a sustainable livelihood, yet the lack of alternatives is affecting marginalized youth attainment of attributes of adulthood through marriage and capacity to support family. Internal and particularly international migration is seen as providing opportunities and markers of success such as land purchase and house construction achieved by some returning migrants who are seen as role models. Uncertainties run throughout rural occupations, and migration is seen as positive uncertainty.

Keywords: (international) migration, adult status, marriage, aspirations, agriculture, uncertainty, Hetosa, Ethiopia

Introduction

Hetosa District is a drought-prone area, situated in the centre of Ethiopia, some 150 km from Addis Ababa, in Arsi Zone of Oromia Regional State. The lives of young people in drought-prone Kebeles are shaped by environmental fragility. In most of the dry season, young people drop out of school, young men migrate in search of pasture land and water, while many young women bear the burden of taking care of elders and children at home. The fragile environment, proneness to drought, and lack of infrastructure add to feelings of marginalization and alienation that are fuelled by lack of access to alternative livelihood opportunities.

Migration in Hetosa District has been conventionally part of diversification strategies used by households to deal with risks such as shrinking land sizes, insufficient agricultural income, or job insecurity in the local non-farm sector. Also, migration remittances appear to be easier to access than other non-farm activities (Asnakech, 2014). Problems of land and livelihood shortages affect young people's transitions to adult status through marriage and independence, and many invest in migration to gain resources. Mobility is a key strategy for marginalized young people in times of uncertainty, and not only takes them to nearby small towns, but to big cities and in some cases to Gulf countries for work. For some marginalized youth, migration has become an almost essential part of a transition to adulthood, to gain attributes of adult status.

The total population of Hetosa Woreda (Hetosa District) was projected to be 156,243 in 2016. The District is primarily rural: less than one-fifth of the population live in towns, the majority in rural areas and depend on subsistence agriculture for a living (see Chapter 4). A 2014 study (Asnakech, 2014) indicated that 67 per cent of households surveyed fully specialized in agriculture, whereas 33 per cent diversified into non-agricultural activities, which mostly consist of low-return activities.

Research was carried out in the rural villages of Guri Debula, Tero Moye, and Hurtuba Denbi with 94 of the most-marginalized youth aged 15–24, taking care to reach a gender balance in sampling, including 40 detailed case studies. The participant sample and criteria of marginalization and vulnerability were developed through the inception and piloting phase of the project, and snowballing used to reach the most-marginalized (see Chapter 3). Participants from Hetosa were predominantly from a single ethnicity and religion as is representative for the area. In addition to young people, adult and stakeholder perspectives on the situation of youth were recorded.

Marginalization, adult status, and migration

Living in a rural drought-prone area, yet dependent on agriculture, youth develop feelings of marginalization and alienation, particularly because of limited basic infrastructure. Interviews show that services of government and non-government organizations in the District are limited and inaccessible for the most-marginalized youth, many of whom consider that living in drought-prone rural areas is itself a characteristic of marginalization.

The environment, limited means of livelihood, coupled with conventions of achieving social status, mean that in order to fulfil attributes associated with adulthood, many marginalized young people must migrate, especially internationally. Those who are further marginalized by disabilities (see also Chapter 18), who have problems accessing school as well as work, may not be able to migrate. The key issue for those migrating is how they return, their reception over time, and then whether they have to re-migrate to gain sufficient capital to achieve acceptance and attributes of adulthood. The uncertainties about gaining adult status influence decisions to migrate, which are then also bound up with uncertainty about travel, destination, and return.

Adult status and marriage

Marginalized youth uncertainties about social transitions to adulthood concern conventional attributes of adult status. Youth consider themselves as suspended between childhood and adulthood due to an inability to attain cultural signifiers of adult social status which include providing support and help to family, getting married, and establishing their own family, and having a means of livelihood. In contrast, migrants are mentioned as attaining adult social status and seen as successful through returning with capital. Migrants are mentioned as role models among the most-marginalized youth.

Youth in Hetosa villages define their status and age depending on social expectations and roles rather than chronological age. The transition to 'youthhood' for boys is mostly associated with outdoor social activities, and for girls with biological changes such as menstruation and changes in physical appearance. At these stages they are also presumed by the community to be youth and marriage proposals from family members of young men are expected. Yet for marginalized youth, early marriage is generally not an option, because land shortages restrict expectations of supporting a family, while conventions such as bride-price are unaffordable. Due to a shortage of resources such as land and escalating bride-price, marriage has become a long-term plan for many. The bride-price in some areas is 20,000 ETB (US$750) which is not affordable for the most-marginalized youth.

Abduction is practised with the consent of young women when young men are not able to cover the costs of marriage. Although the process appears forced, it is dependent on her will. The man then sends elders to the women's family before they open a case against the perpetrator. If the family agrees, the man will pay some compensation money, and they will get time to pay the bride-price. A young man explained how abduction with consent of the woman reduced the bride-price he was expected to pay.

> I met a young girl who lives in a different kebele. We fell in love and agreed to get married. However, I had nothing to give for her family as a bride-price. I talked to the girl and we agreed to bring her to my parents' and made it to look like abduction. I didn't pay for her parents yet, but I have to when I get money. (Muktar, male, 22)

These changes are said to increase young women's agency on marriage choice, although the practice of early marriage and abduction has partly reduced due to lack of economic capital to finance and sustain the marriage, and because of land shortages. As land, a primary resource given for the bride and groom on marriage, is now lacking, that has restricted marriage. The practice of early marriage has changed. Young men are interested in getting married but constrained due to economic problems and inability to fulfil social expectations upon marriage.

> There are a set of expectations from a girl's family side when you propose for a marriage. They expect the would-be husband to have land, money and a house before proposing for a marriage. I don't think I can have these things in the short run. My parents promised to give me 2500 sq/m of agricultural land but it will not be enough for the formation of one's own household. (Yetages, male, 25)

The practices of early marriage and abduction in rural villages of Hetosa are now disappearing. A young man in Hetosa village said:

> Although marriage arranged by parents used to be the norm, families are no longer interfering in marriage decisions of their children. In other terms parents don't force their children to get married young. (Aragaw, male, 25)

International migration to Middle East countries has also partly contributed to curtailing the practice of early marriage. On the one hand, this enables youth to acquire capital to become independent and marry. On the other hand it provides resources for parents and family, particularly when marriage for young women is not benefitting them through bride-price, while migration can.

> Our parents prefer to send us to Arab countries. Because they expect something in return. They hope we will send money. However, if we get married here, they will get nothing in return. They will not be benefited. Hence unlike the previous times they encourage us to migrate than getting married. (Muferyat, female, 18)

Living situation: agriculture, land, work, employment, and education

All farmers rely on rain-fed agriculture on a small plot of land, and without access to irrigated land, most have a poor, unreliable subsistence livelihood, rarely sustainable for young people. Further environmental degradation comes from deforestation, a livelihood strategy of many marginalized youth and their families, who cut down trees to produce charcoal and firewood to sell. Environmental fragility, through lack of annual rainfall alongside deforestation, coupled with shortages and fragmentation of land over generations due to widespread polygamous marriage and large families, has limited agricultural productivity and consequently influenced marginalized young people's choices. Youth opportunities and decisions are further constrained by childhood work, education experiences, gendered household work, and employment in the informal sector, as well as limited information about services provided in the district.

Education and work

Primary schools are located some distance from villages and children have a long way to walk. Marginalized young people in Hetosa District report late enrolment because of parents' reluctance to send children, partly because of their concern children cannot cope with adversity on the journey, that they might be attacked by wild animals or people on the way. Youth see this as a paradox, since children are sent long distances to fetch water and herd cattle at a very young age while being forbidden from going to school. Reluctance to send children to school is also due to the cost, and because their labour was needed at home.

Many marginalized children and young people dropped out of school because of domestic and agricultural work, and through unaffordability of formal secondary education, limited access to a library and availability of books, and some through early marriage pressures. Problems of drought, water shortage, and lack of electricity also lead to irregular class attendance and lack of study time.

> My mother was suffering a lot to feed the family. My father couldn't work and support her. My brothers were very little and dependent. Feeding and taking care of eight family members was the responsibility of my mother. When I was grade four student, I decided to drop-out and support my mother. I helped her for a year. And I re-enrolled in the next year. Though I could attend classes regularly, I wasn't able to read after school. I was the second child and have had responsibilities unlike my little ones. Though it was not mandatory to support my family, I felt pity for my mother. (Lubasha, female, 20)

Youth explained tiresome long-distance mobility in herding cattle, searching for water and firewood, and travelling to market places. From the age of five and above, boys are responsible for herding cattle while girls start helping with household chores. Young women regard domestic work as dragging them out of school as they are missing classes taking care of household chores. They also point to long distances travelled by girls and young women to fetch water in drought seasons. The gendered division of labour is described by many young people to favour young men.

> I grew up helping my parents in house chores. My brothers herd cattle. Boys do not engage in household chores though girls took care of both the work inside and outside. Girls help their brothers in herding cattle and collecting water walking for long distances every day. My parents do not expect our brothers to engage in the house chores. It is hence I used to spend most of my time handling the household chores. I felt these are my responsibilities as I am a woman.' (Muferyat, female, 18)

Secondary schools are located in towns, so youth from poor rural family backgrounds must engage in informal work to cover costs of living there, which gives limited study time outside classes. Many marginalized youth who do manage to combine work with schooling still fail to score a pass mark in the National Exam in grade 10. Some who graduated from higher institutions mentioned unemployment as a critical problem, and that corruption and lack of good governance, such as hiring job applicants based on nepotism, is a challenge for the most-marginalized youth in Hetosa. Formal education is seen as irrelevant by many marginalized youth, with classes thought to lack appropriate content or applicability to young people's daily activities.

Most families in our village have bad attitude towards education. They say there is nothing you can change even if you complete your study so that you better help us with farming activities. I knew students who used to live in rented rooms in a place where there are high schools. Many of them dropped out of school because they were evicted from their rooms by the landlords as their family stopped paying rents. (Aminet, female, 20)

Informal work and mobility

Most-marginalized young people in rural Hetosa are employed informally from childhood. Families with small plots of land use their children's labour for diversifying their income. Young women are mostly employed as domestic workers for economically better-off families in their community, whereas young men are employed to herd cattle. Those young people with experience of domestic and farm work reported violence from employers, denial of primary education, and exploitation by heavy workload with minimal pay.

Informal work starts at a young age helping parents in selling firewood, charcoal, and other agricultural products. Some young women work as a petty trader with their mothers. As they get older, working in the informal sector and contributing income for the family becomes essential for marginalized young people in Hetosa's drought-prone areas. Young people consider working informally important to finance their formal education, provide freedom of mobility to places including nearby towns, and to establish networks with other people and experience urbanized life before moving to towns.

At times of drought, young men migrate to the nearby town searching for water and pasture-land, or engage in informal work, whereas women stay at home to look after younger siblings and older parents. Some young women have experiences of mobility to the nearby town for buying and selling regardless of the season. Mobility for schooling, marketing, fetching water, and herding cattle is common for youth in Hetosa. This may be to the closest town, but some youth engage in rural-rural migration in search of better sources of agricultural livelihoods, especially young men. Young women had experiences of rural-rural migration as a result of marriage. Such familiarity with mobility provides a context for migration.

Migration

Migration is a prime strategy of the most-marginalized youth to escape impoverished and marginalizing living situations, but also aims to provide a means to achieve adult status and acceptance. Migration is a highly gendered phenomenon in terms of local expectations, destinations, and work, triggered by multiple intersecting factors. Young men are over-represented in internal mobility, while young women outnumber them in international migration.

Many marginalized young people have experiences of mobility since childhood, roaming long distances for herding cattle, collecting water and firewood, and visiting markets in nearby towns, including girls. Recurrent drought triggers young men's internal movements and seasonal migration is common. Many young men move to urban places after harvesting until the next ploughing season. Drought is not spoken of as a push factor but presented as limiting opportunities for youth such as their engagement in agriculture, formal education, accessing water, and creating incapacity to socially transit to adulthood. Although youth aspire to leave their fragile environment, migration requires financial capital and social networks.

Peers provide information and networks on migration to nearby towns, and returnees become role models and indicators of material success.

> As I grew up, I observe my friends migrating to the nearby town. They came up with money and wear fashionable clothes. I wanted to be like them. Then I asked myself why I stayed in the rural place while my friends take the courage to change their life to the better. Then I decided to migrate internally. (Nebil, male, 22)

International migration is also influenced by returnees:

> One of my half-sisters was in Dubai. She is older than me. She has now returned, got married and started her own life. I partly became motivated to migrate looking the changes she brought after she migrated. (Lubasha, female, 20)

Saudi Arabia, Qatar, Kuwait, and Dubai have rapidly become major destinations for most young migrants in Hetosa. Although these migrants are predominantly young women, frequently encouraged by families who see the cost as a worthwhile investment, young men are also interested to go, but report lack of parental support and expectation. This is partly because demand for male migrant labour in the Middle East is low and associated costs are high, coupled with high demand for male labour in the agriculture sector in Hetosa. But many returned young men say migrating is better than staying in the certainty of poverty.

> My parents were against my decision to migrate to Dubai. They were against my decision as there was no one to handle the agricultural tasks. I looked for someone to help them and migrated despite their reluctance. My sister facilitated my travel to Duabi. She had migrated before me and has built house in Hetosa. She used to tell me positive information about life in Dubai. I then became motivated to migrate. She covered all the expenses. I have only paid for medical test and passport. (Muktar, male, 22)

Marginalized youth link their migration decision with socially embedded feelings of responsibility to support their poor families and aspire to become successful within a short period. Young people enthusiastically discuss migration decisions in terms of expected success. Both young men and women aspire to migrate and come back with capital: many aspire to buy a plot of land in town from migrating internationally.

There is a common saying among the most-marginalized youth, that 'both staying and migrating are full of challenges, and migration has hope that might turn to be positive'. Youth are aware of abuses and mistreatment of migrant workers in Middle Eastern countries. But the influence of successful migrant workers, who bought urban plots of land and livestock, seems to be considerable, so youth consider migration as means of securing a livelihood. As Aminet explained, migration is an informed decision:

> Currently I don't have any paid job. However, I help my family with harvesting crops as this time is the harvest season in this locality. I am dependent on my family for all of my expenses including food, cloth and shelter. Therefore, in order to improve the quality of my life I want to go to Dubai and work for a certain period of time. From what I heard about the country [UAE] is mostly bad. I heard that people faced many challenges in Dubai. But death is unavoidable and I pray for Allah to protect me so that I can work in Dubai and come back home safely. (Aminet, female, 20)

Marginalized youth report their journeys had hope and uncertainty, and most of the time were and are initiated considering the positive sides of migration. Potential youth migrants gather information about journeys, working and living conditions prior to departure, often from returnees. Young people say that media and returned migrants portray negative sides of migration and exceptional success stories. For rural marginalized youth, uncertainty of migration is preferred to staying in a condition of certainty of poverty. As Fatuma explained:

> It is so difficult to advise people – either to encourage or discourage them about migration to Arab countries. But people usually focus on successful migrants who returned home unharmed and with capital. As a result they don't want to listen to the bad part of the story, they just want to go and see things for themselves. Moreover people tend to interpret 'don't go to the Middle East' advice as being envy of them. (Fatuma, female, 25)

Most young women migrate as domestic workers while young men go through free visas and engage in construction, herding camel, and door fixing works. The cost of international migration for Hetosa rural youth reportedly ranges from US$350 to $1,480. The preference is to migrate through legitimate routes although some young men described experiences of irregular or illegal migration as a particular source of uncertainty in destination countries. Young people with irregular migration status have fear of sudden imprisonment, deportation, and limited access to services. Yared, a 24-year-old young man who had had irregular status in Saudi Arabia, described feelings of uncertainty and strategies adopted to move out of it. Yared worked both in the city and in rural areas. He was paid 600 Saudi Arabia Riyal (SAR) (approximately $120) for herding camel in rural areas, and got paid on average 1,200 SAR ($320) per month wage-earning in gardening and other informal work in the city.

> When you work as an illegal migrant life is uncertain as you can be imprisoned accidentally. So in most cases migrants send the money to their families immediately. I sent the money I made to my families immediately through my friends. In most cases my friends used the money for themselves while some of the money is consumed by my family. I was hoping there will be some money in the hands of my friends and family but it didn't happen. When I returned here there was no money left for me. (Yared, male, 24)

Young women working as domestic employees are more vulnerable to physical violence in the home. They mention restricted mobility and communication with family members. But both men and women are vulnerable to heavy workloads, violations of human rights, denial of salary, and lack of legal protection working in Middle Eastern countries. They are further vulnerable because of language problems and difficulties in adapting to local food and domestic practices.

> Life in Dubai was very difficult. My employers didn't care whether I got sick or tired. I stayed for three years in Dubai in a single household. I suffered a lot since I didn't know their language. They used to take me to the place where Ethiopians live so that I could learn Arabic language from them. I had no chance to call and talk to my family in that difficult moment. After some time, they prohibited me from going outside. I was locked in a single compound for three years. I only went downstairs to dump the trash. My contract was for three years. They requested me to extend my contract. However, I asked them to visit my family and returned back. They called me after I came back. I told my employer that I didn't want to return sooner. It is because Ethiopians are suffering a lot there. I have seen people suffering and got frightened to return back. I am now thinking to continue education. If that is not possible I will start my own business. If the situation is worse, I will migrate back to another Arab country. (Lubasha, female, 20)

Working with other Ethiopian domestic workers helps youth adapt to living and working conditions and pass moments of uncertainty.

> I was lucky; I was working with other Ethiopians in a household I got employed. They helped me to learn Arabic language since they speak better. They used to translate for me too. I was paid 4500 ETB monthly. My employer was a very good person; she even gave me two bags of clothes and some jewellery when I came back. I have found it very difficult to understand Arabic language. We used to communicate with signs and gestures. I also found it very difficult to adapt to the food in

> Dubai. I got very sick. I got gastric irritation. I asked my employer to send me back home as I got very sick. Then they returned me. (Lishan, female, 20)

Although experiences travelling and in destinations are known to be difficult, youth prefer to migrate than stay in what they see as impoverished and hopeless living conditions. Yared indicates a sense of shame in not supporting his family.

> My friends work and live well in Saudi. I wished I have gone and died while migrating than staying here. There is no one who helps me financially. My father is the one who supports the family. (Yared, male, 24)

Return

Reasons for return are wide-ranging, including expiration of working contract, deportation, language problems, illness, and in rare cases achieving one's goals. Forced return before achieving goals often creates uncertainty as it leads to stressful relationships with family and community. Returning before paying back migration expenses is particularly difficult and enhances migrants' propensity to re-migrate. As home-remaining family members invest scarce resources to send migrants away, returning before paying this back worsens the certainty of poverty. A reason for many youth to stay away longer despite experiences of difficulties is to repay money invested in their trip and attain the status of a successful migrant by buying land and a house in urban areas. Youth who migrated through illegal or irregular routes are more vulnerable to returning before attaining their aspirations as they may be turned back or face difficulties at their destinations.

When migrants return, they may become role models for the most-marginalized youth in Hetosa, especially if they succeed in bringing back resources which are seen as local markers of success. In the eyes of most-marginalized rural young people, these markers include starting a business, buying land, having a house constructed in towns, and financially supporting their family. But returned migrants also face difficulties, such as whether they have brought back enough, how long funds will last, and reintegration to the community.

Young returned migrants mentioned their concern over returning before accumulating capital. Some migrants who managed to remit their salary, got their remaining family members to buy a house or open shops in urban areas.

> I brought no money because I used to send all the money I had to my parents. They used some of it and also opened a small shop for me. I am working in this shop now. (Muferyat, female, 18)

Migrants' reception and treatment depends on accumulation of wealth and achievement. They are thought to have potential to positively change the life of their family. Most of the modern houses (with corrugated-iron roofs) built in the community are financed by migrants for their families or for themselves. They also help their families economically before they return. The result of such impact is a positive reception on return. In addition, migrated young women who accumulated wealth are wanted for marriage, and both men and women successful returnees gain social status and recognition within their family and community.

In contrast, migrants returning empty-handed are represented as failed and face rejection and mistreatment. Successful migrants who returned with some money described how their initial positive reception and treatment from family and community changed as time passed and resources were utilized. Yared said his relationship with family and friends changed after his remittance was finished.

> Most people in the community were happy with the fact that I returned back. Everybody received me with a smile on his/her face. I had only a total sum of 300 US dollar when I returned home. This money was finished after sometime and the happiness faded away shortly. (Yared, male, 24)

Reception of returnees is said to vary.

> Reception depends on what you have up on your return. If you came up with money or brought clothes for people in your locality, people warmly welcome you. My situation was a bit different. My family didn't know I was returning. Hence they were worried about my health so they didn't complain though I returned empty-handed. However the people in the community blamed me for spending my parents' money and returned empty-handed. However, my parents defended me when people blamed me. They didn't even allow them to say a lot about my return. (Mina, female, 24)

Their reception has led to aspirations to re-migrate for some returnees from the Middle East in spite of challenges they encountered there. Reasons that trigger re-migration include mismanagement of remittances, unwelcoming reception from family and community, inability to implement skills they brought back, being unable to introduce aspects of the way of life learned abroad, and lack of employment opportunities. Family members and friends who supported youth to migrate, utilize their remittance, and are unwelcoming on their return, also trigger re-migration.

> It's around two years now since I returned back home. I still want to migrate if I get the chance. (Yared, male, 24)

Conclusion: uncertainties and adulthood/status

International migration regardless of routes is still considered a primary strategy for marginalized young people to obtain markers of success in the community, including buying land and a house in urban areas, financially supporting family and being able to attain adult status by getting married and taking part in social activities. The uncertainties around gaining attributes of adult status are provoked by marginalization and environmental fragility. Such fragility may be degraded further by marginalized communities through livelihood strategies involving deforestation, creating further uncertainties. Land shortages and fragmentation over generations through polygamous marriage and large families, and consequent effect of this and poor incomes on marginalized youth opportunities, are changing some social practices, particularly early marriage. Instead marriage is frequently being delayed until young people can gain capital and alternative livelihoods, creating social uncertainties. Resources to provide for family and marriage are sought through migration, especially internationally to the Middle East, but there is no guarantee migrants will return with sufficient funds, or that any new status in their home community is sustainable. The costs of migration, often borne by family investment, need to be repaid. The migration itself is full of uncertainties, regarding the journey, destination, pay and income, and reintegration on return, while the depletion of remittances and funds brought back may lead to aspirations of re-migration.

While the process of migration appears precarious, it is preferred by many marginalized young people, and sometimes their families, to the perceived certainty of poverty if remaining at home. In contrast to migration, formal education isn't perceived to be paying back study time to attain resources and markers of success. The costs of education and failure in national exams for many marginalized young people is contrasted with observed unemployment of many who do pass the examination. The fact of educated youth being unemployed is said to be de-motivating and contributes to dropping out of school. Marginalized young people are disadvantaged in school anyway, because of family need for them to herd cattle and/or undertake household chores from childhood. They later become employed in the informal sector to support family in nearby towns or in better-off households as domestic workers.

For these marginalized young people, agriculture has brought no change in the lives of their family, although long practised as the dominant means of livelihood. Instead, marginalized young people, often with the perceived role models of successful returnees, aspire and decide to migrate in order to support their poor family members and themselves. The decision and rationale to migrate has multiple contributing factors, ranging from economic impoverishment, declining value of formal education, to aspirations of marriage and status, and the land purchases and house constructions of those who successfully returned. In addition, mobility is a strategy to connect with the outside world for many youth who consider living in rural areas as marginalization.

Contrary to popular perceptions of youth being abused and exploited in risky and adverse journeys and destinations, migration is seen positively, as uncertainty that can have either positive or negative outcomes. Many fail to secure the desired objectives of accumulating financial capital and status due to mismanagement of remittances by family members, or rapid depletion of funds on return. They described feelings of an uncertain future and, as with those who do not migrate, many are potentially home-remainers, who are marginalized and stay due to lack of migration-facilitating infrastructure such as social networks and financial capacity. Yet of those depleted and so-called failed migrants, many aspire to re-migrate.

CHAPTER 8
Addis Ketema: Identity and support in street situations

The most-marginalized young people in the sub-city of Addis Ketema are street-connected and involved in informal work associated with the major bus station and the large open market, Merkato. *They face uncertainties throughout their daily lives, in seeking work and protection from discrimination and abuse from others in the community and the authorities. Many have migrated from rural parts of the country, many due to family breakdown, although some still live with family members. Their work ranges from daily labour to peddling to commercial sex work. Their principal identity and main source of support is with other street-connected young people, with whom they share common daily experiences of street situations. Many also share experiences of substance use as a way of coping with street life, but which has detrimental effect on work. They oppose institutional-based rehabilitation and seek intervention programmes based on their own knowledge and local resources.*

Keywords: street-connections, identity, substance use, uncertainty, Addis Ketema, Addis Ababa, Ethiopia

Introduction

In a densely populated slum area of Addis Ketema, a sub-city of the Ethiopian capital, Addis Ababa, marginalized and street-connected young people experience uncertainties in their daily life through making a living and in relationships with authorities and other sectors of the community. Many of these young people are migrants from other parts of the country, whose parents then died, or who moved themselves to escape difficult situations including exploitation in urban settings. Family breakdown and economic problems are the main problems pushing many young people to live in the streets. Street-connected youth survive through begging, food scavenging, commercial sex work, collecting garbage, and other informal activities. They mostly sleep around the train station, on garbage dump sites, in verandas, doorways, and roundabouts. They have a tense relationship with the police. Community labelling, which relates street-connected young people to theft, sex work, and addiction, is common. They may take up, passively receive or resist government and NGO interventions depending on perception of appropriateness. Yet the research generally shows an impressive resourcefulness of street-connected young people in resilience and adoption of survival strategies, indicating how they could contribute and play a leading role in preparation of interventions and projects concerning their life and the local community.

Addis Ketema had a total population of 297,793 (144,954 male and 152,839 female) in 2015. It is a hub for internal migrants from different parts of the country, and youth within Addis Ababa. It has the largest *Merkato* (open market) and *Autobis Tera* (bus station) in the country, which makes it attractive for youth involved in informal sector work and/or street-connected.

Researchers worked with 125 marginalized young people, including in-depth case studies with 40, which form the basis of this chapter, in addition to adults and local stakeholders (see Chapter 3). The young people were selected purposively from different groups living and working in street-connected marginalized contexts (see below). Adults were drawn from community-based organizations, including community policing, *Iddirs* (burial association), and women's development groups. Stakeholders were recruited from governmental and non-governmental organizations working directly or indirectly on issues that influence the life of marginalized and street-connected youth.

The research team considered and involved different groups living on and working on the street, and living in impoverished marginalized contexts. Selection of participants was based on information collected from youth themselves during the co-construction research stage (see Chapter 3). At that time, almost all street-connected young people involved were out of school and engaged in different income-generating activities.

Identity, youth marginalisation and street-connected in Addis Ketema

In Addis Ketema, the concept of street-connection is used for youth who have some kind of connection, strong or loose, with the street and in one way or another depend on the street for their livelihood. They may depend on the street for economic and social benefits. But, as shown through discussion with young people, it is important to note that dependency on the street does not necessarily mean identifying oneself as a person living on the streets.

In the research locations, a connection to the street is mainly linked to poverty and considered the last resort that youth and their family take for survival. Many young people live and work on the street in various ways in Addis Ketema, following various livelihood activities from commercial sex work to peddling. Young people selected for research fall into various overlapping categories as defined by themselves and other marginalized youth, including: street youth, shoe-shine boys, petty traders, school drop-outs, unemployed youth, youth with disability, those in conflict with the law, return migrants, internal and international migrants, commercial sex workers, and beggars.

Issues of identity arose when researchers explored how 'on the street' is internalized among street-connected youth themselves. Commercial sex workers, for instance, were found to have strong street attachment due to the kind of activity they are involved in. However, those who participated in this research did not refer themselves as 'street youth' or 'street-connected youth'.

Shared identity among youth who live and work on the street is created through their daily routine, experiences, and language. As an expression of being part of a group, most street-connected young people have a set of experiences in common, such as receiving leftover foods, begging, working as a labourer or related activities, using tobacco, chewing *khat*, and sniffing glue. The speech they use to express different scenarios in their surroundings and area, their body language and way of communication make them seem different. As their daily mobility and means of survival are distinct and different, other members of the community tend to see them as a group. In turn, as a result of deprivation, street-connected youth feel they are 'marginalized by the larger society'. They say that, over time, the designation by others as *Godana tedadary* (those living on the street) and the perceptions and realities of having a sub-culture, a different way of life, made them differentiate themselves. Feelings of marginalization are exacerbated by reactions of the surrounding community towards them. They say they are perceived as deviants, thieves, addicts, and useless creatures, and are excluded.

> We [street youth] do not get the chance to take part in the affairs of the community. (Suleiman, male, 26)

> There are still some individuals who marginalize street youth. We are mostly taken as suspects when criminal activities are committed. People judge us just by looking at our clothes. (Tamene, Male, 20)

> After I started working as a commercial sex worker, my life became all the same. The payment is very minimal and couldn't bring change way of life. Rather my life became a routine and boring one. This business made my life certain. I usually woke up in the middle of the day, drink coffee and chew chat and when I have customers I will work. (Kokebe, female, 24)

But even with a degree of shared identity, street-connected youth cannot be seen as one group, because of their own diversity in addition to having different levels of attachment to the street. Only some of them live and work on the street, which makes them solely depend on it. Some are beneficiaries of development interventions that help them gain access to different services while living and working on the street. For these young people, the street may not be the only livelihood they rely on. Also, some street-connected youth work on the street and go back to their families at night. They rely on the street to support their families economically although they still have options for shelter and parenting. Thus, attachment to and identifying themselves as street-connected youth differs among groups.

Some street-connected young people no longer have affection for and sense of belonging to their family. Zegeye said the role of family was replaced by the street youth group.

> I don't want to reintegrate with my family. They were not there for me when I needed them the most. There is no cause left to get in touch with them. (Zegeye, male, 23)

It may take just a short time for newcomers to adjust and identify themselves as street-connected youth. For example, Boko, 18 years old when interviewed, from Boditi town in Wolaita Zone of Southern Nations, Nationalities, and People's Region (SNNPR) of Ethiopia, said he came to Addis Ababa and 'settled' on the street recently. He started to feel 'in-group' in a short time, and explained fast adjustment was possible because other street youth helped him cope with the challenges, and that he then lived with many other street-connected boys who had quite similar daily routines.

> I get up early in the morning and look for work. I carry stuff for other people. I eat my breakfast with my friends. If we have money, we buy Injera with shiro [chickpeas/peas stew] for 15ETB and eat together. If all of us do not have money, then we might not have dinner at all. (Boko, female, 18)

Vulnerability and diversity

Street-connected youth are not the homogeneous group perceived by many people in their communities. Rather, different groups have different exposure to the street and different levels of vulnerability, dependent on factors such as age, gender, and length of time in this situation.

Being both street-connected and a person with a disability makes street vulnerability worse. Addis Ketema is home for many young people with disabilities who come from different parts of the country in search of better opportunities. Some work in the informal sector while others work begging. They say some members of the community portray youth with disabilities as incapable of sustaining their livelihood through work. Interviews reflected the negative attitudes towards young people living with disabilities, including community members thinking they are unable to work or support themselves (see Chapter 18 on youth living with disability).

Street-connected female youth are more vulnerable than males. Selam migrated from the south to be a domestic worker, but ended up on the street. She thinks that getting into a relationship with a man is the only way of survival on the street.

> Street-connected females are few in number in comparison to males. When females are new to the street, they are forced to be accompanied by a male from the street. Otherwise, they will end up harassed and in some cases raped by other street youth. I was forced to get into a

relationship not to be sexually abused; however, what I tried to avoid just happened to me and I got pregnant and gave birth to a baby girl. (Selam, female, 25)

The child's father lived on the other side of the city and made no financial contributions.

Income-generating choices for females on the street are restricted, with fewer economic opportunities and consequently less daily income. Those who work in the informal sector are paid relatively less. They often lean on male street-connected youth for food. Females who work and live on the street are mostly involved in begging. Limited options mean many engage in commercial sex work, and further vulnerability.

Street-connected youth are forced to segregate themselves from others as a result of the way certain people or groups target them for physical and psychological abuse. They explain it is common to encounter abuses by police, such as non-judicial beating, torture, forcible round-up, transport to other secluded locations, and, in some cases, imprisonment. They also think most services provided by government offices are not welcoming for street youth.

> We were around 200 street youth. The police took us to a place outside of Addis Ababa without our consent; we didn't know the place before. They moved us during the night for the reason we do not understand. I stayed there for three months in a training centre again without my consent. The food they offered us was not good. I got very sick as time progressed. We didn't receive any trainings. We used to spend the day wandering in the compound. Escaping was the only option for us; but I couldn't dare to do that because of the severity of punishment for attempted escaping. (Mahlet, female, 18)

Movement and migration to the street

While street-connected youth in Addis Ketema share common experiences of marginalization, discrimination, and certain routines in daily life, their diverse vulnerabilities also reflect variety in the ways in which they came into these circumstances. Paths to street situations involve forms of mobility, including rural to urban migration over long distances in-country, and local movement from employment to unemployment, even in the informal sector. Key factors are breakdown in relationships, often through abuse, violence or exploitation. For many, experiences of marginalization and abuse begin before they become street-connected, particularly for those now living on the street. Many have experience of being beaten, sexually abused, and exposed to labour exploitation, being engaged in bonded labour work for parents or relatives, and forced on to the street. Their feeling of marginalization in street situations is not new, but rather a continuation of the deprivation, often at family level, before they go on to the streets.

A major cause of becoming street-connected is family problems and breakdown, especially lack of parental care, including when parents or guardians divorce or die and there is no one to care for the surviving child or children. For example, Zegeye, born in a small village near Ambo town (110 km from Addis Ababa), was raised there by his grandmother after his parents' divorce, and supported financially by an uncle. He was forced to work all day on household chores, limiting his schooling. The death of his uncle drove him out to find support on the street.

> My uncle was the one who supported me by buying school materials. Unfortunately, he died due to a car accident when I was thirteen years old. Things went from bad to worst with my grandmother. I was attending grade five when I was forced to drop out from school. There was no better choice for me to consider at that time but moving to Ambo. I slipped away from home and moved to Ambo that year. I was a small child and the street boys supported me as if I were their younger brother. (Zegeye, male, 23)

Family breakdown was an immediate push-factor leading many street-connected youth to leave home.

> Our step-mother was harsh on my sister and me in the way she treated us. She gave birth to two children from my father in a couple of years. When things become worse, I decided to escape the terrible condition and moved to the city. It was challenging as I didn't know where to go. (Zeru, male, 23)

Mahlet also went on to the street as a result of her parents' divorce and the consequent complicated relationship with her step-mother.

> My parents divorced when I was a child. My mother used to get sick frequently. She used to stay at home as she was not able to work. My father was a soldier who used to stay outside home for so long. We thought he was dead as he disappeared for long. Life was tough for my mother. My uncle used to support us financially. I realized my father is alive and married to another woman. I came to Addis Ababa to live with my father at the age of five. However, it wasn't easy to live with my step-mother. We used to fight day and night. That made my stay at home terribly difficult. My father sent me to the nearby school when I was in my childhood. However, I dropped out of school and moved back to Hirna when my mother died. I stayed there for more than a year and returned to Addis Ababa. My relationship with my step-mother went from bad to worse and I ran away from home. I finally ended up on the streets. (Mahlet, female, 18)

Most street-connected young people are migrants from different parts of the country. Family breakdown and economic problems are part of a push to leave for the city, but some youth also migrate seeking work opportunities.

Transportation may be financed by friends, by savings made while living with parents, or, as one young woman mentioned, stealing from her mother. Some travel with other youth, some with relatives.

> My friends, whom I used to live and work with, told me that they were planning to move to Addis Ababa. They invited me to accompany them. I only knew Addis Ababa from people's narration. I was 13 years old when I arrived in Addis. I settled around the Bus Station, where I slept on the streets. I mostly used to get food from hotels which provide us with leftovers. I also work when opportunities were available. Life on the streets was tough to adapt to. I got used to communicate and live with other youth of my age. (Zekaryas, male, 15)

Netsanet came to Addis Ababa financed by her relatives, but when relationships broke down, ended up street-connected.

> I came to Addis Ababa to live with my grandmother. My uncle, who is the first child of my grandmother, gave us a house in Addis Ketema … We were only taking care of my grandmother and in return my uncle used to support us financially. After my grandmother passed away, things changed completely. My uncle informed us to leave his house and we became homeless. My mother got sick. My brothers and I had never worked before and didn't know how to make money. My mother requested the local administrators to provide us with a low-cost government house on rent; but, she couldn't find. The house rent in Addis Ababa is very expensive which we couldn't afford. (Netsanet, female, 24)

For some marginalized young women, an exploitative relationship with relatives or those who employ them as a domestic worker, pushes them to live on the street, where they frequently become involved in commercial sex work or begging. Meftehe came to Addis Ababa and started living in her relative's house, but went on to the street as a result of abuse.

> I run away from home at the age of 10; I didn't think twice when my friends asked me to go with them to Addis Ababa. We moved to Addis Ababa and I went straight to my relative's house. However, I found it very difficult to stay in my relative's house. Moving away from home was a mistake I made as a little girl. The time I spent without the support of my family was very difficult. It made me hate myself. (Meftehe, female, 24)

Family economic problems made many women engage in informal work that left them vulnerable to abuse.

> I have been engaged in the informal business since my childhood. I didn't remember the time I played as a child. It is a difficult experience to bear a responsibility as a child. The fact that I started working in the cafeteria in my early teens has exposed me to engage in unsafe sexual relations. (Meron, female, 23)

Youth with disabilities who work on the street experience discrimination. They say this starts from placement in schools built for their perceived special needs, and continues through varied challenges in getting access to vocational training or financial support, and in the lack of job opportunities. They say discriminatory practices and lack of social protection schemes make their lives so difficult that some have to work and live on the street.

Rural-urban migration was visualized as a pathway to personal autonomy for many youth who become street-connected. They came in search of work, but ended up on the street because of lack of follow-up support from their parents.

> I grew up seeing my siblings moving in and out of the city. I thought they are leading a better life. I started aspiring for a life in the city due to my siblings' migration experience. (Mistre, female, 22)

Informal sector work and education

Most street-connected marginalized youth have dropped out of school and work in the informal sector. Reasons cited include family economic problems and pressures to be self-reliant or contribute to household income, lack of parental guidance, and perceived pointlessness of school due to high unemployment of educated youths. Kokebe dropped out to help her parents:

> I joined primary school at the age of eight. However, I was unable to attend classes regularly. I was supposed to support my poor family. More importantly, my parents couldn't afford to fulfil my needs. They couldn't buy me exercise books, uniforms, pens and pencils regularly. Finally, I decided to drop-out and support my poor parents by working in the informal sector. (Kokebe, female, 24)

After migrating to Addis Ketema, some tried to enrol in school, but needed documentation they could not get.

> I wanted to complete my education; but, because of two reasons, I am not in a position to do that. When I asked a school to register me and allow me to continue my education, I was told to produce a certificate which shows that I attended school up to grade five. My parents live in Gojjam where I went to school and I couldn't get my certificate because of problems associated with the long distance. Besides, since I have to work during the day, I believe that combining school and work is a challenge. (Beyene, male, 24)

Netsanet attempted to combine work and study but found it too expensive.

> After I completed grade 10, I was placed in Winget Technical College to study IT. However, I heard people talking about the tuition fee. I decided to quit since I had nothing to pay with. Then, I started looking for a

> job and managed to find one in a small shoe factory. I started working in the factory for two reasons: one was to support the family and the other was to pay for college tuition fee. Then, I got registered with Rift Valley which is a private college. I chose Secretarial Science and took courses at the night shift. My salary was only enough for the tuition fees. As I had a responsibility to support my sick mother, I decided to drop-out. (Netsanet, female, 24)

Some street-connected youth attended short-term vocational training but did not get employed, and opted to work informally.

> I have attended short-term training opportunities as a hairdresser. However, I could not find a job and stayed unemployed. Despite the difficulties to find a job as a hairdresser, I did not sit idle. I work as a hairdresser informally in my community and receive minimal payments. That is how I support myself and my daughter. (Meftehe, female, 24)

The scant opportunities open to youth make them choose the informal sector. Addis Ketema is known for large inflows of people from different parts of the country since the open market and bus station are there, and the need for informal sector labour is high. Young people work as petty traders, daily labourers, shoe-shiners, car parking workers, assistants to mini-bus and bus drivers, car washers, brokers and bedroom renters, messengers, and other low-paying jobs. There is a considerable amount of money circulated in informal businesses. But young people said that informal-sector income is not sufficient to survive in big cities like Addis Ababa.

> I do not make enough money for saving. It is from hand to mouth. I depend on my siblings who support me. Sometimes, they give me pocket money. Sometimes I work for others carrying goods from place to place and I make 100 ETB a day. (Donga, male, 20)

Since most street-connected youth end up there as a result of poverty and lack of access to formal employment, in striving for a way out, many take risky steps as a short cut to earn income, including involvement in sex work, also undertaken for the sake of survival. They are prone to an array of severe health-related harms, sexual abuse, physical abuse, unwanted pregnancy, and abortion.

> Working as a commercial sex worker, I couldn't save money to change my life. I always aspired to leave this job and start another one. However, I am still in it. I thought that if I get married to one of my customers he might help me to get out of this work. And I conceived a child from one of my customers thinking to marry him. On the contrary he failed to acknowledge that the child is his. I end up being a single mother. I have tried for the second time from another man but he also disappeared. Now I have two daughters who do not know their fathers. (Kokebe, female, 24)

When the unemployment rate increases, looking for alternative pathways is common among youth. Some are keen to migrate internationally. Street-connected youth mostly have experience of internal migration and this coupled with difficult working and living conditions, escalates aspirations for international migration. But the high costs involved and lack of support from friends and families lead them to stay. Some say that if they had access to funds, they would try a local business.

> Mostly people invest a lot of money to migrate. I do not have the money to invest in migration. Even if I have the money, I wanted to invest it in a profitable sector and work here in Ethiopia. (Tamene, male, 20)

Zinabu (aged 22) said that he always thinks of moving abroad but it is difficult for street-connected youth. He said he is illiterate and that would significantly affect his life if he left the street. Also, he doesn't have the finance and someone abroad to facilitate his move.

International migration is mostly an option only among street-connected youth who live with their families. They have the possibility of raising funds to move and organize the migration chain needed to reach the destination. The pressures of finding income and work are great and some attempt to migrate abroad illegally, which risks deception by brokers and deportation.

> I tried to move to Dubai and Europe both legally and illegally. I tried to move to Dubai many times but I failed. I can travel on a visitor visa but I heard that it's difficult to cope with the pressure of the police. Once a broker whom I approached told me that he could facilitate my move easily. He showed me a company visa online and told me the date of my flight. After paying for his services, I found out that the visa he showed me was fake. (Suleiman, male, 26)

Sometimes funds can be borrowed. Kaleb took credit from the local saving and credit association for work he planned with his friends. After they took the credit, his friends changed their minds and decided to use the money for migration.

> I was shocked when they told me that they were planning to go to Dubai with the money we took from the credit firm. It was a tough decision. They decided and left for Dubai. I stayed as I was afraid of failure. I returned the money. My friends are now in Dubai working illegally. They are paying their credit. I sometimes regret my decision. (Kaleb, male, 22)

Work, services, and the authorities

In addition to problems of insecure work and pay, informal sector work is, in most cases, deemed illegal and measures are taken against young workers by authorities and police. This probably reinforces perceptions of street-connected young people as criminals. Most of them stated they have tense relationships with police.

> The police [officers] make street youth their first suspect for robbery. The mass eviction of street youth from different areas was also mostly coordinated by the police. (Zegeye, male, 23)

> Life on the street is full of chaos. You cannot predict what was going to happen every minute. At night time, the police come and wake us up. They do not allow us to sleep around the bus station in most cases. If we do, they wake us up at least three times in a night. (Zinabu, male, 22)

As they may stay during the daytime and the night on verandas, street-connected youth are suspected of varied unlawful activities committed in the surrounding area. They complained they are victims of suspicion about criminal activities committed by other local youth.

> I have confidence in the fact that street youth have minimal involvement in crimes, especially theft. There are some young people who live in the area who come to the bus station for robbery and fraud as if it were their legal work. They commit crime and go away immediately. Youth from the surrounding have somewhere to hide. We stay here as we don't have places to hide. The policemen come and point their fingers to us. They arrest us and make us suffer on something we do not have any involvement in. (Zinabu, male, 22)

Melhik, living on the street, said that because of abuse from police, he sometimes thought about returning to his family.

> We are usually beaten by police when they caught us either falling asleep or wandering on the streets. That is the difficult face of life on the streets. Now, I aspire to go back home due to this tense relationship between the police and us – street youth. (Melhik, male, 15)

Apart from the police, other authorities and agencies, including government and non-government organizations, make interventions in the lives of street-connected youth, particularly through what are described as rehabilitation programmes. Some of these interventions are viewed with suspicion. Chiquala says efforts to rehabilitate street-connected youth are made in a way that marginalizes street-connected youth. He is suspicious that city clearance operations are implemented in the name of rehabilitation, leading to what he calls *afessa* (forcefully moving street-connected people out of town). During *afessa*, street-connected youth are gathered by police by force and taken to regions outside the capital, in harsh environmental locations, like Afar (an eastern regional state, lowland with a very hot climate), and put in a vocational training centre. He says such operations are often undertaken at night. He says he and his friends who live on the street oppose these government measures and run away when they are aware of them happening.

> When we hear about afessa we run away. During such operation, one has to have money in his pocket to pay for a shared bedroom and spend the night. That is the only way for us to escape the afessa operation. (Chiquala, male, 18)

Mahlet narrated a similar experience. She resents that she was forcefully taken out of Addis Ababa, put into a secluded centre established by government to attend vocational training, and opposes such interventions as done without enough planning and consent. She stayed in the rehabilitation centre for over three months. She thinks that it did nothing good in her life.

However, not all street-connected youth are suspicious of government rehabilitation programmes. Some gained certification through vocational training, such as Yaye who trained as an excavator operator, although he is still seeking employment. Yaye suggested measures needed for street-connected youth to be cooperative with government projects. He suggested provision of start-up capital, creating employment opportunities immediately after training, making youth part of the solution, creating market opportunities for small-scale producers and making vocational schools accessible and affordable for youth.

> We were mobilised and got trained for two weeks in paving roads using cobblestones by the local government. However, we have not yet started working. Although they promised to offer us jobs right away it all turned out to be a lie. As the cost of life is rising, we found it very difficult to pay for house rentals and be able to eat three times a day working in the informal sector. (Meron, female, 23)

Young people interviewed said that in practice government and non-government organizations make few interventions to create employment for street-connected youth. They recognize that due to the mobility of street-connected youth and limited NGO capacity, only a small number benefit from those interventions. But also, they said that youth services are not open to them, and that they are excluded from the design of intervention programmes and social services devised by development practitioners, which further exacerbates feelings of alienation and marginalization.

Zeru escaped from a street youth intervention programme after being forcibly placed there by government. He said views of street-connected youth were ignored when those interventions were developed, which he suspects led to high attrition from rehabilitation centres.

> We [street youth] don't get the chance to take part in the affairs of the community. The local administration does not consider us beneficial group of people. There is a Youth Centre in the woreda. However, street youth hardly go there as they are regarded as outsiders. (Zeru, male, 23)

Instead, marginalized and street-connected young people rely on each other for support.

Dealing with daily life
Support

A basic but most significant support for street-connected youth is other young people who work and live on the street. They work and live together for security, and peer support is also a substitute for love lost from their family. They say they experience psychological gratification through contact with other young people from street situations. But even with support among themselves, finding someone to help them get employment is challenging, so they become involved in informal work activities which do not require relationships or other collateral.

Many indicated that for newcomers to live and work on the street, support from other street-connected youth is vital to help them adapt to the life. Chalachew, who lives on the street, explained how he was received, with an emphasis on the role of mutual support.

> Street children and youth live in a group. It's difficult to survive unless you become part of one team. In my first day, I went to a group of street youth and told them that I had no place to go to. They welcome me to the street. They helped me eat dinner, leftover from the nearest hotel, and showed me place to sleep. I thought they would force me leave the next day; but, they were comfortable having me on their side. We are still friends and live together. (Chalachew, male, 26)

For young women, mutual support from female or male street-connected youth is vital to avoid sexual abuse. Meklit said she sees herself as a local protector for female newcomers to the street. She is concerned about risks females will be exposed to if they are not helping each other.

> I live with three other female street youth. If I am there, all the male street youth will fear to come to our place. We [females] have our own shade and if any of the males comes nearby, I will bombard them with stones. Sometimes, drunken passers-by come in the middle of the night and destroy our plastic shades [wanting] to abuse any of us. But we are already too strong to confront any one at any time. (Meklit, female, 23)

Substance use

Substance use is common among street-connected youth. They consider this as a way of conforming to 'in-group' statuses, so some begin using substances as a result of peer pressure. They say it is also a way of adopting and coping with life on the street. Some assert it helps them to forget grief they have had in life, and helps to calm them for a while. Substance use was often part of their past home life, as some went on to the street as a result of domestic violence fuelled by alcohol use of their parents or guardians. Some left home for good when their families discovered their substance use.

Yet in comparison to youth who live on the street, those who work there and go to their houses at night use substances less often. It was found that a strong support system, especially from friends and families, helped them to have minimal exposure to substance use. But the majority of street-connected youth reported that they have used substances for long periods of time. They explained different actions they took to escape addiction, but failed in most cases. The reason for the failure was related to personal problems, peer pressure, and the availability and affordability of substances where they live.

They use various substances, including glue- and benzene-sniffing, local liquor drinking, *khat* chewing, tobacco smoking, and in some instances marijuana. Street-connected youth relate their use of such substances to confrontation of difficulties on the street. They assert that it will help them forget vulnerability and calm hunger, offer entertainment, provide courage, a feeling of belonging with other young people when using together, and enable sleep without interruption by voices and noises of overcrowding, and the cold weather.

The use of substances greatly affects their life. Reported effects include lack of confidence to seek formal employment, boredom, feelings of shame, depression, and hopelessness, nervousness, sleeping difficulties, sweating, and mental fatigue. According to young people, substances are easily accessible, affordable, and become normalized over time. Relevant stakeholders say they are well aware of these issues. Lack of enforcement of laws prohibiting sale of substances to minors, and unavailability of detoxification and rehabilitation programmes, were mentioned as reasons for perpetuation of problems.

Substance use affects youths' lives and life-decisions. Bereket, who lives with friends around a bus station in Addis Ketema, was a beneficiary of an intervention programme providing vocational training for street-connected youth. He got six-months' training on male hairdressing, attending diligently as it lasted only two hours a day. He then tried, but could not continue, the work found by the organization, because of his substance use.

> I thought that I can last for long time without chewing *khat* and smoking cigarette. However, I couldn't. I left the work and returned to my life on the street. I can't live in a situation where someone would tell me at what time I have to enter and go out. I have had the opportunities to be employed again but I hesitated. I want a work that I can work at any time of the day so that it will not be challenging for me to use the substances I want. (Bereket, male, 23)

Others reported similar stories. Interventions prepared and implemented by different stakeholders were found to be top-down with minimal involvement of street-connected youth, and not designed to be convincing and accessible for them. Interventions by government and non-government organizations on substance use are mostly in institutionalized environments. But most street-connected youth oppose the idea of institution-based rehabilitation services. They prefer interventions to help them harmonize with the community and environment where they live.

Conclusion: uncertainty on the street

Due to their living situation, marginalized and street-connected young people in Addis Ketema face uncertainty throughout their daily life. Having dropped out or failed at school, often without literacy, many migrated from rural areas some distance away, and living away from or without parents, their work opportunities are limited to the informal sector. Much of this work is unreliable, transient, and requires daily planning to find. Due to loose or no interaction with parents they make daily and life-changing decisions by themselves. Awareness of issues such as reproductive health is minimal: most do not have parents with whom they can talk, and those with parents are not in the habit of talking openly about such issues. They rely on peers for support. A shared identity and support is manifested through common daily experiences of making a living and survival, and through substance use.

Uncertainty is also perpetuated by the way the community perceive youth who live and work on the street. Most-marginalized and street-connected young people feel that the community around them, including authorities, perceive them as deviant, in conflict with the law, and liable to commit damage or harm in the area. They are prime suspects for any criminal activity. They feel uncertain about their co-existence with community neighbours. Further uncertainty arises from their living situation which makes street-connected youth more vulnerable to effects of political and economic turmoil, particularly ethnic and political conflict.

Some think they are considered a burden rather than a useful part of the community, a perception reinforced through actions forcibly removing groups to training camps away from the city. Street-connected youth identify themselves with street peers; they stress the need for their views to be heard in development interventions that affect their lives directly or indirectly. The use of top-down approaches, in which interventions are planned and implemented on them without consent, makes them feel insecure and further marginalized.

Although street-connected youth talk about their intention of moving out of street life, most oppose institution-based services and would prefer to be rehabilitated where they live. They are resourceful and have a strong connection with their local social space and environment. They devise different strategies of surviving on the street with increasing resilience over time. The top-down intervention programmes do not take into consideration the resilience, skills, and ambitions of the street-connected youth.

PART 3
Nepal

CHAPTER 9
Nepal: Context and themes

Nepal is globally famous for its mountains and is situated between the two most populous countries on earth, China and India. Its multi-ethnic/caste and multilingual population resides in the mountains, hills, and plains. Conflict since the late 20th century has brought political change, with a new constitution and government leading to reform. Changes in formal categories of ethnic/caste groups are part of broader shifts seeking to change the circumstances of marginalized and poor people. In this chapter, the diverse population and social structures are outlined along with a short background to the present social and political situation. Changes in youth policy and young people's perceptions of marginalization are set against policy definitions. The location of four YOUR World research sites in Nepal is briefly described followed by an outline of key findings from Nepal across all locations.

Keywords: youth, Nepal, marginalization, families, discrimination, education, employment, migration, genderfluid

Introduction

Nepal is globally famous for its mountains and its high altitude, given the presence of the mountain known as Everest in English, सगरमाथा *Sagarmāthā* in Nepali, 珠穆朗玛 *Zhūmùlǎngmǎ* in Chinese, and ཇོ་མོ་གླང་མ *Chomolungma* in Tibetan. The different pronunciations and names indicate the cultural and political significance of the country, situated between the two states with the largest populations in the world, China and India. The mountains provide a political barrier but do not divide, with ethnicities of Tibetan, Nepali, and Indian group identity living on both sides of the border, significant belief and religious commonalities, and cross-border interactions among families and communities as well as trade. Nepal has a distinct history and cultural composition that can pose conceptual challenges to people whose everyday lives are not structured through similar social hierarchies.

Nepal is known for the Himalayan mountain range through extensive tourism for climbing and trekking. But the spectacular environment, along with fragility caused by seasonal rain and landslips, limits rural livelihoods. In recent decades the consequence has been internal and international migration, driven also by issues in social structure and governance, conflict, and other changes. Less well-known is the Terai, plains to the south of the country that extend across the border into India, and the Chure hills that rise from these toward the northern mountains. Despite being flatlands, agricultural use is also limited here. This southern region, in the mid-western part of Nepal, is the site of the birthplace of Prince Siddhartha Gautama (Buddha), who spent his early years in Lumbini in 623 BCE, attaining enlightenment in what is now India. Although Nepal has a substantial Buddhist population, the majority are Hindu.

The population of nearly 30 million is very diverse in terms of ethnicity/caste and language, with over 100 of each. The apparently rigid hierarchies of the past, a complex set of categories forming a political-religious-social structure, is changing both formally and practically, particularly with the constitutional changes in the 21st century. Changes in governance have accompanied conflict, the aftermath of which is still relevant. Constitutional changes and inauguration of a new government during the research period heralded other changes in governance. The country is in the process of transition from a unitary to a federal state, devolving responsibilities to local levels, which will particularly affect the lives of children and young people as they grow older.

This chapter provides a brief background to the diversity and categories of people, languages, conflict, and governance, and situates the research sites, issues, and findings.

People

In 2011 the national population was 26.5 million people (26,494,504), with slightly more females at 13.6 million (13,645,463) than males at 12.8 million (12,849.041) (CBS Nepal, 2012, 2014a, 2014b). By 2020 estimates of the population projected an increase to 29.1 million (29,136,808 on Worldometers website). The national demographic profile is young, with 40 per cent under 18 years in 2016, but population trends show a rapidly ageing society (UNICEF, 2018).

The 2011 census indicated the scale of population diversity, with 129 categories (including foreigners) listing 126 ethnic/caste groups. The group categories involve different styles of identity, for example the so-called 'caste' groupings based on formulation of a hierarchical social structure, while other 'ethnic' groupings include various hill and mountain peoples with separate 'tribal' identities, while predominantly religious categories, such as 'Musealman' or Nepalese Muslim, are also included. The overlay between caste, ethnicity, and religion indicates the complexities of identity that are further differentiated through place of living, migration, and marriage. Changes in the constitution also changed some categories with the aim of eroding discrimination against groups such as Dalit, but also hill peoples now included as indigenous people within the term Janajati.

The main groupings, each with a population of over 1 million in 2011, were: Chhetree (or Chhetri) with 4.39 million; Hill Brahman, 3.22 million; Magar, 1.88 million; Tharu, 1.73 million; Tamang, 1.53 million; Newar, 1.32 million; Kami, 1.25 million; Musalman (Muslim), 1.16 million; and Yadaev, 1.05 million. All groups had more females than males, except for the Muslim and Yadeav. However, because there are separate sub-groups of Dalit peoples (who have faced significant discrimination and oppression over centuries), their population has to be separately totalled. The census categorizes separately groups such as Badi (over 38,000) and Other Dalits (over 155,000). In 2011 these categories totalled 3.6 million Dalit people, 13.6 per cent of the population (and current estimates suggest this has risen to 20 per cent; IDSN, 2021).

In summary, the hierarchical structure putting Dalit people in this position was formalized in the late 14th century by Jayasthiti Malla (1354–95), in the classification: 1) Brahman/Chhetri (priests/warriors); 2) Vaishya (merchants); 3) Sudra (peasants); and 4) Achhut (untouchable) (Sharma, 2004) and codified in the 19th century, in the detailed Muluki Ain law code of 1854 (Hofer, 1979; Gellner, 1989). The past has continued to influence the hierarchic structure of society which has resulted in differential access to education, economic, political, and socio-cultural resources, the marginalization of some groups and continuing inequity in society. Social change is occurring alongside political and constitutional change. In 2005 the major ethnic/caste divisions, drawn from the 1991 census were given as: Parbatyas (Nepali speaking); Newars (Newar or Nepali speaking); other hill or mountain ethnic groups, 'tribes'; Madhesis (groups speaking north Indian dialects); ethnic groups of the Terai; Muslims; Marwaris; and Sikhs (Whelpton, 2005: 9–10). The first two and fourth groupings comprised a range of hierarchical castes; the third grouping a range of hill peoples.

Changes in government and policy (see below) have given greater emphasis to groups seen as marginalized. These particularly include Dalit, Janajati, Adivasi, and Madhesi. The widespread identity of Dalit, previously considered as part of but outside the higher caste framework as *untouchables*, is noted above. The term Janajati is now used across the country embodied in law. Janajati also refers to *Aadibasi* or *adivasi* and means indigenous people, a tribe or community, for example, Tharu, Thakali, Newar, Gurung, Magar, Limbu, Sunuwar, Tamang, Sherpa, or Hyolmo, which is mentioned in the law of Nepal, has a mother language and traditional rites and customs, distinct cultural identity, social structure, and written or unwritten history. The Madhesi are people living in Terai (southern plains), with linguistic and often other connections across the border with India (Ghimire, 2018; Karna et al., 2018). They are predominantly Hindus with some Muslims and Christians.

These terminologies and identities, past and present, are important as the lens through which much of the population sees the world and relationships, and because they are also part of governmental changes to deal with issues of marginalization. In addition to group identities, over 100 languages with native speakers were listed in the 2011 census. Apart from Nepali, with over 11 million, there were four other languages with over 1 million, and a further six languages with over half a million native speakers. Many other languages had speakers running into the tens and hundreds of thousands, indicating linguistic complexity and implications for delivery of education and other services.

Background

A new parliament and government came into power in February 2018 after elections at the end of 2017. In the preceding decade a much larger constituent assembly had been elected in 2008 and 2013 to produce a new constitution. The new government, after elections for all three tiers, local, state, and federal, of the new constitution, marked a 'conclusion of a political transition that began with the signing of the Comprehensive Peace Agreement in November 2006' (World Bank, 2020)

The Peace Agreement itself marked the end of a 10-year conflict, and a long period of change in Nepal politics since 1951 in which the monarchy, now abolished, had played a major role. Nepal was unified in 1788. From 1846, Nepal was ruled by a succession of hereditary chief ministers, *Ranas*, who dominated the monarch and kept the country isolated from the outside world (Whelpton, 2005). In 1951 the *Ranas* were overthrown and the Nepali Congress Party formed the government until 1960 when King Mahendra took control and suspended parliament. After 1962 the King ruled through a panchayat, council system, although pro-democracy protests were held throughout the 1980s and in 1990 King Birenda agreed a new constitution. In the elections of 1991 the Nepali Congress Party won, and in 1994 a Communist government formed which was dissolved in 1995. While the Maoist revolt began in 1996, political instability saw several changes of prime minister (Shrestha, 2004). The royal massacre of 2001, officially reported as the Crown Prince killing the King, Queen, and other members of the royal family, before shooting himself, is still seen as requiring further investigation by some. King Birenda's brother Gyanendra then became King. Conflict over the next few years saw governments dismissed, elections postponed, and in 2005 the King restored an absolute monarchy. Conflict continued until the 2006 peace agreement, followed by restoration of parliament in interim government which agreed the abolition of the monarchy in 2007 (Snellinger, 2018). Conflict persisted in the southern plains, where some groups sought regional autonomy, and in the west. The conflict had led to thousands of deaths and much internal displacement. The government, with varied successive leaders from Congress, Communist, and Maoist parties, formed the new constitution leading to the elections of 2017. In February 2018 the Chair of the Communist Party of Nepal, K.P. Oli, who was prime minister in 2015–16, was again sworn in. At the end of 2020, he dissolved the House of Representatives, amid a tussle for power with his party leaders and called for elections to be held in May 2021. But the Nepal Supreme Court overturned the Prime Minister's decision and reinstated the Lower House of Parliament.

Significant changes came with the new constitution, including a shift to a federal system with more powers moving to seven new provinces, and 753 local governments. This requires new legislation and institutions, with central government now focused on oversight (World Bank, 2020).

Youth policy and marginalization

YOUR World Research works with young people whose age ranges from 15 to 24, but youth policy age definitions differ in Nepal (and Ethiopia). A National Youth Policy approved on 6 October 2015 (2072/6/19 in the Nepal calendar) superseded the 2010 policy implemented during the Constituent Assembly period (MoYS, 2010). Both policies define youth as men, women, and people of the third gender aged 16 to 40 years, but the 2015 policy recognizes that 'The conditions and needs of the youths belonging to different age groups being different, the targeted programs shall be conducted by dividing the youths into two different age groups (16–24 years, 25–40 years)' (article 24). The definitions set out in the policies highlight issues around priority groups, need, marginalization, and vulnerability. They also show changes in languages and concepts, for example to 'citizens' rather than 'men, women, third gender', and changes in the special priority groups.

2015 Youth policy definition:

a. 'Youth' means citizens within the age bracket of 16 to 40 years.
b. 'Youth belonging to priority group' means women *adivasi*, *janajati* and *madhesi* youths,
c. 'Youth belonging to special priority group' means the youth belonging to the community of conflict victims, endangered, physically crippled, marginalized, exposed to extinction, minorities, dalits, Muslims and the youth belonging to Karnali and the backward regions.
d. 'Conflict victim youth' means the youth affected by the armed conflict ranging from the year of 2052 (1994) to Mangshir 5, 2063 (2006) and those belonging to conflict victims' families in the later days.
e. 'Youth at risk' means the youth infected by HIV and AIDS, victims of trafficking trapped in natural disaster, users of narcotic drugs, those involved in sex trade, homeless, those belonging to *mukta kamaiya* (freed bonded labor) families and the youth involved in foreign employment in countries of insecure destination.
f. 'Physically challenged youth' means the youth having confronted by types of physical and mental challenges.
g. 'Youth belonging to marginalized minority community' means the youth deprived of national and non-governmental benefits and services due to geographical remoteness and caste, language, culture, region, class and gender related grounds, marginalized and the other youths who could not come in the national mainstream.

Source: MoYS, 2015

Youth perceptions of marginalization

Discourse on marginalization in Nepal for many years focused on 'indigenous peoples, women, *Madhesis*, *Dalits* and other marginalized communities on the basis of caste, ethnicity, language, religion, sex, class and geographical territory' as indicated by Om Gurung (2009: 1), However, while youth perceptions in this research follow contemporary government definitions of marginalization to some extent, such as including discrimination due to gender, caste/ethnicity,

118 YOUTH AND POSITIVE UNCERTAINTY

Table 9.1 Marginalization: some youth indicators from research locations

Kapilvastu rural and urban	Sindhupalchowk
Gender, caste, and ethnicity	Gender, caste, and ethnicity
Language	Lack of access to public services
Landlessness, no property	Land ownership
Depending on religion – Hindu/Muslim	Family poverty
Lack of access to public services	Alcoholism
Lack of parental care	Conceiving before marriage
Violence and abuse in families	Environmental fragility
Heavy workloads and long hours	
Voices unheard, adults don't listen	
Young women's lack of mobility	
Kathmandu street and slum	**Kathmandu genderfluid**
Caste and ethnicity	Sexual identity
Neglected on the street	Lack of citizenship papers
Called names on the street such as *Khate*	Harassment in school/public spaces
In slums poor health, poor housing, inequality	Workplace discrimination
	Feeling rejected
Poor access to services	Discrimination in health services
Drug and substance abuse	
Lack of employment opportunities	

language, class (as indicated in Section g of the 2015 Youth Policy above), they go further. Youth also include discrimination by services and feelings of rejection in communities. Most marginalized youth who participated in the research had dropped out of or failed at formal school.

Some indicators of youth perceptions of marginalization are laid out in Table 9.1.

Research locations

Research was conducted in two urban and two rural locations, selected through discussion with partners (national government officers, academics, non-government organization staff, youth organizations). These locations were chosen as having been affected by previous conflict and environmentally fragile or prone to disasters. They are particularly impoverished and show diversity in terms of ethnic/caste group and religion, so as to explore how different processes of marginalization and varying vulnerabilities affect uncertainty among young people.

A rural and an urban location were selected in Kapilvastu, in the plains or Terai region to the south of Nepal, bordering India. A very different geographical region, Sindhupalchowk in the hills and mountains to the north, was selected as the other rural location before the 2015 earthquake, which severely affected this area. Parts of Kathmandu were chosen as an urban location, focusing on slum areas of in-migration, where street-connected youth are also to be found. Genderfluid young people were interviewed mainly in Kathmandu.

Kapilvastu rural and urban

Kapilvastu is a district in Lumbini Province, situated towards the western end of Nepal. Lumbini is one of the seven provinces established by the new constitution of 2015. It has hills and a small area of high mountains to the north, and plains to the south. The province is well known as the birthplace of the Buddha in what is now Rupandehi District, to the east of Kapilvastu, both districts having a southern border with India. Before 2015, Kapilvastu was in the middle zone.

Kapilvastu District is in the south of the province and consists of lowland plains and some low hills in its north-west. The plains, known as the Terai, extend into India. The district is moderately vulnerable ecologically, exposed to waves of heat and cold. Although most of Kapilvastu is lowland plains, less than half (48 per cent) is suitable for cultivation, with consequent pressure on the rural population. Rural areas of Kapilvastu remain among the poorest communities in Nepal. Communities have not only been destabilized by poverty but also through periods of conflict and subsequent post-conflict tensions, although they are not now in situations of armed conflict.

Apart from the airport in Bhairahawa, which provides domestic flights to Kathmandu of less than an hour, travel in and out of the district is facilitated by the main East-West Highway connecting Kapilvastu to other parts of Nepal. A northern feeder road from the highway serves adjacent districts, but another feeder blacktop road runs south to India. South-western Kapilvastu (Krishnanagar) is an important transport corridor between the two countries. Seasonal migration to India is important for many rural households to increase their income, and the district is said to be highly dependent on remittances. Since the southern belt of Kapilvastu borders India, the rural economy here largely depends on cross-border commercial links, both legal and illegal. Competition for control of border trade has been a major cause of tension among various factions, including landlords, small political groups, criminal gangs, individual members of the security forces, and political parties (Bhandari, 2008).

The population of Kapilvastu increased by 90,000 in the first decade of the 21st century, from 481,976 in 2001 to 571,936 in 2011 (CBS Nepal, 2012, 2014b). This population is roughly equally divided between male (285,599) and female (286,337) (CBS Nepal, 2012, 2014b). The District's age profile reveals a rather young population, and with many fewer males aged between

15 and 34 years than females. This gender imbalance is common in districts with high rates of seasonal migration.

In recent decades significant domestic migration into the Terai (including rural areas of Kapilvastu) from northern hill districts has resulted in tensions between Terai residents and incoming Pahadi (non-Terai people) settlers, who include Muslims and Hindus of all castes, including landless Dalits. The Pahadis have tended to settle in already established Madhesi communities. In the early 1990s the Government distributed land to some Pahadis (for example in Dipendranagar village, Patthardaiya Village Development Committee, Kapilvastu). Other Pahadis occupy formerly unused public land, such as in Devipur village, Bishunpur village, Kapilvastu. Land issues continue to be a primary source of tension (Bhandari, 2008).

The population of the district is diverse in religion and caste/ethnicity: the government profile of the district describes some 86 castes/ethnicities in Kapilvastu. Caste-based discrimination is prevalent and the rural area of Kapilvastu has experienced communal violence and religious riots. The majority of the District population are Hindu (81 per cent), similar to the national proportion, but with a much larger number of Muslims (18 per cent in Kapilvastu, but under 5 per cent nationally) and the remainder Buddhist and other religions (CBS Nepal, 2014b). In terms of caste/ethnicity, over a quarter of the population are local Terai groups (26 per cent), and other large groupings include Brahman-Chhetri (16 per cent), Tharu (13 per cent), Terai Dalits (12 per cent), along with the Muslim and then smaller groupings such as Gurung/Magar (3 per cent) and Hill Dalits (3 per cent) and others.

In the years 1985, 1991, 1992, 2000, and 2005 different types of conflicts erupted, resulting in fires set on houses and vandalization of property. Subsequent violence in 2007 is regarded as a continuation of such activities. Kapilvastu often experienced Muslim-Pahade communal violence, but after the formation of an Anti-Maoist Resistance group many huts were burnt in 2007 on the accusation that they provided shelter to the Maoists. In that cycle of violence, more than 600 huts were burnt, and more than 50 people were killed. The violence was triggered on 16 September 2007 following the killing of Mohit Khan, a leader of Madhesi Loktantrik Mukti Morcha (MLMM) and a former leader of the anti-Maoist resistance group, in Birpur area (Bhandari, 2008).

Kapilvastu has some of the most rapidly growing urban areas in Nepal. In 2014 six new municipalities were designated, alongside the five rural municipalities in the District. Some of the urban areas on which the research focused were previously, but quite recently, village development communities. A main focus of urban research was Chandrauta of Shivaraj Municipality. The total population of Shivaraj Municipality is 49,988 people, comprising 24,948 males and 25,040 females (OS/DCC Kapilvastu, 2017). The 2011 census found 90 per cent of the district population were Awadhi speakers, followed by Tharu (5 per cent) and Nepali speakers (5 per cent). There are over 13 languages spoken in Shivaraj Municipality, indicating the extent of diversity and in-migration.

Sindhupalchowk

Sindhupalchowk is a district in Bagmati Province, situated in the centre north of Nepal. Bagmati, province Number Three, is one of the seven established by the 2015 constitution. The province runs north to south of Nepal, with the south-western district of Chitwan bordering the Indian state of Bihar, while three districts in the north, including Sindhupalchowk, border Tibet and the government of China. The province has 13 districts, further divided into urban and rural municipalities.

Sindhupalchowk can be divided into two areas: mountains (with elevations above 3,500 metres) and more density populated hilly areas. It has three urban and nine rural municipalities. Chautara, the district headquarters, is located at an altitude of 1,450 m. The population of Sindhupalchowk is 285,770, (149,107 female, 136,663 male) residing in 66,635 households, with a life expectancy of 62 years, and an average literacy rate of around 60 per cent (CBS Nepal, 2014b).

The population of the district encompasses many ethnicities/castes including Tamang, Chhetri, Brahman, Newar, Bishwokarma, Sanyasi, Sherpa, Darji/Pariyar, Majhi, Magar, Gurung, Hyolmo, Thami, Mijar/Sarki, Danuwar, Pahari, Ghale, and others. The dominant languages are Nepali (55.31 per cent), Tamang (31.26 per cent), also with Newari (6.71 per cent), Sherpa (2.86 per cent), Hyolmo (2.11 per cent), Thami (0.99 per cent), and others (0.76 per cent) spoken.

The environmental fragility of the district is indicated by the impact of frequent landslides where the population lives and cultivates at different elevations on hills and mountains. The villages of intense land movements in Sindhupalchowk correspond to areas with high rates of seasonal rainfall, which trigger landslides. The risk of continued land-sliding escalates significantly as the rains begin. This ongoing problem threatens already-affected areas, and extends further through the wash of landslide sediment downstream onto valley floors and floodplains.

Landslides of August 2014 severely impacted agricultural production in the district, and the effects of these problems for the local population were exacerbated less than a year later by the earthquake of April 2015. Some 63,885 houses (two-thirds of households based on the 2011 Census) were severely and 2,751 houses moderately damaged in Sindhupalchowk through the earthquake. Based on government reporting on damaged houses, an estimated 109,000 people were affected, that is 40 per cent of the district populace according to the 2011 Census. Around 90,000 people were in need of assistance based on reporting at village authority level.

Environmental fragility, and low level of agricultural production, mean that nearly half the population (some 45 per cent) are living below the poverty line

(CBS Nepal, 2012). This is a factor in the extent of out-migration for employment and income, which also contributes to trafficking. Sindhupalchowk district has one of the highest rates of human trafficking in the country, where marginalized women and children are particularly vulnerable, driven by factors such as poverty, lack of women's rights and empowerment, gender discrimination, and lack of livelihood opportunities.

Kathmandu: slums and street

Kathmandu is the capital city of Nepal, located in the Kathmandu Valley in Province Three – the same province as Sindhupalchowk. The Kathmandu Valley comprises three districts, essentially separate but adjoining towns, of Kathmandu, Lalitpur (Patan), and Bhaktapur. These together cover 899 square kilometres, although the area of the valley as a whole is 665 square kilometres. The Valley encloses the entire area of Bhaktapur district, but less of the other two: it includes 85 per cent of Kathmandu district and just 50 per cent of Lalitpur district. A government website (in 2021) proclaimed that 'Kathmandu is now the premier cultural and economic hub of Nepal and is considered to have the most advanced infrastructure among urban areas in Nepal. From the point of view of tourism, economy and cultural heritage, the sister cities of Patan (Lalitpur) and Bhaktapur are integral to Kathmandu' (OME Nepal, 2021).

The 2011 population of Kathmandu was 1,744,240, with a high population density of 4,415.80 per square kilometre (CBS Nepal, 2012). The census shows that over the first decade of the 21st century the population growth for Kathmandu, at 60.93 per cent, was far higher than the increase for Nepal overall, at 14.98 per cent. This growth in Kathmandu largely stems from a process of in-migration from other parts of the country, so that in 2011 the city accounted for approximately one-third of Nepal's total urban population which had been growing at a rate of 4.76 per cent per annum (CBS Nepal, 2012). This process also caused an increase in inequality and a rise in numbers of the 'urban poor' strata: this category includes migrant workers, street vendors, and people living in slums. They generally live in deprived economic conditions, are unable to get better occupations, and lack access to social, cultural, and educational opportunities in comparison to middle and upper class people (SS Nepal, 2014; UNICEF, 2014).

The city area has been densely populated for millennia. The Valley was predominantly inhabited by Newar people in the past, but with in-migration and urbanization, Kathmandu's present demography includes most castes/ethnicities, religions, and languages of Nepal. According to the 2011 census, the five largest population groups in Kathmandu are: 1) Brahman, 2) Newar, 3) Chhetri, 4) Tamang, and 5) Magar. This is different from the national profile whereby Chhetri (4,398,179) is the largest population and Newar (1,321,933) is lower. National proportions are: Chhetri, 16.6 per cent; Brahman, 12.1 per cent; Magar, 7.1 per cent; Tharu, 6.5 per cent; Tamang, 5.8 per cent;

and Newar, 4.9 per cent (Mega Nepal, 2017: 9). In terms of religion, most people follow Hinduism (80.01 per cent), Buddhism (15.39 per cent), Christianity (2.33 per cent), Islam (1.25 per cent), and Kirat (0.77 per cent) (Mega Nepal 2017: 295).

According to Pradhan (2003), the number of squatter settlements in the city was increasing at the rate of 25 per cent per year; also, early in the 21st century, Kathmandu city held 7 per cent of the national population but 30 per cent of the urban population. Pradhan showed growth from the 1970s with only 17 squatter settlements in the Kathmandu Valley, to approximately 64 at the start of the 21st century. These 64 settlements were estimated to accommodate 2,600 families or nearly 15,000 people. The conditions of slum children were then more vulnerable compared to other working class people (Pradhan, 2003), which continues. People living there are deprived of basic amenities such as education, health, and sanitation. Unlike youngsters living in higher income urban areas, millions of adolescents in slums go to work instead of school, head a household, and are parents in and outside marriage (UN-Habitat, 2006, 2007; UNICEF, 2014).

Key themes in the research

Key themes emerging from the research in Nepal involve uncertainties around poverty, landlessness, the effects of stigma and discrimination based on caste/ethnicity, gender, disability, living situation, dropping out of school, inappropriate education, having household work and duties from an early age, and consequently the capacities for marginalized young people to fulfil social expectations and family responsibilities. In order to address their own circumstances in the context of family and community conventions, marginalized young people need to make decisions dealing with uncertainties.

The main themes discussed across the following chapters from the Nepal research sites concern families, education, and employment. The theme of families includes issues of discrimination and abuse as well as family support. The themes of education and employment are combined, and also involve migration. These key themes are also discussed in Chapter 19.

Families

Marginalized young people in rural Kapilvastu have grown up with lives structured by discrimination based on ethnicity/caste, religion, age, economic status, and gender, on top of the effects of family landlessness and poverty. Discrimination continues to structure uncertainties of youth and early adulthood, and shape the poverty that limits their education and frequently requires early school drop-out to support family, but differentiates futures of young men and young women.

Many young people, sometimes with their families, have migrated from rural Kapilvastu into the urban area and have different experiences of conflict and integration. Marginalized young people in urban Kapilvastu feel pressures from parents and elders to meet expectations for providing family support and fulfilling obligations. They want to break up discriminatory practices, but retain other social conventions such as supporting family, although shifting patterns of consumption increase pressures on them.

In Sindhupalchowk, because of environmental fragility and poor agricultural yield, many parents have migrated, leaving children and young people with economic and social household responsibilities. They have to work from an early age and will drop out of education partly because of that and inaccessibility of school. They would prefer to stay in the district but face community pressures to migrate to earn an income and support family.

In Kathmandu, in-migrant families form slum communities facing environmental fragility and insecurity of tenure. Young people and their families experience stigma and discrimination from external communities and authorities, but recognize gradations of marginalization within the slum, partly based on the degree of family support as well as associated problems of unemployment: drug use. In the context of in-migration from other parts of the country and forming a comparatively new community, family support is important for youth aspirations and dealing with uncertainty. Many of those who are not successful may take refuge in drug use.

Genderfluid young people often come from traditionally gendered families that find it hard to accept their sexuality, although the research showed increasing acceptance. Many genderfluid youth do not declare their sexuality or feelings due to fear of being rejected. (See Chapter 14 for research with genderfluid youth.)

Education and employment

Across the sites, marginalized young people had dropped out of school or failed national exams: they suggested that formal education was not relevant to their lives. Education is not providing them with the skills they feel they need to gain employment. There was also strong evidence of gender discrimination and lack of understanding of the value of girls' education. Some of the most-marginalized may be interested in education but lack financial means, or girls, especially from Muslim families, do not have the mobility to travel for education beyond primary level.

In rural Kapilvastu, poverty and marginalization mean that children work from an early age and often drop out of school. Social and family expectations and differential gendered mobility mean that young people must cope with different mobilities and uncertainties. Young women face restrictions on movement, even going out of the home, and uncertainties on marriage. The limited mobility of young women places further burdens on and forces young men to face uncertainties of finding income for family.

In urban Kapilvastu many had dropped out of school and been forced to take risky work; many had left home or drifted about because of difficulties and abuse in their families. Much of the abuse and violence they experienced at home was associated with alcohol use by adults. In this rapidly urbanizing area, marginalized young people are developing new strategies to meet uncertainties, through consulting family but also making their own decisions to both find employment and fulfil aspirations to engage with new cultural practices such as music and fashion, through alternative local means, or by international migration.

In all sites, many young people were expected to provide for their families and had to take low paid or exploitative work in order to do so, often migrating within Nepal for education or in search of employment. Although many in the hills of Sindhupalchowk have an interest in staying in the village or in the country, some migrate as a result of community pressures to seek work due to the fragility of the environment and lack of local income and employment.

In Kathmandu slums, education is viewed by some families as important but also not providing appropriate skills for work, and young people often prefer to train on the job. Employment is often difficult to find and secure without support. Unemployment is associated with escape from rejection through drug use and criminal activity, but employment appears essential to rehabilitation. Some youth migrate internationally, partly supported by family, as a means of obtaining housing and small-business capital that is otherwise unavailable.

Genderfluid youth

When YOUR World Research was planned, it was envisaged that 10 genderfluid youth from each country would be interviewed. In Nepal this was possible, through assistance from local partners in Kathmandu, to find youth who identify as being genderfluid or, using local terminology, as third gender. In Ethiopia it was not possible to work with genderfluid youth because at the time of research it was not accepted that people could identify as non-binary or any sexuality other than heterosexual. The research with genderfluid youth in Nepal is important in understanding how they feel marginalized even in a country where their identities are recognized and there are national policies of non-discrimination. (See Chapter 14 for genderfluid youth views and voices.)

CHAPTER 10
Rural Kapilvastu: Discrimination and uncertainty

Marginalized young people in rural Kapilvastu have grown up with lives structured by discrimination based on ethnicity/caste, religion, age, economic status and gender, on top of the effects of family landlessness and poverty. Discrimination continues to structure uncertainties of youth and early adulthood, and shape the poverty that limits their education and frequently requires early school drop-out to support family. Experiences of conflict shaped further uncertainties and left a residue of mistrust and feelings of retaliation and anger, confirmed by insecurity when violence erupts in the community for reasons including alcohol misuse, which is also associated with domestic violence. Most marginalized young people live with parents and support families. Social and family expectations and differential gendered mobility mean that young people must cope with different mobilities and uncertainties. Young women face uncertainties on marriage, and their limited mobility forces young men to face uncertainties of finding income for family.

Keywords: youth, caste/ethnicity, gender, age, discrimination, uncertainty, rural Kapilvastu, Nepal

Introduction

The rural area of the Kapilvastu district in Nepal has experienced communal violence and religious riots and, although not currently in armed conflict, communities have been destabilized by its aftermath and ongoing poverty. Young people are marginalized through poverty and social exclusionary practices based on ethnicity/caste, gender, age, and income discrimination. Children and young people in families that have broken up or become reconstituted following parental death, separation, remarriage or remaining single, face stigma and discrimination and further marginalization and domination in the community. Young women experience unequal power relations due to a patriarchal social structure, particularly in Madhesi and Muslim communities. Discrimination and conventionally expected behaviours of young men and women steer their experiences of uncertainty while restricting their roles and opportunities. Young women are restricted to the household by parents, brothers, husbands, and in-laws. While young women's mobility is limited, young men are expected to support the family and must go out to seek employment, and often need to migrate internally or even internationally.

Kapilvastu is a district in the south of Nepal, bordering India. It is situated in the low flatlands, the Terai, which extend across the border and offer a complete contrast to the hills and mountains further north. International, overland cross-border movement, for trade, marriage, and migration is prevalent in both directions. The diverse population of the Terai includes large Madhesi and Muslim communities, and in-migrants from other parts of Nepal. Both rural and urban areas have experienced communal conflict arising from religious identity, and this, along with issues of language associated with ethnicity, and the significance of gender discrimination, were found to be key themes characterizing the lives and uncertainties of young people.

The total population of Kapilvastu District in 2011 was 571,936 (285,599 male, 286,337 female): projections suggest increases of some 55,000 by 2016. In 2011, Muslims constituted the largest group categorized, around 18 per cent (103,856 people); the majority (81 per cent) were classified as Hindu religion with a small Buddhist population. Larger groups classified in 2011 include: Tharu (70,096), Yadav (57,967), Hill Brahman (48,834), and Chhetri (35,722). Over 30 languages were listed as 'mother-tongues' in 2011, the four largest, constituting 549,144 people, were Avadhi (284,701); Urdu (101,744); Nepali (98,062); and Tharu (64,637). No others had 10,000 or more mother-tongue speakers (CBS Nepal, 2014b).

Selected villages were particularly impoverished and show diversity in terms of religion and ethnicity. Research was conducted in Devipur, Bishunpur, Vudihawa, and Bahadurgunj, all affected by conflict, migration, and environmental fragility. Forty detailed and 20 additional focused case studies were collected from marginalized young people (aged 15–24 years), half male and half female. Detailed case studies included 21 from the Dalit community, two Janajati, nine Madhesi, and eight who wanted to be identified as Muslim in both ethnicity and religion. Thirty-two participants followed the Hindu religion.

The situation of young people

The lived experiences of marginalization of some young people in rural Kapilvastu are framed by inequalities and discrimination, activated through issues of access to land and public services, while the situation of many further depends on family circumstances and relationships. A major factor behind family poverty is landlessness. They live on public land and as a result of not owning it, are deprived of access to many government services such as electricity and water supply. While most marginalized young people were living with a parent, family circumstances structured their lives, because many parents were separated or bereaved, single or remarried.

> I was born in Daldan, Kapilvastu and grew-up with support of my grandmother. My mother left me within a month after my birth. From the very beginning my grandmother cared and supported me. My father

> did second marriage. Hence, I did not get love and care from my parents. My grandmother was old and could not do the work like- collecting water, going for labour work etc. So, I used to cook, collect water, clean house from my childhood. (Lajana, female, 20)

Many most-marginalized young people were living in reconstituted families or with guardians. They had lost one or both biological parents, and grown up with single parent and/or with a step-father/mother. They experienced stigma and domination in the community and feel they are without proper care and support.

> I was born and grew-up in family environment. I spent all the time with my mother. I was closer to my father. But my father's sudden death was uncertain for me. He was sick, his treatment was going on. All of us wished for his betterment but he passed away. He was the head of the family. In his absence now, other people of the community dominate us. (Juhi, female, 15)

Young women shared experiences of abuse by step-parents, and feelings of mistrust and even hate towards parents. They live in communities with social conventions that do not include or encourage children and young people to express their views; they are not listened to or heard, so many problems such as abuse become socially invisible.

> I feel marginalized as I cannot express my wishes or want to my parents easily. My voice is less heard. (Tasi, female, 17)

Young people face heavy demands on their labour from childhood to help support their family. While young women mainly are expected to do household work such as cooking, cleaning, washing dishes, and taking care of cattle, young men are engaged in labour from an early age to support their family financially. Many did not go to school and cannot read and write simple sentences. Others dropped out from school at early age, before completing primary education, because of poverty, home commitments, long distances to school, or the need to contribute to family income. Even when attending school there are domestic constraints and young women especially do not get enough time to study because of heavy home workloads.

Families without their own land are particularly vulnerable to poverty, environmental fragility, and discrimination. Landlessness cuts across their livelihoods, living situations, and social contexts and has heavily influenced feelings of uncertainty. In these circumstances young people generally need to work to help support family, but many also want to exercise economic freedom from an early age, and so prioritize risky work in the informal sector over education. Young people spoke about labour exploitation in seasonal and factory work both in Nepal and in India. A perception that 'earning and saving money in Nepal is difficult' among the most-marginalized young men leads them to migrate to India and other countries. Proximity to India means migration occurs both ways. Young people from Kapilvastu can migrate south for work in India for short or long periods, given the close distance; but inward migration is equally attractive from the other side of the border, and Nepali young people experience wage depression due to the influx of cheap labour from India.

Young people who dropped out from school become engaged in different income-generating activities. When young men can find employment, it tends to be on construction sites or in factories. Young women tend to be engaged in agricultural work on a seasonal basis. To improve employment opportunities, most-marginalized young people, especially young men, try to find ways of learning skills while in informal employment. Accessible skills include driving, cooking, carpentry, repair work, house painting, and sewing, but youth aspire to gain skills suitable for agriculture and factory work, and preferred areas such as electricity, video-making, catering, tent-making, generator-repairing, and cooking. They say that realizing they have skills increases confidence.

Inequalities and discrimination: gender, ethnicity/caste, and age

Apart from family circumstances and relationships, marginalized young people's lives in rural Kapilvastu are largely structured through social inequalities and discrimination. Living with the feeling of discrimination is a common experience among marginalized young people. While discrimination based on ethnicity and caste has framed some social and economic inequalities, and fuelled communal violence as well as armed conflict, gender discrimination plays an important part in the daily lives of young women and opportunities available to them. All marginalized young people experience further discrimination on grounds of age, with their views and voices generally unheard and not taken into account in local decision-making. Inequalities are further exacerbated through discrimination against young people with disabilities. These dimensions of discrimination and associated social and economic inequalities structure the opportunities available to young people, their decision-making in the face of poverty and insecurity, and their responses to uncertainty.

A further component is experience and prevalence of communal violence/conflict that young people perceive to be responsible for their marginalization in impoverished rural Kapilvastu. All youth interviewed in Devipur were found to be affected by incidents of past conflict, when schools and houses were burnt, many people lost their lives, others lost homes and property, and were displaced.

> There was an incident of fire due to Maoist conflict 11 years back. My house and all the community houses were gutted. I was small but ran away to save myself. Then, my family migrated to another location nearby community for shelter. We were back after two years following the construction of home. I saw a man coming from somewhere in the community and burning all the houses. It was very difficult time;

people were mistreated and assaulted. Nobody was able to save his or her home or goods like my family. Everyone ran away here and there. I was afraid and hid myself in sugarcane farm far from my home. Some people died and many injured. None of the children and women died. I still remember all those incidents and feel bad. (Nishaali, female, 16)

Violence to people, damage, and destruction of property involved different communities and ongoing revenge motivations. Observation, knowledge, and experience of these events has affected children's and young people's family life and personal wellbeing, as well as material circumstances, access to education, and other services. Some community tensions continue.

> There is a conflict between Hindu and Muslim in our community. There always erupts fight during the time of Laxmi Puja and Dashain [big Hindu festivals]. (Kale, male, 19)

Ethnicity/caste discrimination

Discrimination based on ethnicity/caste is often interwoven with discrimination based on poverty and economic status. Young people report that because of poverty they experience domination from higher-status people, and do not have the capacity to negotiate and challenge oppressive power relationships because of their marginalized status in the community.

> As I belong to poor family, I have experienced domination from higher community. If I go to someone's house, they ask me to sit outside. If they are seated on chair and bench, I have to sit on the ground/floor. I do not feel that I am equal to them. If I go to work in their farm, there is also difference. I'm supposed to do the things which they say to do, and I have to be happy with money or goods what they think appropriate for us. I feel marginalized as I have no good house, not enough food to eat. Because of which I want to earn enough money and build good house in my own name. Provided I've enough money and good house people will not dominate. (Pankaj, male, 16)

Improving economic status may be viewed as a route out of such discrimination by some, but generally those reporting discrimination based on ethnicity/caste identity hope, but do not believe, the relationship will change. The term and identity 'Dalit' is used to dominate young people:

> I feel marginalized being poor and Dalit. I suffered from childhood. There was no food, no clothes and other things at home. People would dominate even going for work by calling us 'Dalit'. (Pushpa, female, 17)

> Caste-based discrimination exists in my community. I feel marginalized as people use the words like 'low-caste' and dominate us referring to 'you lower-caste'. I can't speak in front of them [higher-caste people]. I feel very bad. (Komal, male, 18)

Pankaj's story (above) shows Dalit are not allowed to sit with so-called high-class people. Also, they are prohibited from touching water and food when visiting houses of people of other castes. Om, Neeta, and Jasmin shared similar experiences:

> I feel marginalized being a Dalit caste. Some of the places and households in my community do not allow us to sit with them. Though, I feel some change at present, but the discrimination still exists. (Om, male, 20)

> I also feel dominated and marginalized being born in a Dalit family. People call me for work, but they dominate me as they do not allow me to touch water and other food items. People even do not give lunch and other food items on their plates. (Neeta, female, 15)

> I am experiencing caste-based discrimination due to which I do not want to go other people's [higher-caste] houses. Our work is useful for them, but they do not allow us to sit there, touch water and food. I feel bad. There is no good/harmonious relationship with upper-caste people. I feel dominated and marginalized when higher-caste people seek our services and do not allow us to touch water, food and any other goods at their home. They ask for work but behave differently which I do not like. (Jasmin, male, 21)

Marginalized young people also experience religion-based discrimination:

> In my community, there is caste-based discrimination among Dalit and non-Dalit. Similarly, there is religious difference among Muslim and Hindu. There is domestic violence in some house. Given all these discriminations and fights I feel bad. (Inder, male, 18)

Many most-marginalized young people speak only the language of their ethnic group which may not only lead to discrimination, but is a key factor in exacerbating marginalization. For example, young people interviewed in Bahadurgunj speak Awadhi, and find it difficult to understand and speak Nepali. They cannot share experiences, problems, and interests with people who do not speak Awadhi. Most-marginalized young people's experiences also show that language means barriers to accessing government services since most office-holders communicate only in Nepali.

> I can't speak Nepali because of which I cannot participate in any kind of discussion and interaction programme at community. I also do not go out from home due to the language difficulties. Some time ago, a few people came to my community from Butwal [a nearby city] and asked about my community. But I could not say anything with them as I cannot speak Nepali. Last time, due to sickness, I went to hospital, but I could not explain about my problem properly. Then, the doctor referred me somewhere else. But I did not get treatment. (youth discussion group participant)

> I faced difficulties while buying things. I went to market for shopping but could not speak Nepali, then I returned without shopping. (youth discussion group participant)

Consequently there is reliance on those who speak two languages for information:

> I can speak Nepali and all of my friends in school speak Nepali. I understand Nepali properly. So, I am helping other and also give information about the programme and or any other public notice to the community people. (youth discussion group participant)

Young people said they wish to learn Nepali and go to school, but are unable to break social and religious obligations at home and in the community, where they feel their agency is limited because of language communication problems. Many young women want to learn Nepali but Urdu is also important for them. Youth want government to provide information in local languages.

Youth experiences of discrimination based on ethnicity/caste, language, and religion have maintained and exacerbated feelings of difference and even anger, generated through experiences of conflict when they were children. Despite the end of armed conflict in 2006, and restoration of peace after the Madhesh movement, it was found that youth who experienced violence in childhood were growing up with feelings of retaliation and anger. This is based on perceptions towards different ethnic groups (such as Pahade vs. Madhesis) and religious groups (such as Hindu vs. Muslim).

The complexities of intersecting identities and discrimination are indicated in tensions over gendered behaviour.

> After the school time, there are always some problems in the nearby pond. The youth [belonging to Muslim community] high on marijuana harass young women. We had been to the police station to lodge complaint and also met with their parents in order to make them aware about their children's behaviour. (Harish, male, 22)

Gender discrimination

Most marginalized young people were living with parents and supporting their families. Almost all marginalized young women were experiencing more discrimination than their male counterparts, evidenced on a daily basis through their gendered role in the household and community.

> I feel difference between the son and daughter here in my family. I also feel difference between rich and poor in the community as poor have to do hard work whereas rich people enjoy property and opportunity. We poor have to give more respect to rich people. (Pushpa, female, 17)

The research found that most young women are living with their families and responsible for all household chores and other work such as taking care of cattle. Family members, including older women, were found to discriminate against young women based on age-gender role.

> I live with my family and do work here in my community. I am close to my sisters and friends here. My mother and elders do ask me for household work which I do not like much. Every time doing the same work at home is boring and difficult. (Nishaali, female, 16)

Many said they get bored with routine work and staying at home.

> I was born here ... and live with my parents, two elder brothers and younger sister. I do all the household works as my parents and elders go outside for work in informal sector leaving me at home with entire household responsibilities. My parents ask me to do all the household work- cooking, cleaning, washing dishes, taking care of goats etc. I feel bored doing the same work every day. If I do not complete the task properly, my mother would shout at me. I feel bad and hurt by the words she uses to scold me. (Khusi, female, 15)

Young women compared their roles and opportunities to brothers, who might be engaged in labour work or had more chance of education.

> I feel discriminated being a daughter. I have to do all the household works whereas my elder brother has gone outside for work. There are differences among girls and boys; as girls have to go other homes after marriage. I do not like such differences and going to other home too. (Khusi, female, 15)

> My parents differentiate between me and my brothers. My parents stopped my study, but they are supporting to my younger brother's study. I feel difference among the son and daughter here in my own family. (Mamata, female, 20)

Families may gender-discriminate even where girls attend school, by differentiating the type of school for sons and daughters.

> There is a difference between a girl and a boy. Girl works at home while boy goes outside. Due to household work girl is not even able to go to school and college regularly. In my home too, my younger brother studies at [private] boarding school in city and we (younger sister and myself) study at [government] community school. (Dipa, female, 15)

Such gender discrimination may be supported as conventional by some older women:

> I got the opportunity to get education up to grade 10 with big struggle in my family. When I was at grade 10 my elder brother asked me to quit the school (before final examination). I cried very much. Later my

> mother and sister supported me, and I continued my study. Sister-in-law also asked what I would be doing after study. She insisted me to do household work. (Balki, female, 18)

Yet generational shifts may be indicated since some marginalized young men noted gender difference and discrimination.

> People mostly give preference to son. Similarly, women have more work at household level in comparison to male. I see the dowry system here has much affected girls; because of which there is early/child marriage. I have also observed teasing of girls in the street and open places by young boys. (Jasmin, male, 21)

Another young man said, 'There is gender-based discrimination' and provided an example:

> My parents sent me to school, but my sister never went to school. Sometimes my parents give me money when I am in school, but they do not give to my sister. (Inder, male, 18)

Gender differences were also found where both marginalized young men and young women had dropped out of school and were working in paid employment. Construction sites, factories, and industries are the major places engaging marginalized young men, while young women are engaged seasonally in agricultural labour.

Gendered mobility

Many young women reported their mobility is gender-restricted.

> If I was a boy, I might have freedom to go anywhere easily. (Tasi, female, 17)

> If I was a boy, I would have been going somewhere for work, study and or any other business. I am a girl due to which it is restricted. (Lasi, female, 15)

The restriction on marginalized young women's mobility is largely based on cultural perceptions of gender roles and behaviours. Young women are expected to do domestic work and not go outside home without family permission.

> I felt discriminated being a daughter. My parents did not allow me to go outside home whereas my elder brothers worked outside home. And, my younger brother goes to school for study. But, neither had I got support to go to school nor had a chance to go for work outside the home. (Mamata, female, 20)

> When my brother comes back from school, he goes to play ball and other games in community ground with friends whereas my sister and myself stay at home and support our mother for all the household works. (Dipa, female, 15)

This discrimination associated with social and cultural values and notions concerns young women's behaviour in particular.

> Based on social and cultural traditions, parents issue orders like 'you cannot do this or cannot do that' for example: do not speak louder, wear kurta etc. They also say, 'you are a girl, should not go alone anywhere'. (Sara, female, 15)

Sara felt marginalized through such instructions and uncertain about going anywhere alone, even for learning and/or shopping. She pointed to how people gossip if a girl walks alone in the community:

> If I go somewhere alone, community people start backbiting and start talking bad things which I do not like. Because of this, I go to market with my parents and sometimes with my sister for shopping. (Sara, female, 15)

If young women decide to go anywhere without consulting family members, they are subjected to punishment. Restrictions on mobility are enforced by brothers:

> There is no TV, no water pump, and no toilet in my home. My elder brother beats me if I go to my neighbour's house to watch TV along with friends. My parents also shout at me if I go out of home. I feel bad but could not speak in front of them. (Nishaali, female, 16)

Young men are seen as part of the problem in their behaviour towards unaccompanied young women. For example, boys gather and tease girls. Because of this, and safety concerns, parents do not allow their daughters to go to the market and other places. Balki described this teasing and added,

> If someone encounters such incidents then, people again blame girls saying that 'the girl is bad'. Because of such situations and environment, I felt insecure to go anywhere. (Balki, female, 18)

Fear of violence and abuse is a major reason behind restriction of young women's mobility. Young women are afraid of rape, sexual harassment, and homicide, which have all occurred in their communities, and feel insecure.

> I do not want to go very far from home alone as the places are not safe. Similarly, there are bad boys in different areas, who harass and tease girls. I am afraid to go market and any other place outside the community alone, as there were many incidents like rape, harassment and murder of girls. (Juhi, female, 15)

Young women described how mobility restrictions continued after marriage, where they are subject to the decisions of their husband or mother-in-law, since women move to their husband's house on marriage – also a source of disquiet among young women.

> I have experienced discrimination being girl at home and community. I do not like the differences, as girls should go to other's houses after

marriage while boys always stay in their birth-place. For work also, male goes outside community to cities [and], India, but female is limited at home and around the community only. (Neeta, female, 15)

Sipa found decision-making changed after marriage:

> If I have to go anywhere, then I must consult with my mother-in-law and husband. Before marriage, I used to decide by myself and tell my parents. But now the situation has changed. I want to visit places since I have developed this habit there [in birthplace]. I ask my mother-in-law to go to market and other places, but she does not allow me. (Sipa, female, 16)

The research found marginalized young women, both single and married, feel oppressed by restrictions on their mobility, on migration decision-making, and on employment opportunities.

Work and discrimination

Poverty and marginalization means young people start work at an early age. For young women this is usually domestic work but, depending on family need, also agricultural labour. Mobility restrictions generally limit young women to home and shopping with others, but also mean they do not migrate. This has further consequences for young men who need to provide income for the family, since only they can go out. Because of the lack of local employment, marginalized young men will, and say they must, migrate.

Early age working

Some marginalized young men do labour work from a younger age because of family expectations to earn money. For example, Inder's elder brother earned money to support the family which pressurized Inder to contribute equally, though at a younger age. Childhood earnings may be required for particular costs, such as education or medical treatment.

> I went for labour work from the age of 11/12 to work in other's farm on seasonal basis. I spent the earnings for the domestic requirements, sometimes, for my own and siblings' education. I earn something on seasonal basis and support my mother, sister and brother too. I wish that my sisters and brother did not suffer like me. I also want to support other children in the community as they are also not getting good education. (Mohan, male, 20)

Komal worked to pay for treatment for his mother.

> My mother was sick, and we did not have money for her treatment. I went for labour work in someone's agricultural farm to earn money. I brought medicine to my mother from my income. I was so happy that I was able to support my mother. I wish for betterment of my family. (Komal, male, 18)

Often most-marginalized young people work from an early age for survival. Some began work before their tenth birthday, out of necessity.

> I belong to poor family. I started doing labour works from the age of 9/10 outside the home whereas I supported my parents in household work from the age of 5/6. As there was nothing at home (food and other essentials), my parents used to go to different places in search of work and food. It was very hard time for us. We have no land to produce the food. Our living depends on work outside home. There is struggle every day. I feel very bad. I sometimes think, if I was born in rich family such problems might not have surfaced in my life. I wish I got some good work (less hard work, good place and no dust) and able to fulfil my family responsibility. (Jasmin, male, 21)

Early age paid labour may involve girls as well as boys.

> At the age of 8, I started working at home to support my mother. I started doing labour work from the age of 10. I earned little money from that age but sometimes, parents would collect all the goods or cash by themselves. (Pushpa, female, 17)

> I struggled a lot from my childhood. There was no food and clothes at my home. I did all the household works from my childhood. I started labour work from the age of 10. I went for agricultural labour work and earned some money. I gave all my earning to my parents. (Lajana, female, 20)

When necessary, and without local opportunities, children migrated, often to India, which usually ended their education.

> I went India at the age of 10 and worked at a hotel. I earned around 5,000 a month and returned home after two months. It was very hard time. I missed my home, parents and everything here. I did not feel like staying there anymore. I remembered the hardship at my home like no food to feed my family, hence I went for work. I worked almost every day, provided I got work. (Pankaj, male, 16)

> I studied in India. My [school] … is 10 kilometres far from here (Bahadurgunj, Kapilvastu). I was enjoyed my study. When I was a child, I had to work due to dire financial condition. I did not have anything to feed myself. At that time, no one in my house used to earn money. I even went to Delhi (in India) to work. I had consulted with my mother to for her consent. But, she denied my idea of going there. However, I went to Delhi. I used to pack breads in a company. I worked there for one year. I used to get 3,000 Indian rupees (4,800 Nepali rupees) as a salary per month. My friend circle was not good over there. They would drink alcohol and engage in fighting, which I did not like. So, I run away from there and came to Krishna Nagar. (Radhe, male, 18)

Marginalization and poverty leads to children's employment under the age of 10 years, a further dimension of discriminating age inequalities compared to better-off families able to keep their children in school and provide education.

Migration and gender

Migration is a common aspiration among most-marginalized youth, but only young men can move in search of work.

> There is at least one person from every household going somewhere outside the community for work and employment. (Sara, female, 15)

Much migration is internal, to urban areas in Nepal, but some migrate internationally.

> Many young men are going outside the country for work. (Juhi, female, 15)

Almost all young women interviewed mentioned young men migrated to India and/or other foreign countries for work since there was no better opportunity in their community. Young women said their own migration was restrained by family members because they were girls, and often pointed to their brothers' migration.

> One of my brothers has been to India (Mumbai) for work and employment for last three years and my two brothers are also in the city (Rudrapur) for work and livelihood as there is no better opportunity in the community. (Sara, female, 15)

> There are many young males going outside the country. My elder brother is also in Saudi Arabia for work. For me, parents will not allow to go. It is impossible for girls to go either cities or foreign country for study, work or employment. (Suni, female, 17)

No young women had migrated internationally, except some visiting relatives in India or moving with their parents or husband. Balki believes she would be working abroad if she was male:

> Many people from the community are going for foreign employment. My father and two elder brothers are also in foreign employment. Though, my family does not allow me to go outside from home and community because I am a girl. If I was a boy, I would have been somewhere in foreign country for work at this time. (Balki, female, 18)

Gender-based discrimination made some marginalized young women very unhappy.

> I feel very sad that I was born as a daughter. I think no one has suffered like me. I wish no one suffered like me. I used to think why I was born. I do not enjoy my life. (Sarbati, female, 24)

Uncertainty

Marginalized children in rural Kapilvastu have grown up with lives structured by discrimination based on ethnicity/caste, religion, age, economic status, and gender, on top of the effects of family landlessness and poverty. Discrimination continues to structure youth and early adulthood, and shape the poverty that limits their education and frequently requires an early school drop-out to support family, leaving an uncertain future. Experiences of conflict have shaped further uncertainties and left a residue of mistrust and feelings of retaliation and rage, confirmed by insecurity when violence erupts in the community, as it does because of alcohol misuse, which is also associated with domestic violence.

Young people face uncertainties at different points in life, for example when they drop out of school and when they seek work locally, especially for boys but sometimes also for girls taking on seasonal agricultural labour out of necessity; and then for young men if they migrate and for girls/young women when they move home on marriage.

> I feel marginalized being girl/woman. I also feel bad going to other's house after marriage. I am uncertain about my future in other's home after marriage. (Pushpa, female, 17)

Aspirations and uncertainties vary for boys, girls, and young people largely due to discrimination and its effects. Most young people in rural Kapilvastu are responding to uncertainty by looking for opportunities to generate income to support household economies. Marginalized young men said they aspire to own a business but recognize the need to migrate to earn income, although they want to return. Girls and young women aspire to work but generally cannot because of their discriminated lack of mobility. Landlessness and poverty require income to be earned to support the intergenerational family, but there are few local opportunities for marginalized young people. Discrimination restricts girls' and young women's mobility and employment opportunities; this in turn requires and places more pressure on boys and young men to find work, to venture further out, and often face uncertainties of internal and/or international migration.

> I was uncertain many times. During my school days, I had nothing for my study but enjoyed being with friends. I wanted to be an engineer and get higher education, but I dropped out from grade 6 which was uncertain for me. I am uncertain about getting the land ownership here as we are struggling to get it for a long time. I am also uncertain about the safety and security in my community due to recurring violence within community. I am the eldest son of my family. If I go outside for work, then there is no one to take care of my family and if I don't go then there is nothing to eat and fulfil the basic needs that also create uncertainty within me. I don't know what should I do? Going for foreign employment in Gulf countries is also uncertain

for me. I am not sure whether I will get good and safe work or not. (Oman, male, 22)

Girls do move, since marriage is patrilocal. They feel uncertainties associated with the move, although many single young women are aspiring to marry and leave their community. Marriage is changing through mobile phones and social media used by young people to connect with friends and start a relationship, sometimes resulting in marriage. Inter-caste marriage is happening without parental consent.

Conclusion

Gender- and caste-based discrimination is prevalent in the lives of marginalized young people in addition to their situation of landlessness, family poverty, and consequential limited education. They do not have capacity to negotiate and challenge oppressive power relations because of their marginalized status in the community. Their circumstances have been exacerbated by experiences of conflict and loss of family members, which have left feelings of distress and, in some cases, of aggravation and potential retaliation. But discrimination further perpetuates marginalization of the most vulnerable young people. Gender discrimination is a key factor in shaping lives, opportunities, and uncertainties of marginalized young people, which are further influenced by discrimination based on ethnicity/caste and economic status. They drop out of school, work from an early age, have little say in family decision-making but are expected to fit into gendered norms. These norms in practice add pressure to require marginalized young men to become the main income earner, often through migration, while marginalized young women have limited education and mobility, must take care of domestic responsibilities in birth family households and later in their husband's home. Political instability and outbreaks of violence make young people feel insecure which for young women is exacerbated by fear of sexual and physical violence in the community, and for some at home, including experience of abuse.

Young people feel uncertainty in finding work, and for young men especially in experiences of migration, and for young women in marriage. Yet, youth retain aspirations for improved economic status through work and migration, in order to form and/or support their family, and generally view uncertainties in a positive way, particularly around migration and finding employment. Girls are more likely to feel insecure about uncertainties concerning their move on marriage, and some wanted change in this area. Yet, despite problems of discrimination and the desire for change in some areas, and the increase in inter-caste marriage which has developed through use of mobile phones and social media, youth value many cultural norms and systems. Although the practice of inter-caste marriage suggests change in some of the younger generations' beliefs around caste, there remains a residue of feeling from earlier conflict, and gender-based discrimination may continue if or when young women move to their husband's household. Whereas young men perceive the uncertainties generated by the pressure to work as providing opportunity to exercise some economic freedom, this contrasts significantly with the experiences of young women. Because of discrimination, even taking a positive view on the uncertainties around marriage and work still means some marginalized young women are found to be frustrated and think that they cannot enjoy their life as a human being.

CHAPTER 11

Urban Kapilvastu: Dealing with change and tradition

Marginalized young people in urban Kapilvastu, one of the most rapidly growing urban areas in Nepal, experience significant change, bringing new cultural and consumption opportunities, while they also feel pressures from parents and elders to meet expectations for providing family support and fulfilling obligations. Marginalized young people often drop out of school and lives are further limited through discrimination based on economic status, ethnicity/caste, religion, language, and, for young women, also on grounds of gender. They want to break up discriminatory practices, but retain other social conventions such as supporting family, although the shifting patterns of consumption increase pressures on them. To face uncertainties, marginalized youth develop new strategies for seeking work and fulfilling cultural aspirations. They consult family but also make their own decisions, aiming to both find employment and engage with new cultural practices such as music and fashion, and do so through alternative local means, or by international migration.

Keywords: youth, change, urbanization, uncertainty, cultural practices, tradition, urban Kapilvastu, Nepal

Introduction

Urban Kapilvastu, in the southern plains region bordering India, has become one of Nepal's highest growth cities, a target for internal migration, and further impacted by globalization. Increased road transport, communication, and new markets have changed lives and particularly the outlooks of young people who are local residents or incomers. They face different uncertainties, vulnerabilities, risks, and opportunities from those experienced by the previous generation in the conflict-affected district. The urban experiences of change offer a contrast to the lives of young people and their communities in rural Kapilvastu, with whom many urban youth are linked (see Chapter 10).

Through their use of social media and networks, and international migration, marginalized young people have become connected with global society. Local changes in consumption and new technology have brought new opportunities for cultural practice and consumption, which has fed youth aspirations. They want to break up some existing social norms and practices including gender and ethnicity/caste-based discrimination, feeling insecure about communal tensions, and violence between different ethnic, religious, and language groups and between local residents and in-migrants.

Young people define and experience marginalization in urban Kapilvastu in different forms from the government categories. Marginalized young people often drop out of school early and have limited local employment opportunities. They also have expectations and obligations to provide support for their family.

Young people's strategies focus on balancing their responsibilities to family and their interests in new cultural practices including music, dance, and fashion. They consult family and develop networks to work towards aspirations by combining different work activities locally or through migration. Gender differences persist, as do other forms of discrimination, but young people are dealing with uncertainties and seeking change in a shifting social and environmental context. Young people are active and energetic in urban Kapilvastu. They have been creating alternatives by themselves for their livelihoods, though in many cases they have migrated into other bigger cities and abroad for employment.

The research in urban Kapilvastu producing detailed case studies was conducted from January 2017 to May 2018, with 50 young people aged 15–24 years from marginalized communities and discussions held with 33 local adults and stakeholders. The marginalization and vulnerability criteria and purposive sampling were developed prior to this (see Chapters 3 on Method and 9 on the Nepal Kapilvastu context). This chapter looks at the living situation of marginalized young people, their experiences and reactions to change, and strategies to deal with uncertainties generated through the expectations of family, their own aspirations, and the opportunities available.

Marginalized young people in urban Kapilvastu

Urbanization and migration

Kapilvastu has some of the most rapidly growing urban areas in Nepal, a transformation of previously rural life recognized by the Government of Nepal in 2014 when six new municipalities were designated. The research focused on the central urban location, Chandrapuata, and the adjoining new Shivaraj Municipality which comprises Birpur, Chainai, Bishnupur, Jawabhari, and Shivapur – previous village development communities. Apart from the urbanization processes experienced by those who had been rural residents, these locations have had substantial in-migration from rural Kapilvastu and especially from other parts of Nepal. Many youth migrated from elsewhere with their parents in search of a better life, and some came by themselves looking for employment and others for education.

These processes of urbanization and migration have brought together diverse populations, including different ethnicities/castes, religions, and languages, interacting to shape social and cultural changes which are particularly noticeable among youth, but are also a source of their feelings of uncertainty.

Marginalized youth experience uncertainty in both negative and positive ways. Family poverty, exposure to violence and abuse, conflict, alcohol and drug use, and insecure living environments are major causes of negative uncertainty. Some young people recalled childhood experiences of the Maoist conflict. Now marginalized youth also report current feelings of insecurity generated by communal, religious, and local–migrant tensions and conflict that have become a feature of life through urbanization and growth of inward migration. They have witnessed communal tensions between Hindu and Muslim groups, and between Terai/Madhesi and Pahedi (people of hill origin who migrated in) groups. In addition, language differences can be barriers to communication. Where families are supportive and relationships and networks are good, it was found that marginalized youth have positive uncertainty and greater motivation in looking to their dreams and aspirations. They want secure living, livelihood opportunities, and access to good public services, but where they find their situation insecure, they want to migrate on to bigger cities and abroad.

> I migrated internally with my mother, elder and younger brothers from Gulmi to Chandrauta, Kapilvastu 12 years ago. My father was a drunkard and he burnt the house. We all became very sad and tired with his day-to-day quarrels, and fights at home. We decided to migrate to Kapilvastu in search of a safe and good place to live. I went to Qatar for work and returned home one year ago after 3 years there. Now, I am preparing to go to another country for work. (Jyaseelan, male, 24)

Living situation and marginalization

Many of the marginalized young people from urban Kapilvastu interviewed had dropped out of school and been forced to take risky work; many had left home or drifted about because of difficulties and abuse in their families. Much of the abuse and violence they experienced at home was associated with alcohol use by adults. In addition, a number of local incidents left many young women in fear of teasing and harassment, violence, kidnapping, trafficking, and rape. Parents and community elders also fear on their behalf, and because of this, young women's mobility and access to education and other services are further restricted.

Young people report the current education system is not suited to their situations because they are also expected to support their families and find future employment, which causes them to drop out. Although they sought information and support when leaving home or dropping out of school, many still fell into vulnerable and difficult situations. Those living in separated and shifting families or working in the informal sector generally lack support yet have aspirations for further education, or craft skills that will lead to employment.

> My father used to drink alcohol and quarrel at home which I did not like. My step-mother discriminated us because of which I felt bad. I felt

> that my parents are not responsible to me. They are not supportive for my education and requirements. (Rameshwor, male, 17)

Although some young people have gained skills such as cooking, carpentry, and house painting, they find this is insufficient to find regular and decent local work. They recounted situations of being forced to work in risky and informal sectors, often on a seasonal basis, such as in construction, otherwise they have to migrate abroad. Some young people are using alcohol and drugs to help cope with their situation.

Marginalized young people interviewed in urban Kapilvastu generally struggle to access public services when they are in need, and especially to find information. Barriers to access include location and cost. Although child/youth club membership, participation, and representation can benefit the future of some young people, very few marginalized children and youth are involved in these clubs.

> I am from a Dalit family. I have faced some challenges and discrimination being Dalit. In my community, there are some practices such as festivals, marriages and other ceremonies that people insist are caste limited. There is almost no sharing of goods, no inter-caste marriage between Dalit and non-Dalit. I even faced discrimination working in a company. I felt very bad and want to fight against such discriminatory practices. (Jack, male, 22)

Where they can, some young people are taking memberships in political parties, sports clubs, and other groups. This provides them with new networks and enhances their capacities to deal with power dynamics.

Their living situation and experiences of being marginalized shape young people's feelings and how they define marginalization. Young people said poverty, social exclusion, insecurity, unemployment, school drop-out, language differences and barriers, caste and gender-based discrimination, and tension in the family and community are the major factors marginalizing them. Young people also perceive and blame a corrupt system that obstructs them from gaining access to employment and services, such as education and health, which they feel marginalizes them further.

Marginalized young people and change

The process of urbanization has brought change in the environment, employment, and opportunities available, and in social and cultural relationships and interactions. Many marginalized young people who dropped out of school found work in local construction – in building work that characterizes the shift to an urban environment. The shifts in young people's perceptions of marginalization, particularly around family and community tensions, languages, and discrimination indicate another strand of change. Older people's views of marginalization emphasize caste- and gender-based discrimination and violence based on their own past experience. Older people recognize this has changed, exemplifying Dalit and non-Dalit people now sitting down together. They suggest that young people have a better life than in the past, emphasizing material changes such as water supply, tractors and machines for agriculture supplanting manual work, and the availability of markets and shops. This also suggests that older people's perceptions are still largely rooted in rural life. Young people implicitly disagree, and have broader perspectives on marginalization, and emphasize the expectations, pressures, and challenges they face now.

Marginalized young people still emphasize discrimination as a dominant feature of life, based on gender and on ethnic/caste/religious, language, and other communal divides, as well as economic status. Young people speak about the importance of poverty and unemployment in the changing urban environment, and pressures on them to find work and means to help support their family. Older people instead suggest these stresses of youth are because the new generation value money, waged income, and employment and have no interest in work in agriculture or the household, so they go to labour on construction sites or in transport related work.

Adults recognized there are changes because of technology and communication, with access to information and social media, but the key to how changes have affected young people in particular is not only through new technology but the presence of shops and markets and what adult stakeholders described as increased consumption. Adult stakeholders believe there is a more materialistic trend in Kapilvastu, through the different consumer goods available in markets. They suggest that young people are attracted by these but will get frustrated without the money to buy them.

The changed availability of goods, new products for sale, and shifting patterns of consumption have had an impact on young people in two particular ways. First, the availability of goods cuts across ages and status in society and increases pressures on marginalized young people to earn and support their family alongside changing household consumption expectations. Second, urbanization and consumption have also brought changes for youth cultures and both opportunities for and expectations of young people themselves.

> I've noticed many things have been changed over the period. I belong to Tharu [ethnic group] and have specific way of celebrating different festivals. Now-a-days, young people do not follow the culture, rituals and customs. We have own ethnic dress and cultural values which are now changed and replaced by suits, trousers, T-shirts, tops, and other western dresses. (Ani, female, 18)

Visible change in youth cultures is oriented around clothes, music, and dancing, along with the use of mobile phones, while consumption of fast food is said to be becoming a new habit, along with an increasing use of motorbikes. New fashions and practices include following trends in clothes, singing, dancing, and new music with DJs, riding motorbikes, enjoying drink, and socialising. These changes may have had some impact on youth aspirations for employment, since some want to be a model, dancer, singer or musician in contrast with aspirations for other vocational training and technical skills, including nursing, while some want to join government services or hope for higher education.

> I do not have interest to go abroad. I do not like to go any other places for work leaving this place. If family permits me, I will go to Kathmandu for modelling. (Sabita, female, 19)

Family expectations, support, and young people's work

Despite these changes and the different environment for young people, certain family conventions continue. Young people remain aware that their parents and elders have their own expectations of them. In turn, young people generally aim both to fulfil expectations, and do what they see as their duty to support family.

> I wanted to learn some skills and work though I have not gotten any opportunity. I want to support my parents as a responsible son. I went to work in a tobacco factory last year. But the environment was not good and my parents also advised me to stop the work. (Meena, female, 17)

New fashions may influence the desire for earning money as a motivating force in young people's lives, but expectations of their family remains an important determining factor. Yet for marginalized youth, often with little education and with work opportunities limited by their status and discrimination, the chances of local employment may be restricted to work in the informal sector that could be risky. Migration then offers both a means of earning increased income and becomes an aspiration since it could offer chances for greater consumption. Some young people aim to migrate internally, particularly to Kathmandu, but many others plan to go internationally. Aspirations vary for different countries: some want to go to Gulf countries for employment and others wish for Canada, the United States, Poland, and other destinations.

> It is difficult to save money from the work here in Nepal. The money is not enough even for food and clothes. My dream is to build own house for which I need money. If I could not get chance to go Gulf country, I will go India. (Sabin, male, 22)

> I am doing a part-time job here and preparing to go to Poland for employment. I feel uncertain and stressed here in Nepal. (Jyaseelan, male, 24)

> I have obtained a passport. I am planning to go to any of the European countries as soon as possible. If that does not work, I will go to Korea. (Vawaraj, male, 20)

While all young people are trying to get good work and earn money to support themselves and family, some aim to both fulfil family expectations but also follow their own interests through a combination of different part-time work. In this they may contend with various degrees of uncertainty. However, the ability to perform this doubling of work appears to depend on reaching a particular level of education and having parental support for their choices. For example, Vawaraj is engaged in sport, youth politics, a part-time hotel job, study, and video-making, and Rameshwor in study, dancing, music, and seasonal labour work. Some young women are engaged in skill development training and study, along with household work and also supporting their parents.

> I earn myself by doing part-time job here in Kapilvastu and manage my study and living expenses. I was uncertain about getting part-time job as I am working as an accountant at a hotel here. I am happy that I am doing something for myself. I am also taking training on radio journalism and doing paid volunteer practices in the community radio. I want to earn some more money and pursue university education in future in Kathmandu or somewhere in big cities. (Hyrai, male, 18)

Young people conventionally need parental support for their decision-making on matters such as employment.

> I always consult and take suggestion from my parents while doing any work and study. (Sabi, female, 18)

> Whenever I have problem, I seek suggestions from my parents. They help me a lot. I trust my father the most. I share my problem with my mother. I do consult with my parents whenever I have to take major decision. Sometimes, they deny my proposal. At that time, I feel sad. (Lila, female, 19)

> Here, in Kapilvastu my in-laws are like my parents and they love and care for me, my son and wife. I also share and consult the matters relating to my life, family and business with them. (Karma, male, 24)

In families where there is domestic violence and/or alcohol abuse, young people may not consult their parents, although this can create further uncertainty and dilemmas, for example:

> I am not much connected with step-mother and father. My father used to drink alcohol and quarrelled at home which I did not like. Step-mother discriminates and I feel bad. I also feel that my parents are not responsible to me. They are not supportive for my education and requirement. My father and elder brother do some work and earn money but they spend all the money eating in restaurant and drinking alcohol. I do not like them due to their behaviour. Sometimes, I could not make any decision and fell uncertain due to the dilemmas. (Rameshwor, male, 17)

There is also increased initiation of action and decision-making by young people alone since they may find themselves in situations that were not available to or known by parents in the newly urbanized environment. The use of technology and social media has also opened up opportunities for relationships that would previously have been difficult. Many young people use social media to connect and build networks. This includes young people making marriage choices and also inter-caste marriage. While some young people have married through meeting on social media, it seems that most marriages begun in this way ended in separation after a few months. Such marital breakdown may reinforce the roles of parents and elders in young people's decision-making. When adults and stakeholders refer to young people sometimes making bad use of technology, it is likely that they have in mind the use of social media to challenge existing practices for forming relationships.

While the need for parental consultation and support continues to be a main convention, so too does the need for young people to support their family, generally now through earned income.

> I am working at a retail shop seven-hours every day. I am earning 5000 rupees per month and support my family. (Tula, female, 20)

> I came to this hotel through a link of my friend. I am a cook. After the negotiation with owner of the hotel, they agreed to pay me 14,000 rupees as monthly salary which is a big help for my family. (Rajkumar, male, 25)

Increased opportunities for consumption in urban Kapilvastu, combined with limited opportunities for employment for marginalized young people, add pressure for them to find ways to earn and push towards migration internally or internationally. Yet, the expectation to consult parents can have implications for young people's aspirations to migrate.

> I wanted to go Kathmandu after completing my SLC [school leaving certificate] but I could not get support from my parents. I migrated here in Chandrauta, Kapilvastu from my home town of Arghakhanchi for study and work. In future, I will be somewhere in big cities of Nepal for better opportunity. (Hyrai, male, 18)

The mobility of young women is further constrained since they frequently face limits placed by family and social convention on their work outside the home and migration. Young women feel restricted in going out of the home, which limits their access to services as well as work.

Conclusion: change and uncertainty

Marginalized young people in urban Kapilvastu face uncertainties created through changes in the environment, consumption, and technology that offer different opportunities alongside continued, 'traditional', expectations of adults and families. Young people must deal with the uncertainties generated through the ambiguities of ongoing discrimination and its limitations, new opportunities for consumption and employment, and what adults and many youth see as traditional family expectations and obligations.

The processes of extended urbanization in Kapilvastu have brought marked intergenerational changes, noted by both adults and young people. The most visible changes concern greater use of technology, particularly mobile phones and social media, and an increase in consumption due to the availability of different goods and markets following urbanization and the reduction in conflict. Yet communal and ethnic/religious/language tensions and violence remains a backdrop to the lives of youth, who must also deal with expectations of family and adults, and new opportunities for cultural activities and interactions provided through consumption of technology, media, performance, and music.

The recognition of change by adults appears to be limited to observation and use of increased consumption and technology, and a perception that the lives of young people are now materially better. Yet adult perceptions also appear to be rooted in a rural environment since they particularly highlight benefits from changes in agricultural technology. Adult expectations of young people's duties to support the family remain high, despite the changed environment, and are exacerbated for marginalized youth because of the demands of increased consumption. Young people still feel pressure from adults, particularly from family and elders, to provide support, which requires earned income. Marginalized young people, who have dropped out of school, with limited education, find fewer opportunities available, particularly because of further discrimination on grounds of ethnicity/caste/religion/language in addition to their economic status. Marginalized young women may face further limitations because of gender discrimination, but this may be overridden by necessity. Consequently, the work available locally tends to be in the informal sector and may also be risky. Their other main option is migration internally or internationally.

Young people also experience other pressures and desires through the changing cultural environment brought by technology, media, and other consumption opportunities. This provides alternatives to previous 'traditional' ways of meeting peers and forming partnerships and marriages, as well as offering different interests and employment opportunities such as in performance and modelling. Some young people want to pursue their interests and fulfil obligations for family support. They attempt this by embarking on the uncertainties of mixing different types of work, to support family and fulfil their personal interests. They have adopted new skills including fashion and cultural practices, which have built confidence to deal with their circumstances and find paths out of poverty. Marginalized youth, with the limitations of discrimination, and frequently of education, may have less scope to pursue interests alongside employment because the work available has the uncertainties inherent in the informal sector.

They instead embark on the uncertainties of migration to earn money to support family and potentially pursue their own interests on return. They are uncertain about both destiny and work in international migration, but develop strategies of seeking information from family, relatives, and friends. Essentially young people aim to take up and adapt new cultural practices and fashions, but also keep up traditions that support them towards their aspirations. They seek to balance the new opportunities and old obligations.

Some marginalized young people, facing several problems and negative uncertainties, are restricted in what they can do, particularly those exposed to violence and abuse, communal tensions, alcohol and drug use, and insecure living environments. Many young women in particular have less confidence, with mobility restricted, and are uncertain whether their views will be heard or considered, and are limited to household work or often risky work in the informal sector. But for other marginalized young people, particularly those with supportive families and relationships, and with good networks, the changes brought through urbanization and new consumption have enabled them to gain confidence and capacities for making their own decisions, often after consultation, and to develop strategies for dealing with opportunities, obligations, and positive uncertainties in the changing context.

CHAPTER 12

Sindhupalchowk: Environmental fragility, youth responsibilities, and migration in rural Nepal

Marginalized young people in Sindhupalchowk experience discrimination particularly on grounds of ethnicity/caste, gender, and being without parents. Their families have often responded to environmental fragility, poverty, and low agricultural yields through migration. They leave behind children and young people with economic and social household responsibilities. Many drop out of school and fail exams, but even those gaining education frequently cannot find employment. The 2015 earthquake destruction exacerbated these problems. Marginalized youth turned to the uncertainties of migration out of necessity, due to land poverty, to repay loans, construct houses, and because of community pressure, to maintain personal status. Many would prefer to stay in Nepal if it was possible to make a living, but they experience shame in the community if they do not migrate to support their family as others have done. Migration also facilitates social change and family dynamics, which affect marginalized young people's lives and local norms.

Keywords: youth responsibilities, status, international migration, change, fragile environments, earthquake, Sindhupalchowk, Nepal

Introduction

Sindhupalchowk is one of the mid-high hilly and mountainous districts of Nepal, with elevations of several thousand metres, and international borders to the north and east with the Tibetan region, and with Nepalese borders including Kathmandu to the south. Subsistence agriculture with some livestock is the main source of livelihood, although yields are low in the hills and affected by seasonal rain-fed landslides. Sindhupalchowk was one of the worst-affected districts of the devastating earthquake of 25 April 2015. Experiences of uncertainty among marginalized young people in Sindhupalchowk are not only influenced by environmental fragility, but also family poverty, poor parental relationships, neglect in childhood, domestic violence, and family separation, which leaves young people responsible for the household economy from a very early age. The district was affected by conflict in the past.

Young people have to work from childhood and young women especially struggle to find time to study due to the heavy workload at home and long distance to school. They find uncertainty in the education system and question its utility in finding employment. In response to natural crises such as the earthquake, many youth opted for migration to help support their families to rebuild houses condemned by the tremors, despite the uncertainties associated with this. Most of them worry about the loans taken from different sources for reconstruction purposes, since the support provided by government was insufficient.

The population of Sindhupalchowk was 285,770 in 2011, with more female (149,107) than male (136,663). The district has many ethnicities but main languages are Nepali (55.31 per cent), Tamang (31.26 per cent), Newari (6.71 per cent), with many others spoken. Most (nearly 80 per cent) of the population practise subsistence agriculture and small-scale livestock, although because of the low-level of production, the majority of households are subject to acute food shortages for a large part of the year. About 45 per cent of the population is estimated to be living below the poverty line. Before the earthquake the vast majority lived in houses made of mud-bonded bricks or stone (CBS Nepal, 2012).

In Sindhupalchowk the research engaged with 70 young people including 40 detailed case studies. The research was carried out in Kiul, Timbu, Ichowk, Gyalthum, and Chitre community of Helambu rural municipality and Talamarang, Chapabot, Kolechaur, and Melamchi of Melamchi municipality. The sites were chosen as particularly impoverished and diverse in terms of ethnicity.

Rural environment/living situation

Marginalization and family life

The mountainous and hilly area of Sindhupalchowk is not easily accessible by road, is highly vulnerable to landslide and earthquake, and some youth mentioned fear of flood as well as annual landslip. Marginalization of youth in Sindhupalchowk partly emerges from difficulties experienced in the fragile environment and livelihood, but is exacerbated through other intersecting status, as identified by young people. The most-marginalized young people in Sindhupalchowk include those with a status derived from ethnicity/caste, gender, having disabilities, relationship issues such as being abused, not having parents, early marriage, being a single parent, and economic issues, particularly being landless and living in extreme poverty. In addition, further problems of marginalization may arise from these, such as being internally displaced, being out of school, and working hard from an early age. Other forms of marginalization intersect and may be experienced through urban migration, such as finding exploitative and/or stigmatized work or becoming street-connected.

> I always feel insecure here since all the houses in my village are on steep slopes. A couple of years back a landslide swept away all our houses. The earthquake caused more destruction. I cannot sleep a whole night during the rainy time. The place is vulnerable to landslide. The roads are

not safe to go to the market or the forests. They are not well built and are vulnerable to landslide. (Senita, female, 16)

While growing up in Sindhupalchowk, many marginalized young people experienced discrimination and domination based on caste, sex, and status of living without parents.

> I was born in Dalit family; it is like a feeling of marginalization. A caste-based discrimination prevails since the birth. I was discriminated and dominated in both school and community. Being a woman, I came across many incidents of harassment and sexual abuse in my community. There was no place where we could express our grievances and no one there to hear us. I felt marginalized. Even during the aftermath of earthquake people in our community discriminated while distributing relief materials. (Muni, female, 24)

Muni showed how young Dalit people are discriminated against in school as well as the community.

> Teachers from so called higher caste would speak rudely to me and other Dalit children. I felt dominated and suffered a lot in my school. There were separate water pot, desk and bench for Dalit in school. I did not feel like entering into teachers' room and library. (Muni, female, 24)

Marginalization and discrimination by gender are prevalent, particularly in education.

> I felt bad, as there prevailed discrimination between girls and boys in the family and community. Parents would send boys to the boarding [private] schools for quality education whereas the girls were admitted in public. Moreover, the girls had to do all the household works. (Lax, female, 20)

> I felt bad and discriminated at home. My parents did not invest on me to pursue technical education after grade 10. If I was a son, I could have opportunity to study whatever I wanted; could have opportunity to go wherever I wanted. If I was a son, my wishes would have fulfilled, and I have a great life. (Manjula, female, 20)

Gender discrimination has been manifested in the segregation of females at menstruation.

> Being a girl, I am following traditional practices entrusted upon me by my parents and elders. During menstruation, I feel very bad. I was 12 years old when I had menstruation for the first time. My parents kept me in a dark room of one of my relatives' home which was in the ground floor. It was terrible, leeches would suck my blood and I even saw small snakes. I was helpless and cried. I was totally lost, but I completed seven days in the dark [room] as per cultural and religious practices. I was

voiceless in front of my parents and family members and felt discriminated just being a girl. (Anjana, female, 18)

I had already three elder sisters, so my parents must have wished for a boy. When I started to menstruate, I wished I was a boy. And, I also wished I was a boy when we girls were not allowed to go around. My parents still lament for the fact that I am not a boy. (Pradee, female, 19)

Orphans and youth living without parents also feel marginalized and prone to discrimination.

I felt marginalized when people dominated me, passed bad words since I was far from parents. When I was living in maternal uncle's home, my cousin sister and brother used to call me 'mouse' which made me feel bad. My parents were not with me that's why they were dominating and shouting at me. In that situation, I felt marginalized. (Thuli, female, 19)

Poverty and family problems are also key experiences. Many marginalized youth grew up in an impoverished family, lacking sufficient food, with limited education materials and often where parental relationships were not good. Problems of alcohol abuse are high in Sindhupalchowk, particularly among older people and young men. Relationships with family members are affected, including links to domestic violence. Young women in particular experience abuse and harassment due to alcoholism. The existence of polygamy may also lead to domestic violence and fragmentation of family. Family breakdown means many youth live with a separated parent.

Some youth feel marginalized because they felt neglected by their parents during childhood. Most marginalized youth have been supporting families in household work from early childhood, often to the detriment of education. Some family circumstances, particularly parental separation, compel many marginalized young people to take responsibilities for their household economy from a very early age, including internal migration for work. Some have also experienced migration with parents in search of better opportunities. Change in living place meant they had to change schools and friends as well, which added to uncertainties growing up. Yet, despite the history of their situation, many marginalized young people, both male and female, perceive that their living conditions, rather than being created, are their fate.

Education

The most-marginalized young people experienced barriers accessing education due to long distance and other factors such as household responsibilities, and eventually dropped out. Adult stakeholders pointed out that for village settlements on hill tops, 'it takes around at least three hours to come to school' situated on the lowland.

I used to go to school every day. My school was nearby home and for secondary education I had to switch school which was far from my home. It took around one hour and thirty minutes to reach school and another two hours to came back home. (Rita, female, 12)

It was found that most young Dalits interviewed had dropped out from school, having been working since childhood, influenced by peers, and many experienced caste-based discrimination and oppression in school as well as the community.

> Dalits are still treated differently in the society. Even the school teacher who teaches social studies discriminates the Dalit students. Let me give you an example; Dhungana sir, who teaches social studies in our school, will not eat with Dalit students (Bir Bahadur, male, 20)

Many Dalits working with parents and relatives from a very early age did not attend school regularly, failed examinations, and then felt embarrassed having to study with younger children in the same class. Some said they were also influenced by observing friends who had left school to work.

> I was studying well but did not feel like going to school. When I reached grade 6, I learnt silver-work skills from my brother. I saw other friends, who were also working in the same field by leaving school. So, along with other six-seven friends, I left school. My teachers had told me to continue study and everybody persuaded me to study. But I did not feel like staying home anymore. (Rohan, male, 22)

A key barrier to school/education for marginalized children and young people, especially girls and women, is their household responsibilities. Children have to work from a very young age and young women especially struggle to find time to study due to the heavy home workload and long distance to school. They find uncertainty in school education and question its relevance to the pursuit of employment opportunities. Many families do not have land for farming, which leads to parental migration in search of employment. Youth speak of poor family relationships, and being unable to seek opportunities outside the home due to heavy household responsibilities when other family members are absent working abroad. For example, Trishana did not get enough time to study at home due to household responsibilities, failed the examination, but continued for one year before dropping out due to family poverty and to care for her mother.

> I studied in my village school till grade 5. Thereafter, I started going to Bhumeshwori School from grade 6. I did not have time and opportunity to study at home as I had to do all household chores. So, I was failed at grade 7. But, I again enrolled at grade 7 and passed the examination as well. I left the school while studying at grade 8 due to the poor economic condition and my mother's health condition. (Trishana, female, 16)

Some parents migrate for foreign employment, leaving behind children and young people who have to perform all social and cultural responsibilities, and take care of homes including any dependant family members and cattle. This leaves them little time for study, they fail exams and feel embarrassed to continue school and study with younger peers. They often drop out, as Wona did:

> I studied at [basic school] till grade 2. Thereafter, I started going to Secondary School in Talamarang from Grade 3. I was studying well. I failed in class 6, but continued my study. While I was studying in grade 8, I had to go to 'Mela' [a tradition that offers supportive mechanism to people/neighbours by helping each other in their work] and also do all the household chores such as cooking food, feeding cattle and looking after my brother's daughter, who was sick then. Many times, I just went to school for attendance [record], and would leave for 'Mela.' I did not get enough time to concentrate on my study. So, I failed the final examination of grade 8. I felt very embarrassed because people used to tease me. I did not want to study with the children who were younger than me because my friends with whom I had studied were already in grade 10. It has been around six years that I left school. Many friends are still studying. Actually, I don't have that mind to study well. I did not have time to study in home since I had to do all household chores in the absence of my mother. (Wona, male, 22)

Wona now takes care of his ailing father and a child of his brother, who also dropped out from school but went abroad for employment.

Some attempted to continue education by earning despite family poverty. For example, her family sent Suna from Sindhupalchowk to Kathmandu to be a domestic worker and continue her education. She found it difficult to study and complete her housework including cooking, massaging, cleaning. She could only go to bed at around 1 a.m. after finishing her homework. Her master even changed school for her saying she was not spending enough time on domestic work.

Although parents say they encourage children to go to school, and blame peer influence for dropping out, youth point to family poverty, distance, and domestic work as causes.

> My parents have no job and no money because they work in the farm. When I was in school, I needed money to buy stationeries. I had to walk one hour to reach school and another one hour to come back home. School did not provide mid-day snacks and my parents could not afford snacks for me. I used to be hungry and did not want to stay in the school. I volunteered myself to quit the school due to the distance of the school and also poverty. Some of my friends who lived nearby the school continued and completed the school education. When I was in Malaysia as a migrant worker, I used to think 'oh I should have continued my education'. But when I came back and found my friends who completed the school education still without any job, I had no regret for dropping out from the school. (Dawa, male, 24)

Many marginalized young people question the value of education without it leading to work.

> I think everybody needs to consider the money factor. If you can't support your family financially, though you receive good education, you are worth nothing. (Sejan, male, 22)

Work, migration, and changing family dynamics

Most-marginalized youth have been supporting their family in domestic work from childhood. In many marginalized families without land or without enough to provide sufficient agricultural yield, parents migrate, often leaving their children with household responsibilities. Most of them further support their family by earning some money in the village.

> In this village, we have to struggle a lot. Life is not easy here. We cannot eat without doing work hard. People basically do agricultural works here, but we not have enough land. (Shrawan, male, 19)

Parental migration to India or the Middle East ('the Gulf') forced some youth to bear the financial burden of their household from an early age. But despite this burden, Muni, for example, is proud of being a daughter able to do something for her mother and family.

> I suffered a lot in home and the community. I did labour work from my childhood. I used to work in other's agricultural farm where I never got respect [in the community]. Now, I am taking all the responsibilities of my family, apparently as a head of the family. (Muni, female, 24).

Their understanding of their family situation from an early age helps marginalized youth navigate strategies to support their families. Given the dearth of employment opportunities in the village, marginalized youth tend to migrate to cities. Many experienced internal migration when younger, for example to Kathmandu, for work and education, and some to learn skills such as metalworking. Although some marginalized young people do follow parents or make their own route to international migration, very few were found to be aspiring to go abroad for the sake of it. Rather, they do not have big dreams other than feeding their family and saving some money for contingencies.

Sugandha's family lacked sufficient agricultural land, and he lost his parents in the earthquake.

> I will do hard work and give good education to my child. If I get support from anybody, I will go to Kathmandu and work over there. If I stay here, I always remember my mother though I like this place. I don't have dreams to earn more money. It would be enough for me if there is an employment opportunity that helps me to feed my family as well as I could save a little. I also wish that I could do some small things in my own village. (Sugandha, male, 23)

He eventually had to migrate abroad for work.

Those whose houses were destroyed by the earthquake and who feel responsibility for their family want to go abroad to earn money. Young men are willing to go to Japan, Korea, and Malaysia, whereas young women look to go to Kuwait.

> I am planning to go abroad. My house has been destroyed by the earthquake. We need to pay back our loan. My father alone cannot manage all these things. I am the eldest son. So, I left my study after completing grade 12. I also tried for Japan, but it was not possible. Now, I am studying EPS [language examination] to apply for Korea. The visa will be only for five years. Then again you have to come to Nepal and do exam to go again. Thereafter, I have not thought about. (Dor, male, 21)

Dor related his uncertainty about this trip:

> I have seen my future outside the country. I've chosen Korea, but I'm pretty unsure what will happen in the future, what kinds of work I will be going to do. I heard that we need to eat everything. One of my maternal uncles was also there but he returned back due the problems on food. He said that we should eat insects and dog meat as well. I have also heard that working there is not easy, you will not get enough time for rest, however you will save some money if you stay for five years. (Dor, male, 21)

Many young people feel shame if they don't go for foreign employment. They think the community looks down on them if they stay at home.

> My dream is to go abroad like Malaysia. Everybody is going abroad now. I cannot earn money here. There are no jobs for us here. I cannot save money with little work in the village as people do not call regularly for work. I will go abroad after completing the construction of my house. But there are some problems. My father has become old now. If he gets sick, nobody will be there to offer him even a glass of hot water. So, I want my brother to get married soon thinking that his wife will stay in home looking after my father and house. Society looks down on me complaining that I stay home doing nothing whereas other young people are going abroad and earn money ... All young people from this village have already gone abroad. Some of them are here but indulged on smoking cigarettes, marijuana and drinking alcohol. (Wona, male, 22)

While some young people feel they have to migrate internationally to earn money, many were not interested in going abroad, and would prefer to stay if there are opportunities locally.

> When I was studying in grade 7, my mother became disabled. Therefore, I had to marry early. I was married at 16 years old ... My house was also

destroyed by the earthquake. Helvetas [an international non-governmental organization] supported us to rebuild the house. The government did not give money to us. My father built the house by himself with the help from the villagers.

My aim is to continue agricultural work. I don't have enough land, but it gives us about 7–8 'muri dhan' (paddy), which is enough for four months only. I am working as a labourer with my father. I did not study well.

I made my passport one year back to go to Kuwait as a labourer in a hotel. I did not appear in the interview since they said that I needed to speak in English language. Then, I returned back from there. Thereafter, I also tried to go to Qatar, but the salary was not satisfactory. It was in chocolate company. They offered 900 Qatari Riyal and food at that time. But I did not go. All young people, both men and women of my community are in foreign countries.

It would be very helpful for me if there were employment opportunities in my own village. Young people would not have to go outside the country if there were industries and factories in the villages. My family members also pressurize me to go for foreign employment, but I tell them that I will go only after scrutinising all the terms and conditions. Therefore, I do check in man-power agencies myself to avoid the middleman. (Akash, male, 20)

The main reasons behind not wanting to migrate internationally were attachment to family and certainty of work in Kathmandu. For example, Pratika belongs to a very poor family, but has no interest in going abroad since she does not want to leave the country and her family who she takes care of as they are physically weak. Similarly, Tina does not want to separate from her family. She was born and brought up in India, and would go there, but only with her family.

I don't like going abroad. Sometimes, I think a lot and feel like going again to India. The most important thing in my life is family, not money. I wish nobody had to separate from their family. (Tina, female, 17)

In addition marginalized young people are aware of their vulnerabilities in international migration. These include being cheated by the 'manpower' agency, physical abuse by the employer and not being able to earn enough money to save and bring back. Most marginalized young people who consider going abroad fear violence, punishment, and torture in countries of destination.

They also know those whose family relationships have deteriorated when members are in foreign employment. Some youth said that they did not get an opportunity to go outside because of their added household responsibilities in the absence of other family members. There are tensions, mainly around family relationships and cohesion, among marginalized young people whose family members have migrated to foreign countries.

Changing family relationships

Both adults and young people suggest that migration has affected family relationships in many ways. Adult perceptions of youth aspirations differ, with adult men suggesting that youth migrate abroad because they consider, 'money is everything' (adult male, discussion group). But one adult migrant woman expressed her frustration that she is working in Kuwait. She has two young children, aged 6 and 3 years and left them with her mother. Her husband is not doing much except some seasonal work. She misses her children very much. She says her husband does not understand how hard it is to work abroad and suggests that all males should be sent to work outside instead of females.

Young people expressed varied views on the impacts of migration in their family. Family members at home worried on the one hand about those who left for foreign employment and on the other hand, about the absence of family to carry out agricultural, household, and community work. As a consequence children are pressurized to undertake family responsibilities and household work, missing aspects of childhood and school, but getting support from those working abroad to buy essentials for living, healthcare, and to build houses (youth discussion group).

> My father is in the Maldives. My mother, two young brothers and myself, are at home now. Since last 10 years, I am missing my father as he comes once in a year, spends few days with us and goes back to work. Nevertheless, his earning is our major source of income for living. We were able to afford good treatment when my mother and younger brother became sick through the money father sent to us. If there was no money, we would not have availed proper treatment for them. (Nanu, female, 20)

Young people described concern on both sides:

> The family at home worry about themselves as well as their beloved who are in foreign countries. And, the person who opted for migration also worry about their family at home. (June, male, 24)

But youth also explained the impact upon them as well:

> My father was in India for work. At that time, I had to do all the works at home and in the community. Because of which I missed school's tuition classes which continued for long. I used to take leave from the school to work at home. There was no one at home to go to community for cultural support and work. If the senior members of the family are not home, then, the pressure comes to young ones and children. I eventually stopped going school from grade 9. (June, male, 24)

Marginalized youth identified tensions in family cohesion when members migrate abroad.

> My brother has left for Saudi [Arabia]. He is working there for last 4–5 years. He comes home occasionally. My sister-in-law [brother's wife] has also left him and the house a year back. Earlier she was fine but later she also went abroad. Then, she changed suddenly. She used to send her photographs with another guy to my brother's mobile phone (in Messenger). Both of them came here after that incident. Now the case is registered in police as well. Still there are some legal challenges for my brother to get married again. I don't know where my sister-in-law is now, perhaps she might have gone abroad. My brother loves his daughter a lot. (Wona, male, 22)

Social change

Changing family relationships are observed by both young people and adults, and reflect the impact of contemporary international migration alongside other social changes. Migration itself is seen as changing from predominantly close destinations such as internally and to India in the past, and now to the Middle East as well as East and South-east Asia. In the past international migration was mainly from the Tamang community but now other castes/ethnicities go. Similarly young women now migrate, alongside it being more acceptable for women to work outside the family now, and adult discussion groups see all these as changing family dynamics. They also recognize there are more educated but unemployed youth who have to migrate.

Other key changes include shifts in attitudes towards caste and gender, particularly towards Dalits, early marriage, and even menstruation. Early marriage has declined through arrangement by older people, but increased through the consent and decisions of young people. Inter-caste marriage has increased among young people. Attitudes towards menstruation, which previously ensured women were isolated in animal and other shelters during their period, are also seen as changing.

> I feel some traditional values and customs are good but not all. I do not like the tradition of keeping women separate for 7 days during menstruation. But I like the old cultures. (Suna, female, 20)

These changes are associated with young people seeking reform in some social practices which oppress by caste and gender, but perceiving some traditional values and cultures to be good and in need of protection. During periods of household responsibilities, when parents had migrated, youth undertook various cultural practices at festivals and other events. Many marginalized young people continue to follow and believe shamanic spiritual practice, *Dhami Jhankri*, which also attributes illness and misfortune to evil power, some say 'fate', but which may also involve costs in mitigation. Some say that it is not them but their family members who continue to believe in such practices.

This may have an impact on attitudes to uncertainty, for example, if means are perceived to be available to redress negative influences and outcomes, and if significant events, such as earthquakes, are seen also as disruptions in the cosmic order.

Conclusion: uncertainties

The uncertainty of marginalized young people in Sindhupalchowk is influenced not just by environmental fragility, but also family poverty, parental migration and separation, household and family responsibilities, changing relationships, and aspirations to gain resources to remain in their communities. This is further influenced by unexpected, uncontrollable events and their aftermath. The earthquake left families displaced and unable to rebuild homes, so that many young people are living on other people's land. Most are struggling to reconstruct their houses, as government support is insufficient, leaving them vulnerable to financial exploitation and recurrent landslides.

For marginalized youth uncertainties such as making an income and livelihood through insufficient land, in times of social and economic change, were manifested through parental migration, while youth also dealt with inaccessibility of school and other services, such as health centres, situated at lower altitudes while they live atop hills. This was then exacerbated by the impact of the earthquake on their material and mental lives. The material impact was manifested through the need for house reconstruction and uncertainty over funds for this and livelihood income, while the mental and spiritual perceptions of insecurity, precarity, and uncertainty were associated with unexpected and calamitous events such as the earthquake coming on top of regular environmental shifts such as landslides.

Untangling shifts in perception and uncertainties during this period involves both what was happening at the time, such as adult migration in response to landlessness and lack of livelihoods, leaving young people behind with household responsibilities, and the added effect of the earthquake. The impact of the earthquake, particularly on house destruction, including some that were newly built and funded through migration, and the perceived lack of government support, led to loans, and further out-migration of adults and of young people, many of whom had assumed household responsibility. The options open to marginalized young people, including migration, were in turn affected by their lives in recent years, comprising household responsibility and dropping out of school. The lack of employment for marginalized youth, even those with education and certification, was seen as a key influencing reason for migration.

Yet marginalized young people often do not want to go. Migration is a dream, but the dream appears rather to be the assumed and expected fruits of international migration rather than the process. Marginalized young people prefer to stay, but the certainties involved in staying are, however, outweighed by the uncertainties involved in making enough to live on. While there are uncertainties involved in migrating, such as gaining requirements, from travel funds to visas and entry certification, these are apparently of less concern than relationships with family and community, and the status involved in relationships. In short, there are expectations to go, and dutiful young people accepting or adhering to family responsibilities will go rather than be shamed.

Yet the uncertainties of migration, and interest in aspects of social change around ethnic/caste and gender discrimination, are balanced by an interest in the certainties of a familiar environment and, for many youth who have had household responsibilities while parents are away, a continuation of their assumed autonomy into adult status. They would prefer to stay and, if not, to return back to live: the uncertainties of the migration are built on the uncertainties of the past, but are seen to offer some opportunity for certainty in a rebuilt home in the hills in the future.

CHAPTER 13
Kathmandu: Environmental vulnerability, slums, and family support

Riverbank areas of Kathmandu with poor dwellings, vulnerable to flood and eviction, are home to in-migrant families from all over Nepal, forming a marginalized slum community. Many have low-paid, insecure, informal sector work, from construction to domestic service. Youth and their families experience stigma and discrimination from external communities and authorities, but recognize gradations of marginalization within the slum, partly based on family support, problems of unemployment, and drug use. Youth find it difficult to obtain employment without support. The rejection experienced through unemployment is often associated with drug use and illegal activities, yet having work is apparently essential for rehabilitation. Although some families see education as important, many find it is failing to provide skills that are appropriate for work, so youth often prefer on-the-job training. To obtain housing and small-business capital some youth migrate internationally, partly supported by their family. Uncertainty runs throughout their lives.

Keywords: youth, environmental vulnerability, family support, slum, urban, Kathmandu, Nepal

Introduction

The Kathmandu Valley, location of Nepal's capital city, is one of the country's biggest economic hubs and in recent decades has attracted flows of in-migration for trading, education, health, and employment opportunities. In-migration was accentuated by armed conflict, limited economic opportunities, and lack of basic services in villages. The consequent rapid urbanization has seen a huge growth in slums and squatter settlements, home to a large number of marginalized youth. Their situation, lives, and opportunities depend to a considerable extent on their families and the nature of any support available, their own responsibilities, and how these determine and affect their own strategies. The nature of family capacity and support is important in a context of in-migration, where new networks need to be established, services such as school and health accessed, and where employment opportunities, although varied, often also depend on skills, experience, and level of education and capital available.

The Kathmandu Valley comprises three districts, Kathmandu, Lalitpur, and Bhaktapur. Kathmandu is the main national centre for many major industries such as carpets, garments, finance, and tourism, as well as health and education services, while there is a lack of essential infrastructure in other parts of the country. Kathmandu alone accounts for approximately one-third of Nepal's total urban population which has been growing at a rate of 4.76 per cent per annum (CBS Nepal, 2012). Rapid urban growth coupled with inadequate government provision has led to proliferation of unhealthy, poorly serviced, and infrastructure-deficient settlements, often on public or marginal lands. Mostly the urban poor, including many in-migrants, settle in these areas (UNICEF, 2014).

The Kathmandu district was chosen as a research site because of significant migration from all over Nepal and increasing slum areas and street-connected young people. Researchers visited five sites in Kathmandu slum areas: Banshighat, Buddhanagar, Gairigaon, Shantinagar, and Jagritinagar. These sites are particularly impoverished, diverse in terms of ethnicity, and can show how different vulnerabilities affect uncertainty. Researchers worked with 41 marginalized young people aged 15 to 24 living in slums, in two phases, who form the basis of this chapter (street-connected youth based in hostels were interviewed separately; see Chapter 17). In slum areas it was found that young people are often either extremely busy or invisible: busy at work and/or study; invisible if they are street-connected, involved with drugs or have migrated. Most of the participants were from Janajati and Dalit communities, some Brahman/Chhetri, and one Madhesi. Many were still studying, nine had dropped out, and completed education levels ranged from degree to primary. Some were married. Most were Hindu, with a few Buddhist and Christian. All but one had migrated internally, but only four had experience of international migration, despite almost half being over 21 years.

Migration, environment, and marginalization

Major, interlinked characteristics influencing lives of youth are family in-migration, living spaces in a fragile environment, and how marginalization is determined by outsiders and experienced within the slum communities.

Migration and living space

The families of most young people in the research had migrated from outside Kathmandu, seeking better employment and services, apparently reflecting the general composition of slum and squatter areas. The nature of family life impacted the lives of children and young people and opportunities available to them as they grow older.

> I was born in village, but later moved to Kathmandu as my father was working as cook here. It created opportunity for our study and to experience city life. All the people in my community are migrated from different parts of the country for work, accessing better services and opportunities. (Manjeela, female, 22)

Yet, living in the slum area, they all face problems with the fragility of the environment and tenure, as well as availability of services including education and health provision.

Living spaces in slums vary from thatched one-room dwellings to more substantial concrete buildings. In general they are very gloomy, uncertain, and insecure homes without tenancy rights, with health and sanitation problems, and vulnerable to disaster. The most-marginalized young people live in slum areas characterized as an illegal squatters' residence.

> I am experiencing some sort of insecurity living in the community as the place itself is not secure to live. Being a slum area, government frequent gives us notice to vacate the place, hence the community people are struggling hard with the government. I am uncertain about living in the community in long run as the house itself is not safe and ownership issues remains unaddressed. Secondly, the house (and community) is situated by the riverbank and there are perils of flood during raining season. There is no proper sanitation. I started falling ill from the age of 9 and still I am suffering with this itching (I have 'chilaune' or allergy problem in my skin, but yet to be cured). (Meeta, female, 19).

Migrants may take any work for their survival, often low-paid jobs. Most are construction workers, labourers, and domestic helpers.

> My parents got into labour-based work which was never a regular job. Our entire family struggled a lot due to economic hardship and the shortage of food and other resources. We apparently had no home in the beginning here in the community. In small shelter, we lived together. We had no money to buy food, clothes and study. Whatever earned through labour works, parents tried to manage household necessities. Now, me and my husband live in a small rented room in the slum community. It is hard to manage everything with his earning. As my husband works in building construction sites, the work is not regular. He has to depend on contractor to get work. He has no education and can't get a good job. (Pari, female, 18)

Although unskilled and uneducated in-migrants may best become involved in regular manual work, and others get by through periodic employment, the inhabitants of slum areas are diverse, and include office workers, civil servants, and skilled labourers as well as those selling snacks and engaged in other informal sector work. The slum area has some families considered to be middle-class by marginalized youth, as well as poor inhabitants, with richer people living in adjacent areas. Young people are aware of inequalities in regard to prosperity as well as vulnerability to environmental disaster. They say there are different categories of land in the slum, and the poorest live in the risky area, that most liable to flooding.

> This place is prone to flood during the rainy season. Not all places are insecure except those which are near to the river. In this area, there are

three layers of families – place where rich people live, land used by slum middle-class, and poorest families live in the risky area. Rich people are also spoiling young people. Young people from rich families spend too much money on new fashions and also indulge in bad habits such as drug abuse and alcohol consumption. They have enough money unlike the young people from slum area ... Sometimes, young people from rich families push them to crimes and sometimes, they try to blame on young people from slum area for the crimes they never have committed. Thus, having rich people around the community is also risky for the community. (Binayak, male, 16)

The fragility of the physical environment, coupled with poor quality buildings, provide a distinct but insecure environment. Young people in the slum are very conscious about their living conditions and the perception of others towards them.

There is domination from rich people to poor people. I wish every poor youth had equal opportunity for services and opportunity. (Love, male, 22)

Many spoke about feeling discriminated against and marginalized by people outside the slum and shared their ideas on what is marginalization.

Marginalization

Young people in slum areas feel marginalized due to their living conditions and status of their spaces. Most are landless and do not have their own homes. Slum dwellings are mostly on the riverbank, always an uncertain, insecure situation, especially in rainy seasons. These are not residential areas legally, so inhabitants always feel threatened by government and legal procedures. They feel the area is neglected with limited public services and jobs. Given these circumstances, and being labelled as 'slum', youth feel humiliated to identify themselves as local residents. They also feel people discriminate against them in job markets and other places once their residential identity is known.

If I tell people that I am living in slum cluster, generally people hate us and they also rarely trust us because of this identity. I feel bad living here. (Indu, male, 19)

Although young people in the slum feel marginalized due to their home, and when identified as 'slum dwellers', they suggest the most-marginalized are those who experience discrimination, who are neglected by their family, who do not have a family, who lack education and are early school drop-outs, who cannot get a job, and who are involved in crimes and drug addiction.

I felt marginalized when I failed in school exam. I feel marginalized that at the age of 18–19, I am not able to support my parents. Some friends have good resources and education whereas I have been facing many challenges for getting education too. I feel marginalized if I come last or lag behind in any work in comparison to others. (Meeta, female, 19)

In my view, people who do not have education, beg around in the street and temple and do not mingle in the community are most marginalized people. There are around 15 households who are migrated somewhere from Terai region. Their major living strategy is to beg (children, young and adult all beg in different places). (Manjeela, female, 22)

Youth recognize overlapping categories and complex situations, which also highlight the importance of factors such as being able to support parents, and problems of gender and early marriage.

Those dropped out from schools and jobless are another segment of marginalized people. Adolescent girls, who opted for early marriage and dropped out from the school are also marginalized. (Manjeela, female, 22)

Discrimination is seen as an important factor, largely on the grounds of living situation and slum-identification, but also on the grounds of poverty by richer people.

We are poor. We have no land and any other property. For living, my parents, elder brothers and myself work in informal sector. I have experienced hard times in terms of shortage of food and lack of household requirements at home. Due to poverty, my elder brothers even stopped going to school. There prevails discrimination and huge difference between rich and poor. I do not like such discrimination and want to shift from this location. (Meeta, female, 19)

Slum dwellers feel they are discriminated against by the public service system, and the community outside, as two young women explained.

I feel very embarrassed to tell people that I live in slum area, because, people immediately look at you with different eyes. (Guna, female, 23)

It is very embarrassing when I have to tell somebody I live in slum area ... When people from slum area go to Ward Office [lowest level local government office] or any other offices, people do not listen to us nor entertain any of our applications. They try to ignore us. Everybody looks down upon us. (Anju, female, 21)

Young women's experiences of gender-based discrimination make them feel marginalized, be it inside family or community.

I have experienced and observed gender-based discrimination at my home and in the community equally. I see everyone giving preference to son saying that 'son will take care in future whereas daughter will go

> someone's house at her young age after marriage'. I see parents always ready to invest and support more to sons than daughters. I feel bad as I could not change the people's thought and such discrimination against daughter. (Pari, female, 18)

Although caste-based discrimination has been experienced by young people outside or before they came to the slum, for some it appears that discrimination experienced from living in the slum may override factors such as caste/ethnicity.

> I experienced caste-based discrimination when I was at my husband's home in the village. As, I belong to Dalit caste, when I was home someone would come to us and talk badly. I felt very bad. But, there is no discrimination in city. All the different caste people live together here. (Pari, female, 18)

This corresponds with a perspective of unity among slum dwellers in opposition to outsiders: that it is the identity of living in the slum that creates marginalization because of the way inhabitants are treated by authorities and other communities.

> I do not feel anyone marginalized in this community. This community is not like other communities. There are people who try to look down upon us, but I do not care. One day we will also get opportunity to look down upon them. (Teju, female, 22)

But slum dwellers distinguish gradations of marginalization, as noted above, essentially for those without family support. Lacking family support in some cases may be related to dropping out of school and lacking employment, but they also emphasize factors such as drug use, suggestive of lacking support and capacity for study or work. This appears to be also based on a perspective that some people do not want to improve their situation.

> There are no such people as marginalized. But those who are drug users seem to be marginalized. They themselves do not want to get socialised. (Chandra, male, 20)

This perspective is also related to problems of insecurity within the slum community, and suggestive of fear of drugs and alcohol.

> Our community is quite safe, but there are areas where the people of the Terai origin are found to be taking illicit drugs and dendrite [an adhesive having psychotropic effects]. These people come from outside and I am worried that children in this community may be badly influenced by them. They do not send their children to school. (Dilli, male, 16)

> Though I do not term this place as insecure place, but feel scared at night to come back from work. I call my father or brother to pick me up. When it goes beyond 7pm, I do not feel comfortable to walk alone. There is a place by this river, where many drug-addicts gather. (Guna, female, 23)

Such problems of insecurity are particularly noted by and for girls and women, and also associated with alcohol use.

> I also feel insecure in community and street as some drunken youth and adult are poised to harass the girls and women. In some cases, young people and children are also adopting bad habit of drugs and alcohol addiction. (Meeta, female,19)

Alcohol abuse, particularly among men, is linked to violence and other problems within the family, affecting the lives of women, children, and young people.

Poverty and family support

Many young people described their childhood as hunger-stricken, lacking parental care, and in an abusive household. In discussions three factors – disaster vulnerability, human behaviour, and people with bad influences – were seen as framing living conditions of young people.

> In the community, some children are not secure. They are not getting good food and care from parents (as parents go for work and in some houses parents have alcohol-related problems such as fights). Some children are not getting education whereas some are subjected to abuse and violence. My father used to drink alcohol and there would happen fight between mother and father. But later my father realized it and stopped taking much alcohol. (Iman, male, 22)

In some families the parents' relationship breaks down and they separate, but children may also be separated from family because of poverty.

> My father works in construction and supports the family of six members. Due to financial crisis in the family, I went to work as a domestic help in someone's house when I was just nine years old. Since then I have not gone back to live with my parents and my family. (Batti, male, 23)

Family life in the slum is governed by the insecure environment and nature of work available. Environmental problems take time and funds to address.

> I have been experiencing regular turmoil from flood as my house is small and situated by the riverside. Every year during the rainy season, we live under the fear of flood and we pray that there should not be heavy rain. My house is built with CGI [corrugated iron] sheet which is old now. If there is rain, water seeps inside home. We community people even made a dam with local resources behind our houses though it doesn't work properly [but the effect of flood is less since construction]. I also experienced earthquake, though that did not affect us as we have small huts. (Meeta, female, 19)

Poor facilities and threat of eviction create further uncertainties.

> I live in the slum cluster, the place itself is unsafe. The place is so close to the road and river, we cannot walk around during rainy season. It is government's land and it may give us notice to vacate the place any time. The shelters [homes] are also unsafe. The locations around the community such as streets and bridge areas have no street lights. (Nima, female, 19)

Family survival is often dependent on low paid, irregular, and informal work, generally insecure and uncertain, leaving them poverty-stricken. There is often parental concern about children's lives and education, but poverty is a major constraint. In turn, young people frequently expressed concern about their parents and were committed to supporting their family.

> When I was a small child, I did not get enough care and food. I started to go to school when I was three years old. When I reached five years, my younger brother was born. Again, the hard time started in the family. My mother used to do hard works carrying my sister on her back. My study was not good at that time. When I passed grade 12, I was very happy. I feel I have become a 'man', so I should be responsible for my family. (Samrat, male, 23)

Family life varies according to relationships between parents and between generations. Young people expressed frustration over family disorder, alcohol abuse, domestic violence, and parental separation, besides poverty. While young people in the slum area see the environment and family poverty as causes of uncertainty, they also suggest key differences between households are founded on support within the family. This is seen as having impact on children's and young people's education and work, and shaping their future, including whether they marry early and migrate. Dilli explained how his parents encouraged study:

> I am living with my parents, one elder sister and one younger brother at Banshighat in two rented rooms. My father is a taxi driver and my mother a house-wife. My parents always encourage us to study hard and I'm doing so. Looking at my results the school board has given me scholarship. My sister has also got scholarship. If we were not given so [scholarships] my parents could not afford to send three children to school. (Dilli, male,16)

Similarly, Indu explained family support amidst hardship, even after his marriage.

> I was born here in Sinamangal, Kathmandu. I live with my family- wife, mother and father. My home (one-room) is located in the riverside alias the slum. There is no facility. My family and myself work in an informal sector on seasonal basis for our living. My father was a traditional musical

instrument player from which he earned a little money. My mother also did cleaning and household work in other people's home. My parents at present are selling foods, goods and different items on the street for living. They do not have regular jobs. I grew-up in such situation where parents despite of hardships, do care and support at each and every stage. (Indu, male, 19)

Education and work

While many parents may want to support them at school, children drop out because of poverty (and to support family), peer-pressure, humiliation, and violence from teachers and an inappropriate curriculum.

> There are many young people in the community who did not have opportunity to go school. They dropped out from school and now at the age of 13–14, they go to catering services for part-time work. Some young people also use drugs. Those who are school drop-outs, working in risky areas such as child labouring and drug users are broadly marginalized. They neither have opportunity nor well-informed how to access services and facilities. (Nima, female, 19)

Many dropped out to work to support family income, while others attempted to combine household work and education.

> I enrolled in the school at the age of seven. I used to go to school mostly on alternate days. My school and household work schedules were shared with my elder sister. One day she would go to school and the next day would be my turn. We both would take care of home and do household works on alternative days. The school was also at one-hour's walking distance and every day we needed two hours to go and come back home. I was not good at study and my elder sister mostly took chance to go to school. Thus, my education was not good. I failed many examinations and repeated different times at different grades. I hardly could read and write because of which I tried to hide myself so that the teachers might not ask any question to me. I would sit at last bench in my classroom. Once, a teacher asked me a question, but I replied wrongly and he beat me badly. Thereafter I deliberately missed his classes regularly. I failed again and again at grade 6 and stopped going school. (Nilam, female, 18)

Some young people found they could not study or struggled to continue.

> I felt marginalized as there was no opportunity for study. I was just shifted here and there with family when I was a child. I had many challenges when I was in school. I rarely went to school. I didn't have homework to do. Sometimes, I was beaten by teacher. (Nima, female, 19)

The key for many marginalized young people was balancing work and education, often to help support family finances and to fund their own education.

> I go to college regularly. I go to market and also help my father in his work. I also work whenever I get on seasonal jobs on daily wage basis. (Love, male, 22)

Staying on at school needs the support of parents and teachers, and finances often gained through working. Many parents are unable to give advice about school having themselves not attended or dropped out. When studying is difficult, some young people have to repeat years. Some followed the advice of teachers but that was not always appropriate to the type of work available.

> I went to school at the age of 8, as I got some support from school. I studied up to grade 6 but stopped going after the school stopped support at that level. I was 15 years old when I was studying at grade 6. Besides, there were two other reasons why I stopped going to school. First, there was no higher grades in the school, so I had to shift to other school, and second, I was already 15 years old while my classmates were in-between 10-11 years, hence I felt shy to sit in the same class with them. (Pari, female, 18)

Some said school did not give them any skills useful for everyday life.

> School education is very much theory based, devoid of practical training. Some private schools have practical-based education, like field visits, but they are also limited to science classes and do not impart skills for livelihood and real life. Colleges also lack practical skills in their education. That is the reason why even the college graduates are not finding any job. (Batti, male, 23)

Many young people instead leave school to work and gain skills.

> I started to earn at the age of 15 after quitting school. I did seasonal and part-time work with different groups in catering as well as other wage-based works like building, painting/colouring etc. I supported some amount to my mother too. Gradually, I improved my skills in colouring and started to receive orders from different areas. Around two months ago, while working (painting the building) I fell down from height and broke my right hand. Now, I am home for recovery of my injury. I wish, I recover soon and resume my work as in the past, so that, I can do something for my family. (Indu, male, 19)

Many preferred skill training:

> Now, I am taking some skill development trainings. I want to be technician, repairing mobiles and laptops so that I can get some work and earn money. I want to work and study on my own as I've become

youth now. I cannot ask for support and money with my parents every time. Now, my parents have also become old and cannot work hard. The household economic condition is very poor. (Love, male, 22)

But much work available in the slum area is low-paid, unskilled, in the informal sector.

> Finding job is quite a problem for young people in this area. There are many people who go to work in party palace as waiter, cook or cleaning help. Many aunties go there. Lots of elder brothers are not getting jobs. They do not wish to do low paying jobs where they are paid 6000–7000 rupees a month. Most 'dajus' [elder males] are in foreign country. Everybody is thinking of going abroad after passing 'Plus Two'. (Guna, female, 23)

Young people often have a variety of jobs and need multiple skills to get employment.

> I worked in many places, from wholesale shop in Mahabaudh to marketing for bicycles. I got interested in repairing motor-bikes. I also worked as a plumber, drove light cars and tried my hands as a mechanic in the garage. I learned a lot of skills after SLC. (Batti, male, 23)

> My friends are also engaged in part-time jobs, like working at hotels, plumbing, cooking and assisting in kitchen, and other skill works. (Chandra, male, 20)

Many are working to help support family as well as earn for themselves.

> I did household work from my childhood. I took care of household chores such as cooking, cleaning, collecting water and firewood. I went for labour work along with my sister and mother at the age of 12 in village. I came to Kathmandu at the age of 16 after dropping out from school. I started working as a domestic help in different houses of Kathmandu. I shifted 3–4 different places within two years. In some houses, people were good and provided me wage, clothes, food on time whereas some houses did not give me wage on time, hence I shifted another place. As I was earning some money, I ate what I liked and wore the dress as per my interest. I was happy and felt confident at least for being able to do something for myself. I gave some money to my mother too. (Nilam, female, 18)

Some who continued in school progressed to degree level, illustrating the variety of work and education undertaken in slums with family support.

> I am living in Tripureshwor, one of the slum areas in Kathmandu with my parents, an elder sister, one elder brother, his wife and two children. My other elder sister has already got married. I am studying a bachelor's degree in humanities. My father works in construction and my mother is rearing sheep. My second elder sister is running a tailor-shop and

supports the household, too. My brother has polio, and has a small cosmetics retail shop. My brother's wife and his two children also live with us. (Anju, female, 21)

But others said education did not help find a job, even with qualifications.

> There is no employment for youths, even to the people who have passed MBBS [Bachelor Medicine Bachelor Surgery]. There is corruption in employment. Without personal link, people cannot access to any job. You need someone to pick you up in the job. For that, you need power or money. Most young people in this community cannot afford that, so they cannot get jobs easily. People get frustrated. Because of frustration, they take drugs or fall into bad company. Peer influence pushes them to high risk. They may start smoking cigarettes or even take drugs. (Binayak, male, 16)

Without work: drugs and migration

Unemployment is seen as leading to drug use and other problems.

> I have friends who use drugs and also sell them. It is because they do not get jobs. (Atma, male, 22)

Lack of work and drug use is also connected with criminal activity.

> I think many young people are wasting their lives, getting into bad habits like drug addiction. Unemployment is the major problem for youths in Nepal … Those who cannot get a good job, fall into the drug abusers' trap. They resort to the illicit drug and some of them also turn into burglars. There are more incidences of stealing of mobile phones, laptops, jewelleries, gold and silver goods … We have so many friends who are drug users. Some of them are still into drugs while some have realized how it impacts their lives … Those who can find job continue it. More they get engaged in the work, less they get involved in the drugs and other bad habits. And, eventually they come out of the bad habits. (Batti, male, 23)

As Batti and others explained, getting or having work is an essential means of getting away from drug use.

> I do not remember much about my childhood. My father used to beat my mother which made us sad. When my father died, I dropped out from school while studying at grade 8. I fell in a bad company and started to take drugs at the age of 14. After three years of drug abuse, I quit this habit and came back to my mother. I realized that was a bad habit and I was in wrong track. My mother was alone. My uncle took me to the painting job. I also worked as waiter and also assisted cooks in party palaces. I used to get 150 rupees per day when I was 14 years. As a waiter I used to get 500 rupees, but I needed to work late at night.

I learned the painting skills, so I work as a painter whenever the job is available. Sometimes, I also work in construction when offered an opportunity. (Himesh, male, 19)

Out-migration or stay

Lack of work and wanting to support or please family are primary reasons for young people choosing to migrate internationally.

> These days, 25 per cent of community youth are migrated for foreign employment. Youth are not certain here in getting employment but they are certain to find jobs in foreign country. In some cases, parents also encourage their children to go for foreign employment to earn money whereas in some cases, successful migrants (including returnee migrants) become role models. Parents and other community people take the example of successful migrants who have nice house, who are able to support their family. (Manjeela, female, 22)

Young people also mention that parents do not trust to invest in them, nor is financial support otherwise available if they want to start some business locally, yet it is available for migration, seen by adults as a means to get a house.

> In many cases, parents refrain from investing a substantial amount if young people want to do something in Nepal. Cooperatives and banks as well as relatives do not trust if someone approaches for loan to doing something here in the country, but they are ready for loan if it would be the case of foreign employment. In some cases, successful migrants remain the role models for them and thus the parents often say to their children, 's/he is doing this and that and s/he has earned money and bought a new house'.(Iman, male, 22)

Some youth see migration as means to get capital to set up in Nepal.

> I want to go out of the country – to some good countries to work in bike workshop. I have also learned carpentry. I will work hard and earn good money. I will then come back to Nepal and open a bike workshop to help young people of Nepal. (Chandra, male, 20)

But many would prefer to work in Nepal rather than going abroad. They think it is better to be with their family and work, than go out and suffer for money. They also think friends who had been to foreign countries are not telling the true story, rather only sharing the good part.

> I migrated to Kathmandu from my village at the age of 16 in search of work. I found work with support of relative here in Kathmandu. I worked as domestic help in different households. I earned some money whereas I also faced some problems. Earlier, I wanted foreign employment but in the meantime I heard about some painful stories of people in foreign

employment. Now, I do not have any interest to go outside the country for work. (Nilam, female, 18)

I do not have plan for migrating out of the country. But, my parents force me to go abroad for work. I tell them that I will work here though I have to suffer a lot. I don't think there will be any difference going abroad. My parents persuade me saying that all of my friends have already gone abroad, why I should be staying back. I know my friends also have to suffer there. But, they don't tell their sad story. We can understand it. I am studying now, so I will do something here. (Samrat, male, 23)

Some see migration as part of a general family movement.

I was born in Kathmandu whereas my parents were migrated from Khotang to Kathmandu in search of good opportunity and work. We live in slum community here. Other people in the community also migrated from different parts of the country. Many youth are migrated to different foreign countries for employment and earning money. My relatives are also in foreign employment. I am also planning to go either Australia or Japan in near future. I am certain that I will be going soon but I uncertain about being in foreign country. (Nima, female, 19)

Early marriage

Many young women married early, had children, separated, and became single parents. It was said that youth, especially girls, married early to escape from uncertainties in their life. Although some marriages were arranged by relatives most were consensual love matches.

I fell in love with a guy in the same community. I got married with him and now live with my own family (husband, daughter and myself). My husband does labour work in construction site. As my daughter is just three months old and there is no one to take care of her at home, I am doing household works now. (Pari, female, 18)

But some marriages became abusive and for young women replaced uncertainty with control.

I am 18 years old now. I was just 16 years when I got married. It was our love marriage and I had met him here in Kathmandu. I have a daughter and live with my in-laws and husband. My husband comes home in a drunken state and starts beating me. We always fight over our daughter. (Juji, female, 18)

My husband works in municipality as a driver to collect garbage. He works from 6am to 7pm. My child is small (too young) for me to go out and work outside the home. My husband does not like me to leave my child and work either. I sometimes make glass bead necklaces at home in my leisure time. They pay me 2–3 rupees per a strand. I can finish 3–4 strands a day ... I do not like my husband's drinking habit, but good thing is that he sleeps after drinking. (Bhanu, female, 22)

Conclusion: slum uncertainties, family support

Poor families live in risky slums. Most parents are labourers, domestic workers or in low-paid construction work. Unlike youth in street situations, young people living in the slum are more connected with their families, and family support is a major factor in their lives. Nevertheless, they shared frustrations regarding constant family disputes, separation of parents and multi-marriages which increased uncertainty and insecurity in the lives of children and young people.

Young people in the slum expressed uncertainties in their physical living situation, marginalization, education, and work options, and emphasized the centrality of support from parents to children, and from youth to family. Their living situation is framed by uncertainties including environmental fragility and vulnerability, poor housing, and insecurity through risk of eviction by government. Limited employment opportunities for in-migrating families lead to poverty, while children's education may need to be combined with work in order to fund it and support family finances. Continuation in education and finding work often depends on family support. This is not always available because of poverty, domestic violence, alcohol abuse, and other problems, creating further uncertainties. Children drop out of school through poverty and to work, but also because education is not seen as appropriate and does not help secure work. Skill-training is often preferred, particularly learning on the job. But work can be difficult to find, although it is an essential factor in supporting unemployed young people to move away from drug use and criminal activity. While drug use may be seen as a response to alleviating uncertainties, early marriage is also seen as a response to uncertainty.

Many slum families are in-migrants from all over the country. Because of where they live, they have a shared identity of marginalization, experiencing stigma and discrimination from communities and authorities outside the slum. Young people perceive gradations of marginalization within the slum community, partly based on situations and outcomes where family support is not available. Family support is seen as important in positive strategies for dealing with uncertainty, such as precarious employment and income, education, finding work, avoiding problems of early marriage, of unemployment and associated drug use and criminal activity, and difficulties of injury and ageing. Family support is important because the communities are disparate, incomers and otherwise strangers must build up relationships, and often have no other or limited kin on whom to call. It is also important because it provides the basic initial network in a context of the uncertainties generated in the fragile environment, vulnerable to disaster and eviction, difficulties in accessing public services, low-pay and exploitative work, and discrimination. It provides positive support in the face of uncertainties.

> Youth are more mature and responsible these days. Youth think about family, community and their own career. For example, I feel more responsible than earlier. I know myself and what I have to do. I should support my parents and my sister, too. Life is all about struggles and experiences and learning new things with enjoyment. It is uncertain what will happen in future. (Iman, male, 22)

CHAPTER 14
Genderfluidity: LGBTQI and third gender in Kathmandu

This chapter focuses on marginalization and uncertainties experienced and raised by youth now living in Kathmandu identifying themselves as members of the LBGTQI community, which has been broadly subsumed under the term 'third gender' in Nepal. Many LGBTQI youth say they felt uncertainty, and experienced tension, fear, problems, and feelings of insecurity since their childhood. Many migrated to Kathmandu, but still live in a situation of uncertainty, some on the street, some alone, most separate and far from family. They point to diversification on grounds of caste/ethnicity, as well as gender/sex identities, disability, and their individuality. Rejection from family, less education, street-connection and/or isolation, and citizenship problems, push them into uncertain and vulnerable situations, including exploitative informal sector work and sex work.

Keywords: youth, genderfluid, third gender, LGBTQI, exploitation, discrimination, Kathmandu, Nepal

Introduction

Rights of LGBTQI people have been increasingly taken up since 2007 and genderfluid identities recognized, although many youth continue to experience stigma, discrimination, marginalization, and exclusion. This chapter focuses on the marginalization and uncertainties experienced and raised by a group of 10 youth now living in Kathmandu, who identify themselves as members of the LBGTQI community, which has been broadly subsumed under the term 'third gender' in Nepal (see below); the complexities of sexual and gender identities are not fully described here (see UNDP/Williams Institute, 2014).

Most genderfluid youth found uncertainties as they grew up in recognizing themselves as different from their assigned gender and/or from the sexual orientation they were expected to follow. Many sought the company of others with similar experiences, as part of understanding, communicating what was happening, and for support, particularly when they felt this could not be discussed with family, peers, work colleagues, or community. Many moved to Kathmandu where local organizations provided a supportive and appropriate environment. Through the processes of changing gender and/or sexual identity, further uncertainties ensued, not only regarding identity and relationships, but in all aspects of the living situation, finding a place to live, to work and earn income, official documentation (particularly citizenship), and especially relationships with public services. Difficulties with health services were noted not only by those making transformations, but also because of attitudes and questioning of appearance and gender when raising health issues.

The term LGBTQI is in general use in Nepal now, although the country has been known for the use of the term 'third gender' (Young, 2016; Chhetri, 2017).

> The term third gender is very vague that does not address the real problem of inter-sex people. (Pariniti, genderfluid, 19)

Changes to the law following the end of the monarchy and a Supreme Court ruling in 2007 identified the need for protection of LGBTQI rights and the recognition of a third gender was included in the 2011 census for the first time. However, the census was not completed well in this respect, not least because of the diversity of identities held, and not all agreed with the use of 'third gender' as descriptor. A later survey of 1,200 individuals (UNDP/Williams Institute, 2014) found 21 different terms in use and just 51 per cent 'used some version of third gender (third gender, third gender woman or third gender man). Thus, even with the most optimal implementation, roughly half of the respondents would have been excluded by the Census' (Park, 2015: 17). Although an indigenous 'third gender' *meti*, assigned male at birth, dressing as female, and with roles in various ceremonies, is well known, this has various complexities including caste/ethnicity, sexual orientation, and gender, as does another South Asian term, *hijra*, which mean it is not a simple category (Reddy, 2005; Park, 2015).

Researchers worked with 10 genderfluid/LGBTQI youth aged 15–24 in Kathmandu. Seven had migrated into the city. Four were Brahman/Chhetri and six Janajati; eight Hindu and two Buddhist. Group discussions and interviews were arranged through the Blue Diamond Society.

Self-knowing and identities

Although some interviewed were born in Kathmandu, most grew up elsewhere, often far away, and all found uncertainties through experiences of self-knowing, recognition of self-difference from assumptions made by others in the family and community of expected gender and sexuality behaviour, and through realizing a difference from their assigned identity. This self-knowledge was often difficult to communicate, or be understood by others, especially close family and other relatives. Family life differed: most mentioned families had often previously been supportive and caring, while some had experienced domestic violence and abuse.

> I was born in Kathmandu. I grew up in a family with love and care. I am an intersex female. I came to know about my identity at the age of 13. I was confused and felt difficulties to go to school and other places. Though, I felt comfortable to be a girl in girl's dress-up. I suffered a lot to understand myself. I felt bad with all the changes and could not manage

properly. It is too overpowering from me, I went into depression. (Didi, genderfluid, 17)

> I faced many challenges in my life. My first challenge was to accept myself, which was hard for me. For example, I was born a as girl, but as I grew up my feeling and behaviour got changed, which was difficult to accept and open up. I could not accept in the beginning. I tried to hide myself and tried to play different role which was difficult to manage. Secondly, as time passed by I tried to accept it but again my family was there. They did not understand and could not accept. I had fear of losing my parents and loved ones. Again, the society was there, who could make my life difficult. (Pappu, genderfluid, 24)

These significant experiences of change and uncertainty of relationships and reactions in family and community in early life caused difficulties, including patterns of marginalization, stigma, and discrimination that would continue at least through youth transitions to adulthood.

> I was born as a girl child. When I was at the age of 13, I noticed myself that I was different than what I was. I liked to be a boy. I liked a boy's get-up, dresses, short hair, play football and I felt attraction towards girls. I started thinking why I was different than other girls. At times, I used to be in confusion. I thought, it might be for short-time and I would be fine tomorrow. But things did not happen that way. My confusion increased day-by-day. Every time, I would be thinking why this was happening? But I did not get answer quickly. When I was studying at grade 10, I became fully uncertain with the things happening with me. (Pappu, genderfluid, 24)

> I was born as an intersex child. My parents accepted me as their daughter and thus I was grown up as a girl. I saw that girls who reached grade six had physical changes on them. But I had mentality like that of boys. I felt tensed as I did not know who I was. (Vabin, genderfluid, 21)

In reaction to this, some youth tried to be, as they said, as 'normal' as possible given their role of male or female in their family.

> I was hiding my identity from public almost all the time but I was having male partners from the beginning when I knew myself ... I was different than other men. Sometimes the girls would kid me but I had no interest in them. The girls would say why this boy behaved like a girl. (Komal, genderfluid, 27)

Living situation

Although some live with parents, most youth in the LGBTQI community migrated to Kathmandu because of their identity (as had most interviewed here). Most said parents cared for and supported them until youth found changes in themselves, and then relationships with family often changed. Some found both support and violence in the family.

> [My brother's] suggestions helped me a lot. I took decision to change my get-up, dress and even cut my hair without asking for permission with my parents. My parents shouted and beat me seeing me in short hair and not asking for their permission. (Pappu, genderfluid, 24)

Others were not accepted in the family or in the community.

> My parents were not able to accept me who I was. As, I was a boy (family son, by birth) as well as the only child, it was hard to convince them. (Pinky, genderfluid, 24)

> I was born and grew-up in Hetauda [another city]. I suffered a lot due to my sexual identity. Because of the attitude of community people towards me, I attempted to commit suicide by taking poison when I was 15 years old. I was admitted in a hospital … [but my father] did not want to go home again and live in the family. I asked my mother to live with her which she did not agree. I then came to Kathmandu and living here since. (Rudip, genderfluid, 24)

Many experienced difficulties including bullying, harassment, in school and elsewhere, lost friends, and becoming excluded by relatives and neighbours.

> Elders bullied, pressurized to behave like a gentleman. Everything was going uncertain. I did not know what I should do. People were not accepting me. I was like centre of attraction for all. (Pinky, genderfluid, 24)

> People started to discriminate me because of my sexuality. The villagers started saying that I should be exiled from the village. (Rudip, genderfluid, 24)

Changes in self mostly led to separation from family and living alone in Kathmandu, but relationships may or may not be continued.

> I think sometimes that may be my parents will not come to see or claim my body after my death. (Pariniti, genderfluid, 19)

> I have grandparents, parents, younger brothers and sisters. I have normal relationship with all of them. I am neither intimate nor I've any difficulties with them as I live alone here in Kathmandu. I go home to meet my parents and relatives occasionally. My family does not know about my identity. (Komal, genderfluid, 27)

Some had a street background and no family.

> I feel bad as there is no one in my family. I do not know anything about my parents. Because of which, I lost confidence. (Aadi, genderfluid, 23)

Due to social and family pressure, LGBTQI youth hide their identity. They do not want to hurt parents and elders by their identity, particularly because this is also related to family reputation.

> I do not want my parents to know about me. They still do not know about my sexual identity. I am afraid that somebody will tell them about me and spoil their reputation. I do not want to spoil my parents' reputation. I thought of sharing with my family, but could not do that ... I also take advice from my parents whenever needed. (Ayur, genderfluid, 24)

Education

Youth in the LGBTQI community see education as important, but discrimination in the family, community, and school caused them to drop out, although some later attempted to resume studies. Pappu got a lower score (76 per cent) than expected in the School Leaving Certificate:

> Due the stressful circumstances, I lost my confidence and got low marks. I knew that my concentration was on my body, not in my education at that time. My teachers and friends in the school noticed my behaviours and some of the friends even started bullying me. They asked, 'what is this, you are like "chhakka/hijada"'. I was questioning myself again and again about my behaviours and activities. I was afraid of the views of my friends. (Pappu, genderfluid, 24)

> With support of my parents, I got education and identity. As my behaviours gradually changed, people, neighbours, relatives noticed all these and discriminated me. I felt bad with all the changes, but could not manage properly. I was confused with certain things, for example going toilet in school. It was too bad for me, I went into depression. When I was in school, my behaviours changed slowly, so teachers and friends noticed. I felt bad as I was close with group of girls, but the friends after knowing my status shied away from me. I had no friends at all. (Didi, genderfluid, 17)

Work

Many LGBTQI youth had been engaged in risky and hard labour work from childhood. Because many dropped out from school, and faced bullying and harassment during transition, they had less education, skills, and capacity to compete for jobs. Most do informal sector work such as in factories, hotels, restaurants, and markets.

> I am also working at some sort of small projects here and there when available. I am finding difficulties to get a decent job due to my low level of education. I have been engaged in small tasks like, data collection, blood sample collections etc. (Ayur, genderfluid, 24)

Komal began work aged 13, and spent eight years employed in hotel, carpet/furniture/sand factories, construction sites, and domestic work. In hotels, then a carpet factory, he worked long hours with little payment, so moved to a furniture factory, and later to a house as a domestic helper expecting to get some education. He got educational support for three years but no pay. When evicted he started work in a sand factory (mine/gravel pit) as a labourer.

Similarly, Ale started working from the age of 9 in hotels and factories, but left due to sickness and discrimination. He found restaurant work, but the owner did not pay him, so he left again.

Many youth are also found in risky and vulnerable work, including sex work in particular.

> I searched for work and struggled a lot but could not get any good work. One hand is also dysfunctional [impaired]. I found a friend and started living with him. I was engaged in sex-work (I played the role of female) for my earning and living. I did other part-time and seasonal works whatever I got in market. I am also working in an NGO as a part-timer. Everything is uncertain for me. If I get good job, I will not do sex work. (Aadi, genderfluid, 23)

> I struggled a lot from my childhood. I was engaged in different types of work in informal sector. When there was no other work, I did the sex-work too. Now, I am suffering from HIV. I feel bad and marginalized as I have nothing to sustain myself. (Komal, genderfluid, 27)

> My partner also did not get a job. She works as a sex-worker. I want her to take another job, which she also likes, but there is no other job available. We need money to support ourselves and my mum. This job is very risky. Once I was taken to Hattiban. I was raped there and returned home without been paid. A lot of straights and gays, including foreigners do not like to use condom, so there is high risk of HIV/AIDS and other diseases. (Ale, genderfluid, 24)

> Due to poverty, exclusion and struggles some LGBTI people engage in sex-work which is more risky. I have got information that some are infected with HIV/AIDS and suffering from other chronic health problems. Some of them are disabled ... They have no work and no any other support. (Pinky, genderfluid, 24)

Although many had moved to Kathmandu, there appears to be little onward migration for work.

> I thought of going out for migration work, but trans-genders are not allowed to go out for work. (Ale, genderfluid, 24)

Two LGBTQI youth had migrated to the Gulf, one to Dubai, hiding their identity for a year before returning, and the other to Saudi Arabia, where they were sexually harassed and fired after refusing to comply with their harassers.

Citizenship services

Genderfluid youth often face challenges accessing public services. Citizenship cards are a major concern, essentially a national identity card needed to access services and government benefits (health, education, driving licence) and often obtained at the age of 16 to18 years. In many cases, at this time, LGBTQI youth are still considering and do not open up about their sexual/gender identity, and the card information does not match them.

> My citizenship card and educational certificates endorse me as a girl. Due to which I faced problems seeking services from government and other offices ... as the photo in citizenship card did not match with me in the real life. (Pappu, genderfluid, 24)

Some later want to change their cards to their present identity.

> My biggest desire in the life is to correct my citizenship. There my name is different. Because of this, I have to face several problems while trying for employment as people don't trust me. There are complications in availing health services as well. Also, I am not being able to make a driving licence. (Vabin, genderfluid, 21)

> I went to Kavreplanchowk district where I born to make citizenship card. But they [officials at District Administration Office] asked me to present my sex-change certificate. They ignored my application by saying that this [trans-gender citizenship] was a new issue and they did not know about it. I showed them the legal provisions such as Article 12, Article 18 and Article 42 of the Constitution of Nepal and also explained about the verdict of Supreme Court. But the office secretary threw away all my documents ... I became a subject of laugh for them ... I also discussed this issue with some people in authority here (in Kathmandu). But they also accused me of making fake documents to receive a citizenship. (Pariniti, genderfluid, 19)

But there are families who accept their children as they are and support them, and some youth obtained a citizenship card corresponding to their identities with the support of parents.

Health services

Genderfluid youth report problems accessing health services. Some who have or are transitioning, with particular needs including gynaecological issues, experience discrimination and marginalization when staff do not understand their problems and expectations.

> If I go to hospital there will arise problem. I look like man but my original name and sex organ are that of a female. There is problem where to stand in queue for ticket and check up. Generally, I (transgender-man) have problems such as menstruation hygiene, surgery/operation of uterus,

> problems in breast (I use binder vest which presses breast, with high chance of cancer and other reaction) etc for which I have to seek treatment. Doctors and nurses do not know about my sexual and transgender things and ask such questions which are not relevant. Similarly, they also start gossiping with other persons. (Pappu, genderfluid, 24)

> Health centre/hospitals also discriminate us. When the doctors figure out our sexual orientation, they get quite confused and give up examining us. They skip us by saying that there is no medical equipment to check the third gender. (Ayur, genderfluid, 24)

Violence and support

Genderfluid youth experience violence from childhood, being beaten, abused, and bullied in their homes, schools, and community, including fights, harassment, and rape. Many work and walk in groups, limit the places they go, and aim to support each other (notably through the Blue Diamond Society, known internationally (Young, 2016)).

> Some boys came on motor-bike and abused me. They also attempted to rape me, but I shouted for help. Later, when a vehicle with flashing lights approached they ran away. That was a police van. Next day, I made a complaint at the police station. But the police did not accept to register my complaint and said that I would be in trouble if I made a police case since the boys were belonging to powerful group. I felt that my freedom had been taken away. I felt insecure at that time. I did not feel anything good. (Pariniti, genderfluid, 19)

Conclusion

Many LGBTQI youth say they felt uncertainty, and experienced tension, fear, problems, and insecurity since childhood. Many migrated to Kathmandu, and feel they continue to live in a situation of uncertainty, alone, most separate and far from family, some on the street. They point to diversity in caste/ethnicity, as well as gender/sex identities, disability, and their individuality. But rejection from family, street-connection and/or isolation, and citizenship problems, push them into uncertain and vulnerable situations including informal sector and sex work.

To enhance self-esteem, promote their identity, and find support, many participate in beauty contests and other events and organizations, as well as use of social media. Their aspirations include supporting peers, dreams of being open about themselves safely in public, establishing their own businesses or getting decent work, getting the correct citizenship identity, and particularly acceptance in their family and society.

> We should feel and enjoy equal freedom and humanity as other citizens do. (Didi, genderfluid, 17)

PART 4
Policy themes

CHAPTER 15
Policy themes and impact: Introduction

The research aimed to be used to make changes to support marginalized youth circumstances and strategies, and policy and practice ideas were produced through facilitating engagement between youth, research findings, and government at different levels. In both countries, local and national seminars involved youth as part of verification of findings and also as a means of engagement with government. Youth declarations were signed by representatives. Comparison across countries points to key themes emerging in the research and many structural similarities in experiences of marginalized young people. These themes intersect in many ways indicating the importance of holistic perspectives and approaches rather than segmenting youth lives to suit policy or practice disciplines, departments or organizations. Underlying problems of marginalization, which provoke issues around education, early childhood work, later employment in the informal sector, migration, and becoming street-connected, are central and should not be ignored, in particular discrimination and oppression based on ethnicity/caste, gender, sexuality, and disability.

Keywords: policy, impact, youth declarations, research uptake, partnerships, government, comparative research, Ethiopia, Nepal

Introduction

An important issue and essential concern in research with marginalized youth is how their experiences, and the issues and problems they raise, can feed into policy and practice to make changes. Social, economic, and environmental change is already affecting youth lives, as indicated in findings from all sites in Ethiopia and Nepal, but marginalized youth have little control over change and must make the best of limited options open to them. Changes in environment through disaster such as drought and earthquake affect rural livelihood options. Some limited income-earning activities open to poor families may worsen environments through, for example, contributing to deforestation. Social practices such as land inheritance, marriage, local hierarchies, and status also affect children's, young people's, and families' marginalization and future options.

Distress within families, abuse, alcohol misuse, and domestic violence not only particularly affect the lives of children and women at the time but also shape their future. Processes of urbanization change landscapes and livelihoods. In urban areas marginalized youth are often restricted to work in the informal economy that is exploitative and even dangerous.

Migration has increased in order to provide funds, capital and for survival, but is not a strategy for sustainable rural or urban living. These concerns and issues run throughout marginalized youth experiences in both Ethiopia and Nepal. There are questions of how to address the issues and causes of marginalization, and how to make use of social and environmental changes in a way that is beneficial to youth, their families and their futures, communities, and society.

Action for research findings uptake was built in through initial partnerships with local and national organizations working on relevant issues in communities, and with involvement of youth in local and national engagement with government. In both countries a change of government brought renewed interest in and engagement with youth policy.

This chapter provides a brief introduction to the processes of research uptake and comparison across countries on issues of migration, street-connection, and disability that follow in Part Four. These were three of the key themes that emerged across both countries and were discussed in depth at national seminars that also provided some youth recommendations for action. Other significant issues, such as education and employment, are noted below. These are headings indicating key policy themes, but youth lives cannot be simply boxed-off in this way, and interconnections between issues, and holistic experiences of living, must be considered in any policy, practice or other analysis of research. These few topic themes are used here to illustrate aspects of marginalized youth's lives, rather than limiting spheres of interest and experience.

Research uptake

There are gaps to be bridged in supporting marginalized youth who have difficulties accessing services and who experience discrimination, even when adults in communities freely discuss rights and claim willingness to listen to them. There are also gaps between the rhetoric of policy-making and the reality of marginalized youth gaining rights and access to services. It is often necessary to create spaces where views of the most-marginalized may be heard, and build partnerships for action to follow (Johnson and West, 2018). In this research, spaces for dialogue included Provincial and National Youth Seminars in Ethiopia and Nepal, where government and non-government representatives came to listen to the views of young people, and youth prepared declarations for them to discuss, and which they signed to demonstrate commitment to action.

Follow-on action from such engagement depends on organizations and partnerships (see Chapter 3; also Martikke et al., 2018). Trustful relationships, ownership, and commitment help contribute to effective societal change, as explored by the research team and partners (Johnson et al., 2019a, 2019b). Indicators of successful partnership derived from different contexts of the research include: histories of interpersonal relationships; shared vision and motivations; building ownership; shared platforms and spaces for dialogue; and flexibility to respond to shocks and changes in context. Recognizing the power and politics of partnership can help support high-quality, rigorous research while creating impact at local, national, and international levels (Georgalakis and Rose, 2019). Other mechanisms built in to help create impact included local academic research leads and capacity building for national teams, co-construction of methodology, involvement of national organizations from the outset, and regular communication that enabled ongoing work during difficulties including environmental disaster, states of emergency, and conflict.

National youth seminars and declarations

In Ethiopia and Nepal, in February–March 2019, local youth seminars at research sites were followed by National Youth Seminars in Addis Ababa and Kathmandu. These aimed to create opportunities for policy-makers to understand youth strategies and the support needed. The seminars provided a process and space for young people to be in dialogue with policy-makers and practitioners to influence youth policy. The National Youth Seminars brought together youth representatives from different locations, senior representatives of government and NGOs, academics, and practitioners. At a meeting following the Ethiopian National Seminar a participant noted:

> This research will change the lives of youth across the country in years to come. (Matiyas Assefa Chefa, Ministry of Youth and Sports, Director General for Youth Participation, Ethiopia)

In both countries, youth in research locations and nationally compiled a Declaration, presented to and signed by local and national government. Examples of two national declarations are given below.

Ethiopia national youth seminar: declaration example

Youth prepared Declarations on street-connection, youth justice, and disability. The disability declaration follows (see also Chapter 18): young people who were street-connected and with disabilities identified day-to-day problems, categorized them as severe, less severe, or mild, and suggested solutions.

Ethiopia youth declaration: policy needs by young people with disabilities

1. Formulation of laws and establishment of implementing institutions that support and assure persons with disabilities' mobility for work.
2. Considering persons with disabilities in the country's budget allocation.
3. Considering persons with disabilities while formulating law.
4. Formulation of laws that protect the rights of persons with disabilities and establishing an institution to safeguard them.

5. Facilitating discussions on the issues of disabilities.
6. Provision of assistive devices for persons with special needs.
7. Considering persons with disabilities in construction work and their need for an inclusive environment.
8. Protection to persons with disability from law enforcing bodies.
9. Participation of persons with disabilities on social, economic, and political issues.

Nepal national youth seminar: declaration

The Nepal National Youth Seminar was grounded in local seminars held in Kapilvastu, Sindhupalchowk, and Kathmandu. The national seminar was attended by 54 young people (including three genderfluid), the Rt Honourable Chair of National Assembly (Upper House), officials from the Ministry of Youth and Sports, Ministry of Labour, Employment and Social Security, National Youth Council, practitioners, youth rights advocates, civil society leaders, academics, and journalists from local and national media. Youth helped verify research findings and produced a 12-point declaration, outlining suggested policy and practice interventions.

Nepal youth declaration demands

1. Allocate at least 10 per cent of the total national budget for the holistic development of young people.
2. Ensure the meaningful representation, participation, and leadership of marginalized young people at all levels of the state mechanisms.
3. Ensure the easy access of young people in comprehensive sexuality education, sex and reproductive education, and services.
4. Develop the appropriate mechanism in each local government to provide guidance, counselling, and information to young people.
5. Ensure the fulfilment of basic rights of street-connected young people through their legal documentation.
6. Ensure the access of all marginalized young people to quality technical and vocational education.
7. Implement employment-oriented trainings and skill-development programmes from the local level for marginalized youth and youth at risk.
8. Make arrangements for seed money and soft loans for promoting youth entrepreneurship.
9. Take appropriate steps to end all kinds of social problems and harmful practices related to youth such as child marriage, drug abuse, *Chaupadi* (menstruation discrimination) etc.
10. Ensure the participation of young people from 'sexuality and gender minorities' and their right to marriage.
11. Ensure young people living in slums access to public services.
12. Ensure the safety, decent work, and right to freedom of youth who are in foreign employment.

POLICY THEMES AND IMPACT 197

Impact

Examples of some initial actions taken by youth, government, and non-government organizations.

- *Youth action.* Some young people wanted to get going before policy-makers reacted. For example, in Kathmandu youth organized to access services from local government and government-certified skill development training from HomeNet Nepal. In Addis Ababa, youth with a history of substance abuse asked the research team to help them access training so they can set up small businesses.
- *Non-government organizations.* In Ethiopia, CHADET and MCMIDO, two local NGOs, committed to developing programmes and designing interventions with marginalized youth based on the research findings. In Nepal, ActionAid Nepal, along with HomeNet and NMES, two local NGOs, developed strategies focused on marginalized youth based on the research analysis.
- *Local government.* In Nepal, elected local government representatives in Kathmandu, Sindhupalchowk, and Kapilvastu expressed interest in developing youth programmes based on the research. In Ethiopia, the regional representative from the Ministry of Labour and Social Affairs in Bahir Dar asked for advice on training for marginalized youth. These initiatives were then strengthened at Provincial/Regional and National Youth Seminars in Ethiopia and Nepal.
- *Regional and national government.* In Ethiopia, the former Ministry of Youth and Sports, now part of the reconstructed Ministry of Women, Children and Youth, revised the draft 2018 Youth Status Report and Indicators of Ethiopia based on the research findings. Technical, Vocational, Education Training (TVET) asked researchers to inform a regional training module for training marginalized youth. Representatives from Ministries and TVET jointly held an inclusive national youth seminar in Addis Ababa, to create a space for marginalized youth to inform development of youth policy. In Nepal, the under-secretary of the Ministry of Youth and Sports pledged to develop programmes targeting youth, based on the research findings. The Child Welfare Board met with the research team to inform ongoing strategy.

Findings across countries

Cross-country comparison of findings and issues for marginalized young people are a means of identifying key similarities and differences, but also contribute towards thinking about broader responses to common and global problems. Chapters on three key policy themes identified in both Ethiopia and Nepal follow: migration, street-connection, and disability (see Chapters 16–18). Although they are laid out as individual themes, they are interconnected, and it is important to look at these themes as a starting point in consideration of marginalized youth issues, and to adopt holistic perspectives on marginalized youth's lives and concerns, from their own viewpoints.

Internal migration, from local seasonal mobility to rural-urban and urban-urban movement, is a major strategy for marginalized youth in both countries. Increasing urbanization is accompanied by increasing urban migration, from rural areas or smaller towns, but the work available for most-marginalized youth is in the informal sector and often exploitative. Many become street-connected and those unable to secure regular income may turn to substance abuse. Migration is understood to be gendered, with marginalized young women having different social mobility and work opportunities from those of young men. Disabled youth, often less considered, also feature in these interconnections. Their marginalization is often exacerbated, and they may be isolated, although also wanting to migrate and similarly risk being street-connected.

International migration is endemic for marginalized youth, particularly, in both countries, to the Middle East. This may signal a break with earlier migrations to neighbouring countries, but is also gendered, and clearly linked to youth provision of support to their family and sense of family obligations often reinforced in their communities. The importance of family support, sense of duty and obligation, is prevalent across both countries, albeit manifested differently in the details, but broadly through migration, and often difficult work. Breakdown of family support and relationships, through domestic violence, abuse, and alcohol use, contribute to migration and particularly to street-connection, and to isolation of disabled young people.

Additional common themes and experiences include problems in education, finding employment, informal sector work, and processes of marginalization.

Education, employment, and the informal sector

Apart from family dynamics, poverty, and structures of marginalization, the bedrock of future strategies and many problems lies in education and employment opportunities. Some aspects are considered here, and some youth suggestions for policy and practice given below.

Previous studies, such as 'The Youth Survey' Nepal 2010–11 conducted by Save the Children and the British Council with Association of Youth Organizations Nepal (BC and AYON, 2011), found that education has failed to engage the most-marginalized and more needs to be done to ensure education is meaningful and relevant to the realities of young people's lives and to support youth into community peace-building development initiatives.

In Ethiopian contexts, research from Young Lives has also shown that to meet high educational aspirations, poverty and structural disadvantage needs to be addressed. Here too, more work is necessary to engage most-marginalized youth and support their aspirations and capacities.

Across all sites in both countries, formal education was found to have failed many marginalized youth through lack of relevance for their lives and circumstances, costs, and pressures of combining domestic work and school. Many dropped out of school or failed national exams.

> I felt marginalized as I have no home, no land, no property. Me and my family live in a small hut. Me and my family do not have sufficient food and other requirements for a good home. I have no good education, no good skills to get good and decent work. I have to do whatever I can get, even risky work to earn money. I do hard work and earn some money. People can't even see that and try to dominate me and react badly to me. (Moti, male, 16, Kapilvastu)

In both countries marginalized children work from a young age, on household work but also agriculture/livestock work in rural areas. Many begin paid work, particularly girls as domestic workers, before they are teenagers. This arises from combinations of costs of school, the need to support family, and education not being seen as a route to employment – both countries report unemployed educated youth. Migration is a strategy to find employment and income. Instead of seeing formal education as a means of finding a job and meeting adult expectations to support their families, young people, especially in rural Ethiopia, see international migrants as role models.

> As there are no educated role models in the Town and there are many uneducated youth, I lost interest in formal education. (Ayalew, male, 19, Woreta)

In Nepal there was strong evidence of gender discrimination and lack of understanding of the value of girls' education. Some of the most-marginalized may be interested in education but lack financial means. Girls, especially from Muslim families, do not have the mobility to travel for education beyond primary level. In Kathmandu young people want skills-based training to support their work in the informal sector and often feel pressure from families and peers to find work, even on the streets, rather than stay at school.

> I started to work from the age of 10/11 though I never received money/wages in my hand directly as my elder brother collected money from work providers. As I grow and become a young man, family expectations have been increasing. (Inder, male, 18, Kapilvastu)

In both countries the most-marginalized youth (seen as such by peers and community) had dropped out of school or failed exams. Continuously trying to encourage them back into formal education is not a realistic option. Youth definitions of marginalization are important because they illuminate their reasons, experiences, feelings, and processes of marginalization in different contexts, including intergenerational family dynamics, relationships with other significant peers and adults, and varying cultural, environmental, and political contexts in communities. These experiences are often part of their school life, if or when they attend, and seeking work. The processes of marginalization effectively exclude many most-marginalized youth from education and define their work options.

Two areas of policy and practice that marginalized young people seek to be reformed encompass relevant education, and support for their work strategies.

- *Providing education and training that is relevant.* Marginalized young people see peers who continued at school, passed examinations, still unemployed. Many seek and prefer work offering on-the-job training and skills that enable them to start enterprises or easily find work. They often have aims or obligations to support families and different education and training could help them find better employment.
- *Supporting youth strategies and avoiding criminalization.* Some of the most-marginalized youth dropped out of school and rely on internal and international migration strategies for survival and to provide for families. Many do not have identity cards, especially the most-marginalized and those in street situations. If working on the streets and/or international migration for the less well educated is made illegal, rather than stopping these trends, it may criminalize hard-working, hopeful, marginalized youth. Their strategies need support, and alternative, relevant education/training developed.

Conclusion

In order to bridge the gaps between the rhetoric of concern for the rights of marginalized youth and making changes to support them, engagement of youth, research findings, and government at different levels produced ideas for policy and practice. In both countries local and national seminars involved youth as part of the verification of research findings and as a means of engagement with officials. Youth declarations highlighted policy suggestions.

Comparison across countries points out key policy themes emerging in the research and many structural similarities in experiences of marginalized youth. Yet these themes intersect in many ways, indicating the importance of holistic perspectives and approaches rather than segmenting youth lives to suit policy or practice disciplines, departments or organizations. Underlying problems of marginalization, which provoke issues around education, early childhood work, informal sector employment, migration, and street-connection, are central and should not be ignored. For example, gender, sexuality, and disability discrimination, as well as that based on ethnicity/caste are key experiences of marginalized youth. Young people identified varied forms of marginalization, discrimination, and exclusion, more comprehensive than official perspectives. They provided analysis, for example, of what they could see in their families and communities and how peers needed to support each other, invariably saying these issues of inclusion should be taken into account in youth policy and practice in order to achieve improved wellbeing, education, and employment opportunities for young people. Youth facing intersecting structural inequalities were looking out for each other and their families.

CHAPTER 16
Youth and migration

Internal and international migration is a major part of life for most of the marginalized young people across all research sites in Ethiopia and Nepal. They migrate with families or most go by themselves, aiming to support their families. Most of those who have not, and who are still living near their first home location, are expecting to migrate, or have close or extended family members who have migrated. Everyone seems to know people who have left or returned in their community, and who are often held up as role models. Mobility is largely gendered, particularly in rural locations, but most youth have experience of internal movement. International migration, especially to Gulf countries, is a goal for many marginalized youth in both Ethiopia and Nepal, and is often expected by communities and families, which adds pressure on marginalized young people, some of whom would prefer not to go.

Keywords: youth, escape, hope, return, international migration, Gulf, role models, intergenerational, Ethiopia, Nepal

Introduction

Internal and international migration is a major part of life for most of the marginalized young people across all research sites in Ethiopia and Nepal. Some have migrated with families, but many have gone or will go by themselves. Most of those who have not, and who are still living near their first home location, are expecting to migrate, or have close or extended family members who have migrated. Everyone appears to know of people who have left or returned in their community, and who are often held up as role models for migration.

Although some internal migration of youth by themselves is for education and training, most is undertaken to seek work, get income and/or build up capital to use for house-building or starting a business. Some migration is prompted by a need to escape abuse and violence in particular, but also discrimination and poverty in the family and community. Much internal migration of children and young people with parent(s) or relatives is a strategy for escaping poverty and improving family income and prospects. In this research, migration was understood within the context of intergenerational contracts, youth agency, and also vulnerability in their decisions about whether to stay or leave (Huijsmans, 2012). The way in which networks of kin in communities and internationally shape youth decisions to migrate was also important (Thorsen, 2013). Many youth are mobile within an extended local range, to seek employment seasonally or for longer periods, principally to contribute to their families. Much of the employment gained is in the informal sector, insecure and often exploitative. In some locations, such as the southern plains of Nepal with its proximity to India, international migration across this land border is easier than moving longer distances within the country.

International migration is a significant part of all migration in both countries (see, for example, Sharma et al., 2014 and MoLESS, 2020 on Nepal; Emebet, 2002 and Asnake and Zerihun, 2015 on Ethiopia). Rural migrants may move to urban areas, often following linked-chain mobility before finally making international departures. Others plan their trip abroad, visas and other arrangements, through networks or brokers. Such migration often requires considerable investment, and returns are expected by those who put up the money, often members of the young person's family. Other, illegal routes are followed by some, with anticipated greater benefits but increased risks, including deportation and loss of pay, although problems of unpaid wages also occur in legal migration. Although the destination and other characteristics of international migration, criteria of success, return, and other features vary by site and country, the Gulf region is a significant goal for marginalized youth from both Ethiopia and Nepal. The key differences are rather the gendered nature of international migration. Young women are especially sought for domestic employment, and are more likely to be 'invested in' by family to migrate. Young men seek to go because of the potential income and benefits from this in supporting their family, gaining a degree of independence, and attributes of adult status. The extent of international migration provides cover for trafficking in both countries, also aligned with gender (for example, Abebaw, 2012; Asman, 2016).

Nepal

Marginalized young people in Nepal migrate internally and internationally, but processes and decisions vary by location and context. Internal migration includes movement for education, to attend secondary school/college, for skill-training, for work, and to escape poverty, abuse, exploitation or family problems. International migration has more usually followed on, or has been determined from the outset, and aims to provide income for self-survival, capital for development, or to support family. Yet location and context make a significant difference, such as between rural parts of Sindhupalchowk and Kapilvastu, and between these and urban areas of Kapilvastu and Kathmandu.

In Nepal, the research period (2016–2019) followed the 2015 earthquake which provided an additional set of problems and reasons for migration. Many marginalized youth already migrated to gain education and skills, and did so now also in the hope of returning to help rebuild communities. Although many in the hills of Sindhupalchowk have an interest in, and would prefer staying in, their village or in the country, they migrate due to the fragility of the environment or lack of work. Some migrate depending on caste and ethnicity as this is traditionally expected. For example, young women from the Tamang community have gone to India to engage in sex work (Asman, 2016), while Dalit youth have moved to learn metalworking skills in-country (exemplified in this research).

In rural Kapilvastu there appears to be less resistance to migration, less wish to stay, and it was reported:

> There is almost one person from every household going somewhere outside the community for work and employment. (Sara, female, 15)

Much of this mobility is internal, even locally to urban areas of Kapilvastu, at least as an initial move. A family may have one child migrated internally and another internationally, or have siblings along with one parent gone to different countries. Reasons for going are largely economic, to support family – parents, siblings, children. Many say they do not want to migrate, but feel they have no choice. International experiences vary, partly because of the range of countries involved.

In contrast to Sindhupalchowk, with its international border in the Himalayas, the location of Kapilvastu in southern Nepal on plains bordering India, means that migration to India is comparatively easy and frequent. Some families have relatives on both sides of the border, and there is inter-country marriage. International migration here also works in reverse, with Indian citizens crossing into Nepal to work. Although some youth in Kapilvastu find work from Indian employers in the Terai, other say they must leave because incoming Indian migrants are employed in Indian-owned factories, and local people claim wages are undercut. But there is much migration from Nepal to work in different parts of India. Sharma et al. (2014: 75) found that 'India still remains the top destination for foreign employment' although this may be changing.

Young people migrate because they have insufficient livelihood, and a lack of opportunity and employment in their own communities, particularly to support their family or to earn and save enough to start a business. They often feel school and education has been irrelevant.

> While I was in Malaysia, I used to think 'oh I should have continued my education'. But when I came back and saw my friends who completed the school education are still without any job, I felt good that I left the school. (Milan, male, 24, Sindhupalchowk)

Young men from Kapilvastu reported being sent or going by themselves, or with relatives, to work in India from early childhood, especially from the age of 10–11 years. For example:

> My mother died when I was 10 years old. After 8 months of my mother's death, I went to Delhi along with other 5 boys from the village. I worked in Delhi for one and half year. I used to cook food in a company. (Sonu, male, 17, rural Kapilvastu).

Radhe left Nepal before he was aged 12 and worked in different parts of India packing bread and selling clothes. Now back in Nepal,

> I felt very bad that I could not continue my study. Though I have studied up to grade 8, I cannot read the sentences written on this [Information Sheet]. (Radhe, male, 18, rural Kapilvastu)

Apart from India, young people (including some from Kapilvastu) migrate to South-east Asia, particularly Malaysia, and to the Middle East, particularly Qatar, Kuwait, Dubai, and Saudi Arabia. These countries are preferred because migrants can earn and save more. But the process of migration is more complicated and they sometimes faced problems of brokers taking fees without helping them, long delays in getting visas, and failing required medical tests. As an example of brokers' costs, one migrant took an initial money-lender loan for 95,000 rupees (approximately $874), and paid back 135,000 rupees (approximately $1,242) including interest amounting to some 38 per cent. They say they face difficulties in destinations because of language problems, and not knowing what was expected.

> In the first two months in Kuwait, I felt difficulties. I did not know what to do, how to do, how to speak ... I did not understand the language, I did not know even they were shouting at me. (Sugandha, male, 23, Sindhupalchowk)

But young women complained that parents prohibited them from migrating.

> There are many young men going outside the country. My elder brother is also in Saudi Arabia for work. Parents will not allow me to go. (Suni, female, 17, rural Kapilvastu)

> If I am boy, I would be somewhere in my age and working like other young of the community. (Tasi, female, 17, rural Kapilvastu)

> My father and two elder brothers are also in foreign employment. My family do not allow me to go outside from home and community because I am girl. If I am boy, I would be somewhere in foreign country for work at this time. (Balki, female, 18, rural Kapilvastu)

Migration without a spouse may cause problems in relationships, particularly in cases of early marriage. Although Tanura, a married 17-year-old, and already with a young child, had visited her husband abroad, she was left behind to live in rural Nepal, and needed to seek an income for herself in the absence of regular remittances.

> My husband is working in India and I have no regular contract with him. I do not have any hope for future. I just want to do any work to earn money for myself and daughter. (Tanura, female, 17, rural Kapilvastu)

A main reason for going is simply to find work and income.

> Here, in Nepal, no work, no employability; youth are even not getting support and opportunity for skill development. The main problem of youth like me is employment. Thus, I am planning to go foreign employment. I am sure that my parents and relatives will support [invest] for this. (Iman, male, 22, Kathmandu)

Such need to migrate may involve several members of a family, who consequently see very little of each other, although they are all contributing to maintaining the household and, in Sindhupalchowk, also the rebuilding of homes. A young woman explained the distribution of her family migrations that had been undertaken due to poverty. Her mother had been working in Kuwait and was now in Lebanon, one brother was in India, another in Malaysia, and she herself had just returned from Kuwait. She was about to meet her mother for the first time in over a decade, because her mother had first been away for a long period, then the daughter migrated, and they come home at different times.

> Now we are meeting face to face after 16 years. She is now with us on her 4-month leave. (Kuntee, female, 22, Sindhupalchowk)

Such absences may distort family relationships and children's learning and development as they grow up.

Concern about childhood is sometimes a partial reason for migration, when family members leave to support others through school as well as providing a household income.

> I have my father and brother working in foreign countries at some points. There was a financial crisis in the family. We even go hungry sometimes ... They supported me to study up to 10th grade. (Chandra, male, 20, Kathmandu)

Some children and young people migrate internally because secondary schools are in far-off towns, or to attempt to combine work and education to pay school costs.

Yet the main reason for migration is to support family and household. Marginalized youth particularly want to support their parents, and provide for their own and their family's future.

> I wish to have good house for my parents and establish a business after return back home from foreign country. (Nima, female, 19, Kathmandu)

Apart from house construction, many migrants want to return with enough funds to use as capital to set up businesses in Nepal. Many youth are also interested in making provision to help community development, partly so that others will not have to migrate.

> I will come back and open a bike workshop to help young people of Nepal. (Chandra, male, 20, Kathmandu)

Although adults interviewed, including stakeholders, often believe youth aspire to migrate, and many young people also speak as though that is their dream, the aspiration arises out of necessity, and is actually more for the expected or perceived fruits of migration, or simply because there is no alternative. Many would prefer not to have to go. A young man who had at last got a visa after two years waiting, said:

> I enjoy here ... I do not want to go now, because I am enjoying the work in bike repairing (Atma, male, 22, Kathmandu)

Jyaseelan, who had already migrated to Qatar, concluded:

> I am certain for migration [again] and it would be better ... I will earn some money and will return back home ... I wish to do something which is benefit to me and others too. (Jyaseelan, male, 24, urban Kapilvastu)

Ethiopia

Internal migration, particularly for work was, and still is, a common practice in Ethiopia, with a long history. Some argue that internal mobility was an important factor in Ethiopia's social formation in the late 19th and early 20th centuries (Feleke, 2006; Bevan and Pankhurst, 2006). But the pattern of movement, such as rural-rural, rural-urban, and urban-urban migration, has been changing over decades, along with the profile and motives of migrants and the drivers of internal migration. The 21st century saw a significant increase in rural-urban migration and a decline in rural-rural migration (Pankhurst and Dom, 2018). Land scarcity is a problem for youth especially (Bezu and Holden, 2014), but also rural food insufficiency (Tegegne and Penker, 2016). Most rural-urban migrants are reported as engaged in the informal sector.

> Migration is a strategy for moving out of poverty that is accessible to the poor in rural Ethiopia. It is often a risky investment, it has low short term returns, has the potential to end in disaster, exposes migrants to exploitation, hard work and abuse. However, in many cases, it is the only investment opportunity available, and the only opportunity some of the rural poor have to change their lives (Atnafu, 2006: 6).

Seasonal and internal migration is often a main feature of the lives of marginalized youth and families across Ethiopia: for example, seasonal migration from and to Woreta town and areas with large-scale commercial farms. In drought-prone Hetosa the fragile environment combined with social factors has increased youth migration as an escape out of the area. In Fogera, young people increasingly migrate out for employment in plantations in the north of the country. Some internal migration involves youth escaping abuse and violence within the family, and many of these become street-connected. Youth migrate internally to seek work, for example from Woreta and Fogera to Bahir Dar, a popular destination itself and also a link in a chain migration route to the Middle East. Young women have gone to Bahir Dar for domestic work, and been told the workload is similar but the pay lower compared to abroad. But they may resist and prefer internal migration because of negative experiences of international migrants.

> I don't want to live in my home town 'Woreta'. Neither have I preferred to migrate to the Middle East. People who returned back from the Middle East are psychologically disturbed and experience high levels of anxiety. I don't want to be like them. I want to migrate and live in Bahir Dar. (Lidet, female, 18 years, Woreta)

Although young people in Ethiopia migrate internally, now usually rural-urban or urban-urban, international migration is especially significant. Many want to migrate internationally themselves, and others are sent by their family. Middle East countries are the main preferred destination, fuelled by pictures on social media, observation of remittances sent back and used by local families, and stories and funds brought back by returnees.

Ethiopian labour migration to Gulf countries increased from the 1980s. Asnake and Zerihun (2015) suggest this passed through three phases. First (1980–91) migrant workers reportedly went to Saudi Arabia for Hajji and Umrah (Muslim religious pilgrimage); second (1991–98), most domestic workers legally went to Lebanon (Emebet, 2002); and third (1998–2014) they went to Saudi Arabia to fill gaps caused by the refusal of the Philippines and Indonesia to supply Saudi Arabia with domestic workers (Asnake and Zerihun, 2015).

Despite problems experienced by many international migrants, recounted to peers and siblings, even including advising them not to go, many youth still want to migrate, and many families still want their children, particularly daughters, to go. Underlying tensions within families around international migration are varied, particularly in the light of experiences brought back, and so drivers for youth can also vary. These drivers essentially vary from youth themselves being the initiator to their parents, siblings or uncles being the prime motivator and often main investor – the source of the necessary start-off funding. There are suggestions that international migration is inevitable, whoever initiates the move, not only because it is possible, but also because it is enticing, potentially offering significant rewards, and there are no other options as promising.

> Youth who came back from Dubai were able to buy land in urban areas and construct houses. They have their own housing units and lead a better life than others. They were also able to buy cows for breeding and run their own business on their own premises. I am hopeful that I will be among the successful ones than those who faced problems. (Aredo, male, 25, Hetosa)

Many youth migrate for reasons of education or family. Education concerns either the push of school failure or the need to raise money to continue study, and to attend college. Many feel they have to go because of dropping out of school, or failure in the national examination.

> I failed in grade 10 national exam. I became unemployed person ... I saw people from my village moving abroad which encouraged me to follow suit. (Yared, male, 24, Hetosa)

But the most pressing rationale is often the need for work, or for better-paid work, and particularly a need to support family such as parents and siblings, or their own spouse and child. Poverty and family responsibilities push young people to migrate.

> Our level of income was hand to mouth. I have two younger brothers. After I joined high school, schooling became morally impossible for me. I preferred moving abroad and help my family. I moved to Beirut and stayed there for five years. (Wagaye, female, 23, Addis Ketema)

For other youth the rationale was mixed and key factors included education, unemployment levels, and migrant role models.

> Due to the limited opportunities for education I don't know a person from our locality who got employed by succeeding in education. My role models are those who went abroad, work and improve their family and their own life. This holds true not only for me but also others in the community. As the opportunities in the community are minimal, people take the option of migrating as a means of improving their standards of life. (Yonatan, male, 16, Hetosa)

Whatever the reason for planning to go, potential young migrants generally need the support of parents, including approval for the decision as well as initial funding for brokers, travel, and papers. Some parents are willing to invest, but others need persuasion. Because the initial funding is often seen as an investment, the migrant then has obligations to fulfil in terms of both paying back capital and the returns expected by their family.

Brokers often facilitate rural-urban and international migration, both legal and illicit, for a fee. They may encourage young women to migrate as domestic workers both in-country and abroad. Kalayushi ran away from home at the age of 8 and stayed on the street for a week. She met a broker who facilitated her move to Bahir Dar and there she was employed as a domestic worker (Kalayush, female, 19, Woreta). Another young woman, forced to migrate to Bahir Dar at an early age, was employed as a domestic worker with the help of a broker. But she was raped and forced to work first as a domestic worker in another household and then as a commercial sex worker (Menen, female, 25, Woreta).

The possible benefits to be gained from international migration mean that some youth go because their parents want them to go. Much depends on perceptions of those who have returned, and often social pressure from community can influence or reinforce parents' or young people's own views and ideas.

> Returnee migrants are not marginalized. Those youth who hang around for too long are pushed by the community to migrate. Youth who choose to delay their migration to the Middle East are considered as irresponsible and careless ... My parents convinced me that I better migrate. (Kelemua, female, 15, Hetosa)

Potential remittances are attractive, and for parents with daughters, sending them abroad is seen as perhaps providing greater rewards than early marriage.

> My uncle and my elder brother used to push me to migrate to the Middle East. My uncle has sent my elder sister to the Middle East. She sent money through him which made him think that he made the right decision ... [he] convinced members of the whole family to push me to migrate to the Middle East. (Metaya, female, 23, Addis Ketema)

Some parents prefer daughters to take risks involved in international migration, than remain nearby and be abducted (often a consensual love match, see Chapter 7), where the bride-price is reduced.

> My parents would like me to migrate instead of seeing me get abducted for marriage. When my elder sister was in Dubai she sent money to my parents. (Demitu, female, 14, Hetosa)

Other young women also pointed to how parents benefit more from daughters' migration than marriage.

> Our parents prefer to send us to Arab countries. Because they expect something in return. They hope we will send them money. However, if we get married here, they will get nothing in return. They will not get any benefit. Hence unlike in the past today they encourage us to migrate rather than to get married. (Mufeyat, female, 18, Hetosa)

Benefits from international migration are well known, although remittances not always used as intended.

> Mostly the head of the family, especially fathers, send their children to Arab countries for their own sake. Those in the local area talk, 'Mr Bekele's daughter goes to Arab country and brings this much money. Why don't you send your daughter there?' ... After their children go there and begin remittance the fathers use the money for alcohol rather than putting it for the future of their child when she returns back. They finish all the money. When she come here there is nothing changed in her family and the money is already gone. (Zeru, male, 24, Woreta)

Some young women managed to reject family pressure.

> I had started to work in the informal business. I was able to fulfil my basic needs and that gave me the strength to reject their advice. It wasn't easy to live there rejecting his advice. I became very uncertain in life. And I started looking for support from people around. I decided to get married and move out from my uncle's house. Accordingly I did that. (Metaya, female, 23, Addis Ketema)

Life in the Middle East is known to be potentially difficult from returnees' stories, and some young people are fearful about going. Problems cited include difficulties of the work, because of learning both the language and the tasks required, including different ways of cooking, cleaning, and house facilities. It is known that some experience violence from employers, including beating but there are also accounts of attacks with boiling water. There are stories of attempted rape by men and by police, and fear of rape is said to be constant among young female migrants. Problems experienced in some domestic work situations make some migrants leave their first arranged workplace, and go into illegal work, which pays better but carries the threat of deportation (and greater likelihood of losing pay). These dangers are well-known but seen as a necessary risk for many youth and their families.

> The fact migration is a chance made me feel hopeful. I was hopeful despite the uncertainties ... hence I decided to go to a place where I do not know what was going to happen. You will die here, but either you will die or survive there. (Meriyem, female, 20, Hetosa)

Key messages for policy and practice in Ethiopia and Nepal

The Ethiopia and Nepal national youth seminars (see Chapter 15), involving marginalized youth, government, and practitioners, looked at suggestions around migration for policy and practice. The main areas include issues concerning education and employment, particularly for youth who do not want to migrate or do not want to go abroad, and issues about information, safety, protection, and legality for those who do undertake international migration.

- *Education.* Many young people want to stay, or only move internally, and find work outside the informal sector. They find formal education is not relevant or helpful in getting employment or providing skills, even for migrating internationally. They want appropriate education and vocational training.
- *Employment.* Local unemployment is an international push-factor, particularly in rural areas, along with often limited options in the informal sector for marginalized youth in urban locations. An increase in rural employment and industries, and associated skill-training is

wanted, also support for youth development of small business, both rural and urban.
- *Knowledge and information.* Youth want information about migration, the possibilities and pitfalls of different destinations, what sort of work is available, and what skills and capacities are required, to assess whether it is appropriate for them. They also want to know what resources and opportunities are available locally. Parents and guardians need to know about migration and its realities.
- *Remittances.* Migration is a livelihood strategy, for supporting families, and as a future resource, for example, setting up a business or building a house. Mismanagement of remittances limits or consumes all their gains. Training and support for youth and families on the best use of remittances is wanted.
- *Safety and protection.* Migration needs to be safe, both internally and internationally. Brokers and services need regulation so that international migration candidates are provided with full and appropriate information, and suit skills and capacities required at their destination. Migrants need protection from abuse, exploitation, and discrimination, which requires international cooperation.
- *Legality and avoiding criminalization.* Government and NGOs need to recognize that a main strategy for most-marginalized youth is to migrate internationally to support families, and that while remittances are needed at home, their labour is wanted abroad. They need support to migrate legally, including international liaison to negotiate and maintain conditions at their destinations. Making and enforcing laws that restrict the most-marginalized youth is counter-productive, increases social burdens, and ignores the fact of their often necessary strategies. Migration is important as a survival strategy, and as a benefit to the sending and receiving places, which means that policies and practices need to understand the realities of youth lives and avoid criminalizing them. National policies with international connections around migration need to be formulated in the light of youth experiences, needs, and strategies.

Conclusion

Internal mobility locally and in-country migration is experienced by many marginalized youth, sometimes moving for education, but mostly for seeking employment and income to support their family. Mobility is gendered to a large extent. Although in some rural communities, young women's movements are restricted, even on marriage, many are sent off for domestic work in better-off homes or in other towns and cities. Young men's migration is often necessary because of a lack of income-earning opportunities in rural areas, but since many marginalized youth have dropped out of school, they usually end up working in the informal sector, and risk exploitation.

Key similarities in Ethiopia and Nepal revolve around international migration to the Middle East. Young women in particular are sought after for domestic work. Young men's international migration to these countries is often more speculative, with employment in construction being a major area of work. The dynamics of international migration vary, partly due to the proximity of the Gulf, but also for reasons of social and family relationships. International migration is seen as the only way of making money to use as capital for business start-up or constructing houses in some areas, and young people only go as a last resort and want to return to their home communities, particularly in parts of rural Nepal. In parts of Ethiopia some parents see it as an investment bringing returns and preferable to marrying off daughters at an early age. In some communities there is pressure on youth to migrate, fuelled by perception of supposedly successful migrants. Yet the welcome accorded to returning migrants often depends on how long the capital brought back lasts and what it is used for, assuming remittances have not been expended before their return.

International migration in particular is used as a means of developing and supporting rural economies but does not appear to be sustainable nor produce sustainable changes in those economies. Interventions in policy and practice are needed not only to safeguard migrants but also to address their goals for their local communities.

CHAPTER 17
Youth in street situations

Street-connected youth are evident in capital cities and other urban areas of Ethiopia and Nepal. They form a diverse population in terms of age, gender, ethnicity/caste, sexuality, and dis/ability, and come from various rural and urban backgrounds, live with or without parents, and for them the street is a focal point in some or all aspects of living. Many are involved in a vicious circle of substance use/abuse to alleviate life's hardships and ward off hunger, but find this also limits their ongoing search for employment. Policies towards street-connected youth have recently changed. Youth in street situations want to work but often can only find limited, precarious, exploitative, even dangerous employment in the informal economy. They face discrimination from local communities, are prevented from using services, wrongly accused of criminal activities, and experience violence from authorities and police. Yet, when taken into partnership by local services, communities as well as street-connected youth find they benefit.

Keywords: street youth, justice, substance use and abuse, discrimination, institutional care, Ethiopia, Nepal

Introduction

The number of young people who are street-connected or in street situations, and the problems they face, as well as local community perceptions of them, were found to be a major issue in both Ethiopia and Nepal. A main concern among street-connected young people, as well as local communities and services, is substance use and abuse. Many youth find substance use staves off hunger, exclusion, and boredom, but in a vicious circle also prevents them continuing to seek income and employment. Although youth being in street situations is predominantly an issue of capital cities, they had often migrated from rural areas, indicating aspects of diversity of street-connected youth. The terms 'street situations' and 'street-connected youth' (see below) are used here interchangeably in recognition of the multiple dimensions, characteristics, backgrounds, and lives of young people for whom the street is a focal point in some aspect of their regular living.

This research was conducted in rural and urban sites during a period when policies towards street-connected children and youth changed in both countries. This affected how research could be carried out in street situations, and influenced practical strategies towards working with street-connected youth. In Nepal, changes in government policy (see below) prohibit contact with youth currently in street situations, and research was conducted with young people who were street-connected but now placed in a training centre. In Ethiopia, policies to provide shelter for youth in street situations has only resulted in youth sometimes feeling displaced from the streets, while they still hope that authorities will listen to them rather than presuming they know what actions will be beneficial in their lives.

This chapter provides a brief account of who are street youth and what is meant by street-connected and street situations, particularly in relation to international policy and practice. It then provides an overview of youth in street situations in Ethiopia and Nepal. It goes on to look at the views and declarations of street-connected young people from the National Seminar held in Ethiopia (see Chapter 15), and concludes with policy and practice issues raised through the research and by youth across both countries.

Street situations and young people

The term 'street children' has long been in use, since the 19th century, and carries with it a set of pejorative connotations regarding the children involved, for example, as either victims or criminals (West, 2003). Both public perception and services, and some policy-making, can swing between seeing children as alone, desolate, helpless, homeless, and who are separated from parents to devious, wilful, hardened wrongdoers to be feared. In both extremes, the policy and service outcomes are often similar: placement in institutional accommodation where they are provided with education and generally not allowed to leave. The diverse reality of cause and effect is very different, and many agencies have sought to change the term and shift the categorization to reflect the breadth of backgrounds and circumstances. The problem of 'street children' being out of place, and their rights frequently violated, has been recorded often (for example, Ennew, 1994, 1995; Connolly and Ennew, 1996; West, 1999, 2003; Thomas de Benitez, 2011a, b), yet the term and connotations persist. This provides a significant challenge for service delivery, policy-making, and practice that will actually alleviate the situation, provide support, and opportunity for children and youth, and realize their rights. In many ways street-connected youth, that is older children and young people around the ages of 15 to 24, are in a particularly difficult situation where, because of their age (especially young men), they are seen as a potential threat in public places.

Instead of 'street children' and 'street youth', the terms 'street situations' and 'street-connected youth' are preferred (see OHCHR, 2017) and are used here. These terms aim to recognize the multiple dimensions, characteristics, backgrounds, and lives of young people for whom the street is in some ways a focal point of their daily life or their means of survival or making a living. Street-connected youth are not homogeneous: they include young women, men, youth of third gender or genderfluid, and disabled youth, who are of varied ages, ethnicities/castes, and backgrounds. Their street situations vary, from sleeping and living on the street, to employment or work based on the street, to use of the street for daily survival, then becoming exploited and eventually often misusing drugs. They may be living alone or with peers, or with families, for example in slums, temporary dwellings, or even in suburbs. The reasons for their circumstances vary. Many who are separate from family have escaped physical and sexual abuse and violence at home, from parents and other family members, or at school. Others have attempted migration and have made unsuccessful attempts to find employment to support their family. Apart from experiences of abuse, which is found to be extensive, their backgrounds may also include family poverty, difficulties at school, and status discrimination on the grounds of ethnicity/caste, disability, sexuality, or religion. Their experiences and situations are often highly gendered. When they are in street situations they experience further marginalization, stigma, and discrimination and are vulnerable to violence from peers, adults, and local authorities including the police. They are likely to be pushed into exploitative work in the informal sector or hassled when attempting to develop their own small businesses, vulnerable to commercial sexual exploitation, and to drug and other substance misuse. Their lives in street situations are often mobile, changing, insecure, and uncertain (see Heinonen, 2013 and Kassa, 2018 on Ethiopia; Castle et al., 2012 and Ryckmans, 2012 on Nepal).

Research findings, in both Ethiopia and Nepal, show the diversity of young people involved and reflect academic and policy attempts to shift public, services, and policy understanding and conceptualization of the lives of 'street children and youth'. The United Nations defines children in street situations as:

> (a) children who depend on the streets to live and/or work, whether alone, with peers or with family; and (b) a wider population of children who have formed strong connections with public spaces and for whom the street plays a vital role in their everyday lives and identities. This wider population includes children who periodically, but not always, live and/or work on the streets and children who do not live or work on the streets but who regularly accompany their peers, siblings or family in the streets (OHCHR, 2017: paragraph 4).

Street-connected youth in both Ethiopia and Nepal were of different ethnicities/castes and religions and identified as young women, men, genderfluid or third gender, and as disabled youth. For some, becoming street-connected involved escape from abuse and discrimination within families and communities. Others felt heavy expectations to provide for their families in the face of high unemployment, landlessness, and environmental fragility or simply sought to emulate role models who are successful migrants.

On the street, young men and women can feel insecure, out of control of their lives, uncertain of how to earn a living, or just surviving day-to-day. Some youth living and working on the street find it hard to survive on low incomes and turn to exploitative work, for example commercial sex work and/or the use of substances to relieve their difficulties.

Nepal

In Nepal, government policy (see below) prohibits contact with youth currently in street situations, and research was conducted with some youth who were recently street-connected but placed in a shelter/training home run by non-government organizations. In Nepal, many young people became street-connected in Kathmandu through migration from other parts of the country or from home in the city, mainly to escape family or community violence, abuse, and poverty. Some initially enjoyed the freedom found in street situations, such as a social life with peers and escape from family. But they also rapidly experienced and/or became concerned about fear of violence and rape, exploitation, vulnerability to trafficking, and violence from authorities. Because it was often difficult to find work, some became involved in begging and petty crime to survive. They experienced exclusion, stigma, and discrimination, and many began to use and misuse various drugs and substances to alleviate their situation, which exacerbated some problems.

Many had left their family as a child, to escape abuse at home. Tara ran away from violence and poverty at the age of 10 years, and spent periods in street situations and in shelter homes before settling in a home.

> In the street I stayed for two years, at that time I was only 10 years old. My father used to drink alcohol and beat me a lot ... Both of my parents did not care for us, they have neglected us, so I learnt to go to the bus and started begging over there. (Tara, female, 17, Kathmandu)

A 16-year-old young man, Kamel, left home in the Terai (southern plains) at the age of 5 years with his older brother after their mother died, father remarried, and they were neglected. When NGOs rescued and returned them, each time the neglect continued and they left again to travel, even to India, and survived through begging, until their father and step-mother died and they could not be returned again. Another 16-year-old young man, Sajan, left home at 8 years because of being beaten in the community and under threat of further violence, after he stole a copper wire from a shop.

Most street-connected youth and those living in slums questioned the relevance of formal education, and some gave up school.

> I dropped out from the school with friends and started to live in the street for five years. (Laxmi, female, 15)

They saw the lack of work available, and did not see how schooling would help earn a living. Jay's family migrated from eastern Nepal to Kathmandu, but:

> My family are poor. No money to fulfil daily necessities and requirements, and parents used to fight and drink alcohol. There was no care or concern for me. (Jay, male, 16)

A few preferred street situations to family life.

> Friendship, network and peer enjoyment in the street without any hesitation was the main attraction to children in the street. (Mahesi, male, 16)

> Life in street is quite free and we enjoy a lot, although there are some uncertainties. Sometimes no food and no place to sleep. Sometimes, people feed us. (Binita, female, 20)

In street situations, youth face exploitation from peers, adults, and authorities.

> When I was in the street, there was fear that an older group maybe they capture all the money from me. (Jay, male, 16)

Both young men and women reported being forced into sex by men who found them on the street.

> Once, an adult man took me somewhere in hotel room and forced for sex too. It was very hard time for me. Though, at the end, I run away from the hotel. (Kamal, male, 16)

Many mentioned fear of rape:

> There are many problems, including clothes to wear and fear of rape. (Rajani, female, 15)

They also reported fear of trafficking and violence.

> Possibility for trafficking, elder domination, child labour, child abuse and fighting in the street are major insecure areas. Similarly, children and young people used to have dendrite, drug etc. Rape, harassment and sexual harassment are major insecurity areas. (Mahesi male, 16)

Most feared the police:

> Police used to beat us every night when we were in the street. (Sagar, male, 15)

> I felt insecure seeing police in the street as they sometimes hit me. (Kamal, male, 16)

But one young woman said,

> Police is not a threat to us, because they are also like friends to us. (Rajani, female, 15)

Alcohol and drug abuse is increasing as marginalized young people seek to escape insecurity and experiences of abuse, exclusion, and rejection.

> I felt marginalized and dominated when people used the word 'Khate' when I was in the street. I saw there was other vulnerable children who

are working as domestic workers, as conductors, drug users etc who need support. (Jay, male, 16)

The main substance used is dendrite, a type of glue/solvent.

> Whenever I took 'Dendrite' I did not use to feel hunger. It used to make me 'Jhyap' (Dizzy) ... With our own money, we did not buy good food instead, we used to go to the glue shop and buy 'Dendrite'. (Sajan, male, 16)

The solvent is known for hallucinations, but also reducing hunger pangs and cold.

> Gradually I took it and it became habitual. (Sagar, male, 15)

Experiences of street-connected children and young people in Nepal include problems at home, with family, such as abuse and violence, and similar experiences but also violence from police in street situations, as well as the use of alcohol and substances to alleviate life circumstances. The current policy of placing street-connected children and young people in institutions limited the research to the views of those already taken in. Some noted that, before this policy, they had come into residential care but left, finding it unsuitable. The shift in policy (see below) does not address prevention, in terms of the issues such as violence and abuse that push children and young people to separate from families. Nor does it address the pressure to provide for families, or the actions and effects of discrimination, exploitation, violence, and abuse many experience in the processes of becoming street-connected, or the lives of those who are living with their families in street situations.

In 2015 the Central Child Welfare Board (CCWB) of the Government of Nepal produced 'Street Children's Rescue, Protection and Management Guidelines', piloted over the next three years before full implementation. 'The model was to rescue children from the street, place them in a Drop-in Centre for a maximum of three months, followed by transfer to a Socialization Centre for a maximum of 18 months', which was supposed to lead to rehabilitation with family and society (CWIN, 2019: 1). In practice children were picked up by police and placed in these centres, and individuals and organizations not associated with implementation of guidelines were prohibited from contact with children and youth on the street. Long-term assessment of the policy was still under way, but interim evaluation was undertaken and reported in 2019. Aspects of the initiative were welcomed, such as a dedicated budget, attention to problems of street-connected children and youth, developing a systematic process, better information management systems at CCWB, resources, and getting children off the streets (CWIN, 2019: 2–5).

However, a number of challenges and problems were identified. These include the focus on rescue and short-term, insufficient facilities and service providers, lack of involvement with non-government organizations, problems with forced admissions and the effect on children, collection of the wrong children (such as those truanting for a day), and limited facilities for detoxification. In addition, a high drop-out rate (around 50 per cent) was reported from training centres alone. It was also found the intervention did not work effectively for various groups: older children, older street girls especially, and children with disabilities; also those who were habituated to the street, and those who had found a way of earning a reasonable income although street-connected. There is concern that the issue has been 'driven underground' or made invisible, especially with lack of prevention work, but there are also problems in repatriation with families and support for families (around half of those placed back with their families had returned to the street). Other issues cited include reductions forecast in budgets, concerns over commitment of local government, and frequently changing staff (CWIN, 2019: 5–15).

Ethiopia

In Ethiopia research was conducted with young people in street situations in Woreta and Addis Ketema. Across both sites it was found that young people's street-connection often involved their families in two different situations. Many youth had run away from physical and/or sexual abuse by their family, but others moved or ended up in the city in seeking work to support and contribute to families. In both cases, their experiences may include migration, problems in finding work, exploitative employment, and generally grappling with extreme poverty, discrimination, and marginalization. All of this is exacerbated by lack of support, opportunities, employment, and access to services. Substance use and abuse is widespread as a means of alleviating their situation (see also Birhanu et al., 2014). This in turn becomes problematic and creates further difficulties for them.

Many urban marginalized youth grew up in towns or cities or migrated to them in search of better futures. Some of those who migrated to urban areas of Woreta and Addis Ketema went to find different ways to meet adult expectations and support their families. Successful migrants are often viewed as role models by young people, and some youth migrating to the city sought to emulate them. By migrating they were not seeking to break family and traditional community bonds, but rather fitting in with expectations as well as aspiring to success and wanting to contribute. But some young migrants felt they were carrying a burden of heavy expectations to provide for families in the face of high unemployment, landlessness, and environmental fragility.

When young people reach urban sites, by themselves or with family members, they often find it does not meet their expectations. Some try to survive on very low pay in informal work such as hotels, or on the streets; they may then find more lucrative but exploitative employment, for example as commercial sex workers, or become involved criminal activity such as pickpocketing and theft. Other youth find solace in substance use that can turn into addiction, or to drink that may become alcoholism.

Yet, most street-connected youth came into this situation as a result of abuse, discrimination, and problems in families and communities. They receive their most significant support from peers in street situations, often working and living together for security and support, which provides some substitution for love lost from families. They say they experience psychological gratification through contact with other youth in street situations. They feel and effectively are excluded from life in the community and from local services. This includes services specifically set up for young people, such as youth centres:

> We [street-connected young people] don't get the chance to take part in the affairs of the community. We are not taken as benefitting group of people by the local administration. There is a youth Centre in the Woreda. However, street youth hardly go there as they are regarded as outsiders. (Zeru, male, 23)

In street situations, youth feel insecure, out of control of their lives, and uncertain how to survive day-to-day, let alone earn a living. They are marginalized and feel alienated from everyday social and economic life of the community. They suffer from widespread discriminatory social labelling of youth in street situations, being referred to and seen as thieves and drug addicts. Particularly around the large market and bus station in Addis Ketema, but also elsewhere, street-connected youth find they are often regarded as primary suspects for any criminal activity. They reported non-judicial torture and imprisonment.

Even when street-connected youth have support among themselves, it is difficult finding help to get employment. They often have to become involved in informal activities which don't require relationships or other collateral. Some turn to exploitative work, for example commercial sex work and/or use of substances to relieve difficulties.

> After I started working as a commercial sex worker, my life became all the same. The payment is very minimal and couldn't bring change to way of life. Rather my life became a routine and boring one. This business made my life certain. I usually woke up in the middle of the day, drink coffee and chew khat and when I have customers I will work. (Kokebe, female, 24, Addis Ketema)

Government and non-government organizations have schemes for supporting street-connected youth and vocational training, but there are still problems of finding jobs, very limited employment opportunities, and no guarantee of work for them on completion of training schemes.

> We were mobilised and got trained for two weeks in paving roads using cobblestones by the local government. However, we have not yet started working. Although they promised to offer us jobs right away it all turned out to be a lie. As the cost of living is rising, we found it very difficult to

pay for house rentals and be able to eat three times a day working in the informal sector. (Meron, female, 23)

Various substances are used as a way of coping with life on the street, including glue- and benzene-sniffing, local liquor drinking, *khat* chewing (leaves of the *Catha edulis* plant), tobacco smoking, and in some instances marijuana use. Street-connected youth say that such substances help them forget their vulnerability, reduce hunger and cold, offer entertainment, provide courage and a feeling of belonging with other young people. But they also explain how use of substances has detrimental effects such as losing confidence, boredom, feelings of shame, depression and hopelessness, nervousness, sleeping difficulties, sweating, and mental fatigue. According to young people, substances are easily accessible and affordable despite laws prohibiting sale to minors, and there is a lack of detoxification and rehabilitation programmes.

Many street-connected young people become involved in the justice system, often because of discrimination in communities and by authorities towards them. Some report violence from policemen, even if they are innocent or have only committed petty crimes.

> I have confidence in the fact that street children have minimal involvement in crimes, especially theft. There are some youth who live in the area who come to the bus station for robbery and fraud as if it's their legal work. They commit crime and go away immediately. The policemen come and point their finger at us. We will be arrested and suffer for something we don't have any involvement in. Youth from the surroundings have somewhere to hide. We stay here as we don't have places to hide. (Zenabu, male, 22, Addis Ketema)

On the other hand, some youth were very appreciative of community members and police who were trying to work with them to minimize crime in their area.

> The security condition of the vicinity was fragile before. Now the community is working very closely with the police. The youth are part of the effort to minimize criminal activities in the area. The local administration allows the youth to work in temporary parking lots in the evening. The youth also patrol the neighbourhood while watching over the cars. (Yaye, male, 26, Addis Ketema)

Ethiopia youth seminar

The National Seminar held in Ethiopia in March 2019 (see Chapter 15) included a one-day workshop involving some 40 street-connected youth aged 15–25 years. These included some 20 young people who work and live on the streets, 13 who work and sleep on the streets, and seven disabled youth who tend to be street-connected much of the time. The young people prepared a declaration, and a set of messages for policy-makers and practitioners, to show what they felt should be changed (see below).

They identified the severest problems of street-connected youth as: lack of shelter; disagreements with the police over sleeping on the street; addiction; and shortage of food. They identified four more severe problems: high rates of inflation; not having an Identity Card or documentation; not being able to save enough money to go back and visit their family or the city they came from; and fighting with authorities over the need to have a business licence to do small businesses like shoe-shining. One further problem they raised is the increasing number of street youth and the resultant decreasing number of job opportunities.

Declaration by youth who live and work on the streets

Declaration produced by 40 street-connected youth at the National Seminar in Ethiopia, March 2019.

1. The government should revise the current street-connected institution-based intervention programmes.
2. The current institutionalized intervention programme, in which street-connected youth are taken away out of the city for training in the regions, creates fear among those who work and live on the streets.
3. Provision of opportunities to work: employment opportunities for street youth should be created by taking their financial and mental capacities into consideration.
4. Provision of seed money for those who want to go back and reunify with their family. The family may not have the capacity to provide the basic amenities for youth. The government and NGOs who work on reunification should consider giving the family of the youth input so that their lives are more sustainable.
5. Awareness creation for the community about the life of the youth is vital. The community think of street-connected youth as burdens, drug addicts, and thieves. There should be dialogue and community conversations that show street youth are no different from any other youth in the community.
6. Capacity building, and empowerment of youth through the provision of different services and facilities, is vital. However, they should always be supported by employment opportunities as without this there will be no visible change.
7. Managing food price inflation: street youth assert that it has become difficult for them to eat three times a day due to food price inflation. The inflation of food price forces them to eat leftover food collected from hotels and restaurants.
8. Provision of life skills training is vital for street-connected youth.
9. Ethnic-based division among youth is also negatively affecting the life of street-connected youth. The government should find solutions to help with the problem of ethnic-based group clashes among street youth.

Messages for policy and practice in Ethiopia and Nepal

The national seminars in both Ethiopia and Nepal, but particularly that in Ethiopia which included a special focus on street-connected youth as one of three main themes, looked at key messages for policy and practice. These were drawn from research findings through discussions with academics, practitioners, and policy-makers, and from workshops and input of street-connected young people themselves. The findings and messages for policy and practice generally show much in common in the lives of street-connected youth in Ethiopia and Nepal, despite certain differences in policy.

- *Employment.* Once young people are on the street, services need to take youth perspectives into account to engage with, and find ways to work with, the most-marginalized, and to ensure provision is non-discriminatory and inclusive. Employment support in the informal sector could offer alternatives to street-connected youth and their families. If young people return to communities having not succeeded in employment or migration, mediation may be important in mending broken family bonds so youth can feel that they belong.
- *Shelter homes.* In Nepal, additional policy considerations involve the need to further develop policy and practice around the concept of transitional homes. Shelter homes have collected street-connected children and young people and been used by them for many years. Children have often not engaged with them and some experienced moving many times between homes and street situations before settling in. Shelter homes are providing safe environments for street-connected young people and basic education. But young people feel insecure about leaving shelter homes after their designated 'two years' period. Youth in Nepal recommended providing support and after-care policies and programmes along with life skills, livelihood, and vocational skills training.
- *Substance use.* In both countries there is need for appropriate policy and practice to address drug and substance use, which is not limited to youth in street situations. This needs to ensure that youth perspectives on their lives and circumstances are understood, why they use substances and what would help them to overcome use and addiction. More research is needed towards youth-centred policies that will work.
- *Prevention.* Policy and practice needs to look at prevention, for example in terms of education, through family and community life, and diversion practice before young people enter and once they are in the youth justice system. Many young people become street-connected because of abuse and violence in the family, at home, and in communities. There is a need to develop policy and practice to address problems of violence, abuse, and exploitation particularly within families, providing support for youth and families. Services should include social support schemes for orphans and disintegrated families, and

engage with children and young people through developing their participation in communities.
- *Education*: The relevance of education and school for children and young people should be reviewed to both address problems of dropping out and to make the curriculum useful, with attention to vocational training. Many youth in street situations become involved with the police and justice system and this requires significant attention with the aim of diversion. Authorities such as police need training in working with young people to understand their complex realities.
- *Recognition.* Street-connected youth should be engaged, involved, and valued as members of the community. Experiences of abuse, discrimination, vulnerability, and pressures on livelihoods can alienate street-connected youth from the local community in which they live. It is important to recognize the value and potential contributions of all youth to communities. Services should be designed to engage with young people in street situations and support them to connect with local residents and local government, developing mutual relationships with peers, becoming involved in development work, and participating in their community.
- *Youth policy*. Government policies to clear the streets of street-connected youth and support them in institutions can be counter-productive in supporting youth agency and innovation in their strategies for moving out of poverty. A main strategy for the most-marginalized youth in both countries, in order to survive, and to try to support their families, is to work in the informal sector. If they are working hard on the streets and sometimes needing to sleep and live there, then authorities need to work with them rather than assume they are anti-social and involved in criminal activities. Their small enterprises and creative survival ideas need to be supported and they need help to move out of exploitative and illegal work through alternatives for paid work.

Conclusion

Many similarities in the lives and experiences of youth in street situations are evident from both Ethiopia and Nepal. In both countries, problems of abuse and violence in families and communities have been push factors in children and young people becoming street-connected. Their lives in street situations show various parallels in discrimination and even violence from communities, services, authorities, and police. They find difficulties in obtaining employment except in the informal sector, which is often dangerous, exploitative, and precarious. Particularly in Ethiopia, but this is also evident in Nepal, young people migrate to urban locations with aspirations to find ways to meet adult expectations and to support their families. Those who escaped from abuse to street situations also have aspirations and a desire to contribute. The difficulties of marginalization, violence, and discrimination faced by youth in street situations further exacerbates any previous experience of abuse and the pressures to meet family expectations. Policies and practices of institutionalizing street-connected young people fail to prevent initial problems, or address their circumstances, experiences, and aspirations. Solutions require the participation of young people themselves in policy and practice at all levels of government, as well as in communities, services, and non-government organizations. Failing to listen to, and work with, the children and young people involved, and to understand their diversity and their changing circumstances and needs, will continue to promote public stigma and discrimination rather than provide solutions.

CHAPTER 18
Youth and disability

Across Ethiopia and Nepal, marginalized disabled youth experience problems in education, access to healthcare and services, lack of employment, and issues in migration, experiences of isolation, lack of support, stigma, and discrimination. Their problems, not only for youth living with a disability themselves, but also youth living with family members with a disability, are often side-lined or ignored, and many young people feel isolated. Many problems of education, employment and income, access to health and other services, as well as discrimination, are experienced by most-marginalized youth in various forms, but the situation for disabled young people and families with members with disabilities, is generally further exacerbated through various social barriers, stigma, discrimination, and other difficulties, as shown in marginalized communities and settings, both rural and urban, in Nepal and Ethiopia. Policy and practice issues emerging from the research, local and national seminars, and expert workshops are included.

Keywords: youth, disability, marginalization, discrimination, policy, practice, Ethiopia, Nepal

Introduction

Disability was found to be a major concern for youth in both Ethiopia and Nepal. The importance of understanding the varied dimensions and implications of youth being disabled themselves, or living with family members with disabilities, emerged in the research in both countries. Disability was highlighted as one of the biggest indicators of youth marginalization, echoing international research on youth and disability (Groce, 2004; Groce and Kett, 2014).

Disability is an umbrella term encompassing subgroups of disabilities, and varied categories of impairments, including physical, visual, hearing, mental and intellectual, which intersect with other socially defined diversities, such as gender, ethnicity/caste, class, sexuality, wealth, and income status (UN, 2008). These variations may increase marginalization and difficulties experienced, for example for disabled women, people with multiple disabilities, people with severe disabilities, disabled people who are poor, disabled people who are street-connected, and others. The term disabled youth/young people is used here following consultation with disabled colleagues and young people, rather than for example always using the term 'youth living with disability'.

Disability, poverty, and marginalization are known to reinforce each other. People with disabilities face exclusion, vulnerability, and marginalization to a higher degree than their non-disabled peers (Banks et al., 2017; Abualghaib et al., 2019; Banks, 2019). The most-marginalized youth experience problems of accessing education, employment, health and other services, as well as discrimination and exclusion. Individuals and families living in poverty often cannot access or afford necessary services, including education and health, and frequently also experience marginalization. While the aspirations of disabled youth may be similar to their non-disabled peers, disabled youth face additional challenges in achieving them (Groce and Kett, 2014: 4). It is clear that disabled young people face intersecting disadvantages through various physical and social barriers (Groce and Kett, 2014), exacerbated for those marginalized, stigmatized, and discriminated against for additional reasons. While this has been generally left unacknowledged in most development and poverty reduction initiatives, recent shifts have seen disability move onto various policy agendas. For example, where the Millennium Development Goals did not mention disability once, the Sustainable Development Goals that superseded them mention disability 17 times (Groce, 2013, 2018). Yet this new focus does not often translate into empirical evidence gathering or programmatic action (Banks et al., 2017; Abualghaib et al., 2019). This chapter aims to contribute to both.

The research in Ethiopia and Nepal shows how young people (also older people and children) are disabled through lack of provision as well as social attitudes, discrimination, and oppression, which accords with the social model of disability (Oliver, 1990, 2013). This underlines the importance of understanding these social effects, contexts, and their implications for youth with disabilities or youth living with family members with disabilities. While disability is often individualized in the way it is described, the broader impact on family and society needs to be considered. Disability also affects households, families, and individuals who are considered non-disabled.

Key findings across Ethiopia and Nepal for disabled youth include their feelings of lack of access and support and discrimination in education, healthcare services, and employment. They also raised difficulties they experienced in migration and experiences of isolation in communities. Many problems of discrimination in education, employment, and earning income are experienced by the most-marginalized youth in various forms, but the situation for disabled young people is generally further exacerbated through various social barriers and experiences of stigma, as shown in examples below from Nepal and Ethiopia, and in accordance with other research (such as Teferra, 1999; Kassa et al., 2016; Nidaw et al., 2018; UNICEF et al., 2019 in Ethiopia; Eide et al., 2016; Thapaliya, 2016 in Nepal).

> In our area there is a blind woman. Her family hesitated to take her out of home for a walk let alone sending her to school. Now she is 17 years old, but she doesn't have the chance to go out and experience the outside world. The marginalization begins from her family members themselves. (Yared, male, 24 years, Hetosa, Ethiopia)

Nepal

In Nepal, key issues for disabled youth emerging from the research include healthcare, employment, and income, as well as stigma and discrimination. The problem of disability, multiple marginalizations, and discrimination was highlighted in Kathmandu.

> There is no secure place for the people who belong to Third gender with disability. Among Third gender also, person with disability is more dominated and discriminated. (Aadi, young person, 23, Kathmandu)

The research showed broader societal and family impact and implications of disability discrimination in addition to the consequences of the conflict of recent decades, disasters, and accidents.

Disabilities arising from the conflict caused uncertainties for young people and their families, and led to internal migration, to various places, to seek income and treatment.

> My father was injured in Maoist conflict (12 years ago). It was very difficult time for me (I can't explain it). He was fully injured ... There was no huge money, treatment also not working. All the family shifted different places here to there, sometime Khotang, Udayapur, Kathmandu. I was with my parent here and there, no fixed place to live and do anything. (Nima, female, 19, Kathmandu)

Some injuries sustained during the 2015 earthquake caused longstanding disabilities.

> The house was destroyed due to earthquake. My mother was injured and taken to hospital. I cried a lot. Still chest bones and legs are broken. My father has also stone problem. (Tina, female, 17, Sindhupalchowk)

Young people also reported family disabilities caused by accidents, which brought financial and other problems.

> My father is in Malaysia for another three years. My mother was married at 20 years old and now she cannot work after an accident. (Binayak, male, 16, Kathmandu)

Following parents becoming disabled, youth then take over supporting the family and household.

> I am earning for my family and supporting them fully. My father can't do any work as he became disabled after accident. My mother did hard work when I was child and feed us but now she is also sick and could not work. (Oman, male, 22, Kapilvastu)

Youth described the impact of disability across a marginalized household, intersecting with other social stigma, as well as poverty. For example,

> My father cannot see, and my mother cannot walk properly. When I was 10 years old, I felt sad as I came to know that my father cannot see

> properly, though he got that problem before his marriage. His eye was very weak and then after the devastating earthquake, perhaps due to the shock of earthquake and thinking of societal taboo attached of having only daughters and lack of nutritional food during his childhood, he became completely blind. (Pratika, female, 15, Sindhupalchowk)

This broader family impact was also highlighted in urban Kapilvastu. Sabita was studying at grade 11 but then wanted to work, as her father, disabled through an accident, cannot work and needs money for treatment. But despite wanting to support her family in line with social conventions, Sabita faces parental disagreement and, she says, gender discrimination.

> Now my father is sick. We don't have money, so I cannot study. My mother and father always tell me to study, but I don't want to study. They shouted at me whenever I say that I want to work in the factory. We need money for the treatment of my father. When my father becomes ill and we don't have money at home then I think that if I were a son, then we would not have these problems. (Sabita, female, 19, urban Kapilvastu)

Disabled young people faced interconnecting problems, for example getting access to healthcare and treatment, being frustrated they could not earn, and reported becoming isolated.

> When I was 3 years old, a motorbike hit me, I was severely injured. Thereafter I suffered with the diseases called Harniya ... I think the health is important for life. If you have good health, then you can earn money. (Sijan, male, 25 years, Kathmandu)

Problems of access to and cost of healthcare for marginalized families, and lack of satisfactory answers from the medical system, mean families may seek help from various practitioners. For example, lack of access to health systems may reinforce belief in and use of shamanic spiritual practice and healing such as *Dhami Jhankri*, which also attributes illness and misfortune to evil power, some say 'fate', as an alternative explanation.

> I fell in sickness time to time in my childhood. My parents did domestic treatment (dhami/jhakri) only. I did not get good hospital treatment as my parents are poor. (Nita, female, 15, urban Kapilvastu)

Some who can afford it, and get access, mix different health practices, but also describe circumstances of lacking support.

> I have a very strange disease, called 'Chhopne' [a patient becomes unconscious temporarily, traditionally believed as done by some bad spirits]. It started when I was five years old. When it happens, I feel as if the person who is talking to you or scenario fades away slowly and then faints. Or sometimes, I keep on talking to myself, but I am not aware. It stays for a few days. My parents have consulted

Dhami-Jhankris [shamans]. I was also taken to big hospitals and had done CT scan of my head. Nothing was found. I have also taken many medicines, but they did not work. There is no specific time, place or reason so I do not know when it happens. It may happen right now talking to you, or sometimes, while walking on the street. It is very unpredictable. So I do not feel comfortable going to school. It also has happened many times in the school, too. (Teju, female, 22, Kathmandu)

Those who can afford it, may migrate to seek treatment with families or by themselves. The experience of one young man, who went to India for work and treatment but returned within three months because of leg problems since childhood, illustrates efforts and frustrations.

While I walk I got pain in leg from my childhood. I went for treatment at local health post as I did not have money to go far and get good treatment. That gave relief for short period. Five years ago (at the age of 16) I was suffering with the pain very much. I went to India with the support of parents. I got good treatment as my health is improving now. Though, there is some pain still ... I felt very bad as I did not get good treatment due to lack of money in time.

He also mentioned experiences of isolation:

No one there for me to support if I fall on any bad situation. I have to live myself alone if I get any painful situation. (Jasmin, male, 21, rural Kapilvastu)

Other problems were mentioned, such as frustration due to the desire to work and support family. For example, Teju wants to work, has limited mobility, and needs support, but because provision of the necessary support is generally lacking, does not even want to go out as she is fearful of risk.

Mental health, particularly depression, was experienced as a disabling condition which Meena described as the worst time in her life.

I fell sick [depression] at different times, which is problematic time for me. Last year, I fell sick which was biggest problem in my life. I went for treatment and slowly improved. I am taking medicine now also. (Meena, female, 17, urban Kapilvastu)

Other social problems lie behind some circumstances of youth disability, such as family dynamics, violence, and abuse, but this needs further exploration, as do issues of mental health and services available.

There was no food and clothes at my home. I did all the household work from my childhood. I went for labour work at the age to 10. I was beaten from my step-mother and my hearing capacity was lost [in left ear from being hit]. I have no such dream except living safely with family. (Lajana, female, 20, rural Kapilvastu)

Ethiopia

In Ethiopia, key issues for disabled youth from the research include education, migration, isolation, and lack of support as well as stigma and discrimination. These experiences have implications for mainstreaming disability issues and policies across all areas.

Youth living with disabilities mentioned the absence of informal support at home, at school, and at community level. Disabled young people from rural Fogera and Hetosa particularly highlighted difficulties in formal education, because of problems of physical access in schools, marginalization in classrooms, lack of awareness of teachers about disability, and bullying from peers.

> I can't hear the teacher when he teaches due to my hearing problem. As it's a rural community most of those whom I talked to about my problem didn't appreciate it. Instead of proposing solutions they laughed at me. It was difficult to continue my education as there was no special support for those who have hearing disability like me. (Yetages, male, 25, Hetosa)

Most public services are inaccessible for disabled youth who may have particular needs that need provision, and require at least organizational awareness and a supportive environment in order to use them, including health and education. Lack of support, awareness, and appropriate provision for students with disabilities at both the community and school level pushed them to drop out and stay at home. Young people with disabilities in Hetosa say they have no provision for their needs. Most young people live far from primary and secondary schools, making them inaccessible for many youth with disabilities. The few that do manage to get to school speak of experiences of marginalization due to poor understanding of disabilities and lack of assistive devices for their needs.

Difficulties that disabled children and young people experience in school are reflected in their effective exclusion from local policy and decision-making, as well as being cut off from other services. Yenen, a young man from Fogera, spoke of problems at school due to physical disability, but also about his frustration that he was not included in local government meetings, and that services were inaccessible.

In rural communities some young men and women living with disability feel they are discriminated against and spoke about how others stigmatize them and call them names, but also how this is seen as the local norm.

> Some people in the neighbourhood insult me. They referred to me as senkalla [crippled]. I get angry with them. I feel bad about it. However, I often listen to such insults and keep quiet. My father also told me that I should expect that such things can happen to me. (Betehon, female, 23, Fogera)

In rural, drought-prone Hetosa, where disability is locally perceived as being caused by evil spirits, young people with physical and hearing disabilities spoke of feeling marginalized. Stigma and discrimination, and such local beliefs, may add to pressures on disabled young people to seek help. Some young people sought traditional healing and herbal medicine said to cure ill health and disability, but all talked of lack of access to other medical services.

Many disabled young people found their identity as a disabled youth prevented them from navigating varied livelihood opportunities. Youth from rural areas talked about wanting to migrate like their peers but feeling trapped because of their disability.

> If I was able-bodied like my friends I could have migrated to the city and not suffered here. I always get frustrated as I can't go somewhere as I wish because of my disability. (Regasa, male, 20, Hetosa)

Migration to small towns and big cities has become a livelihood strategy for some disabled youth and family members, but at their destination they often experience high levels of discrimination and stigma due to poor public understanding of disabilities. Migration to urban areas by young people with disabilities has various consequences, not only including dropping out of school and not accessing services, but also moving into street situations in order to survive.

If disabled young people have moved into a town or city they often lack contacts and feel isolated. They reported services were hard to access, and they often felt alienated from those services they could find locally. In addition, some mentioned barriers such as not having identification cards or school certificates for their new lives in the city. On the other hand, some are linked with friends and showed how having a supportive peer group and good contacts is beneficial.

> What brings the five of us together is that we share common problems. One of them is an Oromo and the rest of us are Amharas. Three out of the five of us have disabilities – leg injuries. At times when the two of us are not on good terms then another one of us serve as a mediator and try to help others reconcile. I share my happiness with another person with disabilities who is a Paralympics who is very good at sports and has a better working space given by the local government. (Tarekegne, male, 28, in Addis Ketema)

Being a street-connected youth and a person with disability exacerbated the usual vulnerabilities on the street. Addis Ketema is home for many young people with disabilities who came from different parts of the country in search of better opportunities. Some persist in working in the informal sector while others opt for begging. Yet they say that some members of the community still portray youth with disability as incapable of sustaining their livelihood through work.

> The overall attitude of the community towards persons with disabilities is not that bad. However, there are some people in the community who

think that persons with disabilities are not able to work and support themselves. That perception negatively affects my feelings. There are people who lost both of their legs and are in a wheelchair who are more affected than I am. When I saw people in a wheelchair who are struggling to climb up a hill, then I realized that I am in a better position than they are. That gives me strength to do more. (Beyene, male, 24, in Addis Ketema)

National seminar recommendations in Ethiopia

In Ethiopia, a group of disabled young people ran a workshop as part of the National Youth Seminar in March 2019 (see Chapter 15, including Declaration) held in partnership with the Ministry of Women, Children and Youth.

Disabled young people identified the *most severe* problems of youth with disabilities as:

- lack of support provided for disabled youth from different sectors;
- lack of support from law enforcement bodies for disabled youth;
- lack of response for issues and questions of people with disabilities at different levels of government;
- absence of assistive devices for special needs;
- lack of involvement and participation of disabled people in policy-making.

They also identified three less severe problems:

- service-providing organizations are not comfortable for persons with disabilities;
- lack of support for disabled people in employment;
- lack of psychological support for disabled persons.

They also identified two other problems: first the lack of awareness-raising programmes and events about disability issues; and second that organizations are not interested in employing disabled people.

Key messages for policy and practice in Ethiopia and Nepal

Key policy and practice issues from the research and local and national seminars held with marginalized youth across Ethiopia and Nepal, particularly including responses from disabled young people, are outlined here. Many of the problems of access to healthcare, lack of employment opportunities and income, as well as discrimination and feelings of isolation and stigma, are experienced by all most-marginalized youth, but the situation is generally exacerbated for young people living with disabilities.

The broader impact of disability on families and communities as well as individuals has implications across all areas of policy and practice. A key message is for mainstreaming disability issues and responses across all levels of government, organizations, and services. Government and non-government organizations and departments need to consider and take into account the effect of their policies, services, and practices on disabled people of all ages, particularly for the environment in which disabled children and youth are growing up, and make provision for similar oversight in the private sector.

Mainstreaming of disability issues requires specific actions to address key problems experienced by disabled young people, for example, as set out below.

- *Education.* Experiences of disabled youth in education include marginalization, alienation, isolation, lack of support, poor treatment by teachers, and bullying by peers as well as barriers in access to, and the layout of, schools. Many drop out or fail examinations. Major changes are needed in training and attitude of teachers and other personnel, including dealing with bullying, and in the social environment of schools. Problems of access to schools need to be addressed along with design and changes to buildings where necessary.
- *Employment.* Youth report difficulties in gaining employment because of their own or family disabilities. Government and non-government organizations can lead in changing employment practices to ensure disabled applicants are welcomed and appropriately supported. Other employers need encouragement and oversight to address disability issues, such as incentives to guarantee disabled youth inclusion and an equal chance in the job sector (for example, rewarding businesses hiring a substantial number of people with disabilities).
- *Healthcare.* Disabled youth report problems accessing healthcare services because of cost, distance or location, in addition to their need for relevant information. Accessibility of healthcare needs to include mechanisms to deal with treatable diseases that are increasingly seen as the cause of a variety of disabilities. Disabled youth are at higher risk of contracting diseases where they are restricted from accessing information and gaining appropriate knowledge for prevention and early treatment. This includes contracting HIV and other sexually transmitted diseases, and being excluded from sexual and reproductive health classes.
- *Infrastructure.* In many places buildings, roads, and transport are not accessible or effective for disabled people and have a particular impact on disabled children and youth needing to attend education, find and take up employment, and travel to health facilities and other services. Changes in existing infrastructure and new developments need to specifically take account of the requirements of disabled people.
- *Participation.* Disabled youth report being excluded from participation in local decision-making and policy-making. Development of participation practice for youth, including involvement in community and government policy- and decision-making needs to specifically include provision for participation of disabled young people.

- *Support.* Disabled youth report lack of support, including psychological support, in various aspects of life, particularly in education, employment, and health services, as well as in participation in public life. Services and provision are needed to address support for disabled youth, which should include particular attention for those who have migrated.
- *Law enforcement.* Disabled youth are engaged in a variety of situations and work, including being street-connected. They report lack of support from law enforcement bodies. Attitudes and practices need to be addressed and changed to provide attention to, and positive support for, the needs of disabled youth in communities.
- *Stigma and discrimination.* Experiences of marginalization, stigma, and discrimination against disabled youth often extend to their family and household. Shifting and changing attitudes towards disability need to be taken up through awareness-raising and behaviour-change programmes within public, government, and non-government services, in communities and the private sector.
- *Data collection.* Data is needed on disability issues in order to respond to the needs of, and properly provide for, disabled people of all ages. Disaggregated data collection is necessary, along with a programme developed for this, led by government across departments and services.

Conclusion

The lives of disabled youth, especially from marginalized groups in both Ethiopia and Nepal show experiences of further marginalization and exclusion in communities and services. In both countries these problems are faced by youth with disabilities and those who have family members with disabilities. They need additional resources and support in daily life as well as in facing problems of stigma and discrimination. This demonstrates the importance of those carrying out research and formulating inclusive policies to listen to poor and marginalized young people and their families (following Wickenden and Elphick, 2016).

Problems of access to education, because of costs of work and the need to support the family, are further exacerbated for disabled children and youth because of access, attitudes of teachers and peers, problems of stigma and discrimination, and lack of provision. As in all areas of their life, these issues of access may be further exacerbated for marginalized youth who have family members with disabilities, who need more support and provision. Lack of education further disadvantages disabled youth seeking employment, which may already be problematic for marginalized groups facing limited work opportunities. Problems of stigma, discrimination, and lack of support run through the search for work, as in other aspects of their lives. They also want to or need to support their families, and in circumstances where local employment is lacking also want to migrate, but this is also difficult. Destinations may further stigmatize and discriminate against disabled in-migrants. Many disabled youth who do migrate end up street-connected, and depend on peer support. But for many disabled young people the key experiences are isolation and lack of support, exclusion from communities, from services, from businesses, and often from policy and practice.

PART 5
Conclusion

CHAPTER 19
Conclusion: Listening to marginalized youth on uncertainty

In varied, environmentally fragile and conflict-affected environments in Ethiopia and Nepal, YOUR World Research provided large-scale qualitative evidence about lived realities of the most-marginalized youth. Key strands include: listening to marginalized youth; aspiration, education, employment; youth negotiating social norms and finding new futures; positive uncertainty and youth creativity; migration and street-connection; and processes for research feeding into policy and practice. Their stories are not often sought or heard, but research findings show the significance of listening to marginalized youth about the complexities of their lives, decisions, and their creativity in navigating uncertainty in transitions growing up and in uncertain contexts. Particularly in fragile and conflict-affected environments, it is necessary to understand how fast changing political, economic, and environmental contexts influence young lives. Youth proved resilient and sensible in confronting difficulties, embracing and navigating uncertainty in a positive way, demonstrating what can be learnt from them in uncertain or difficult times.

Keywords: youth, positive uncertainty, social norms, migration, street-connection, gender, Ethiopia, Nepal

Introduction

The research across Ethiopia and Nepal demonstrated that marginalized youth are experts on uncertainty in their lives, but their creativity in fragile contexts needs support, and ultimately many young people want to feel that they are respected and belong in their families and communities. The conclusions provide key messages about child and youth rights, support for youth agency and understanding their situations through youth-centred research, using for example the change-scape approach (see Chapters 2 and 3). Their agency is understood as relational and strategic or tactical; this is discussed with reference to discourses in childhood and youth studies. Youth perspectives on marginalization, aspiration, education, and employment are summarized, and the learning on street situations, migration, and living with disability re-emphasize the importance of listening to their perspectives.

Uncertainty as a trope of our times is discussed with particular reference to the perspectives of youth on uncertainty in being stratified and as potentially positive. Adults would do well to gain insights from marginalized youth on their navigation of uncertainty. Youth are experts in uncertainty both in their experiences growing up and in fragile environments. The book concludes with the important issue of how research can inform policy and practice through trusted partnerships with national civil society organizations and universities. The change-scape approach applied in this research provided mechanisms so that, throughout the process, national research teams engaged with different stakeholders and provided space for marginalized youth to inspire others with their energizing and innovative ideas.

Listening to marginalized youth: a change-scape approach and agency

The change-scape as modified for YOUR World Research takes account of young people's agency, their shifting and multiple identities as they grow up, and how the most-marginalized young people differ from adult and other youth perspectives in research sites. It includes some mechanisms that may need to be built into policy and practice for voices and strategies of the most-marginalized to be understood and incorporated in community development (Johnson and West, 2018). The youth-centred approach in this research fits well with an approach to rejuvenating communities, alongside input from field experts and a living archive of documents (Johnson et al., 2020a). It also fits with 'Youth-scapes' conceptualized in Africa to explore youth lived experiences, their fantasies and realities, in precarious and fragile environments, and changing technological and cultural youth landscapes (Christiansen et al., 2006). Listening to youth can provide different information from reliance only on adult perspectives, in addition to new insights and creative solutions for the future (Chambers, 1998).

The concept of 'living rights' concerns how youth rights are realized in practice and translated from universal rights on paper, to take into account complexities of the realities of young people's everyday lives. This re-conceptualization of child rights has three pillars: living rights; translation; and social justice (Hanson and Nieuwenhuys, 2013). This approach was an important feature for YOUR World research teams who were working within fast-changing political contexts that included shifting notions of rights. It provided a basis to explore lived experiences of marginalized young people and the strategies they use to help access their rights. The terminology and discourse of rights needed to be employed with some discretion in contexts where rights are more difficult to openly discuss, as was the case during the previous government in Ethiopia until 2018.

Going into the research, this approach of 'living rights' proved useful as discussions on youth rights and agency were considered as contextual, with youth agency embedded within family and community dynamics (as noted by Abebe, 2013 in Ethiopia). Recognition that youth have their own individual perspectives, ideas, decisions, and actions, as suggested in the sociology of childhood, was also taken into the research, but other nuanced conceptualizations of agency are relevant. Oswell (2013) provides important guidance in analysing agency of children and young people. Relational agency in the research took the form of peer support in decisions regarding youth action and futures. Corsaro (in 2003, cited in Oswell, 2013) suggested that the maintenance of continued peer interaction can result in peer cultures that interact with families, schools, and communities. Such peer interaction can help to filter and support intergenerational negotiation in decision-making that is key to settings in this research where social norms that privilege adults are persistent. Also relevant here is Oswell's (2013: 55) account of hegemonic negotiation that takes into account institutionalized and cultural power dynamics. Peer support and interaction among the most-marginalized will also be essentially different to seeing youth generationally and as necessarily all having similar aspirations and strategies. Oswell discusses Honwana's (2005) notion that youth tactical agency helps to negotiate context and social norms, which provides a good framing for the innovative strategies and tactics of youth found in this research. It also fits with findings of this research that shift from Bauman's ideas of youth breaking social bonds with family and community, in seeing that this is temporal. In applying these ideas, it can be seen that youth in this research did work with peers and where possible with support from adults to negotiate social norms and fragile contexts. They would need to be strategic or have tactical agency in order to do this, and their embracing of uncertainty has an element of temporality as they ultimately want to feel that they belong.

Intergenerational cultural transmissions have been identified by anthropologists and geographers over many decades. This research and book have taken account throughout of how youth consider adult expectations, and how these are entwined with young people's aspirations and feelings about how they may fit into families, communities, and cultures. Notions of a generational gap and issues in, as well as concerns about, intergenerational transmissions have been raised since the mid-20th century (for example, Mead, 1970) and fed into more recent discussions about intergenerational transmission of poverty (for example, Moncrieffe, 2009). In this research, youth perceptions of tradition, social norms, and adult expectations provided a basis for intergenerational analysis, alongside looking at young people's perspectives on generational differences in aspirations, uncertainty and strategies available. Oswell's (2013) discussion of negotiating hegemony is helpful in considering how youth in the research discussed with sensitivity and creativity how they would try to weave their way through social norms, but also have to reject those that were thought of as harmful to young people, particularly early marriage (for example in Hetosa, Chapter 7).

Youth on marginalization

Youth analysis of marginalization in the research went beyond NGO or government definitions, for example, extending beyond gender, caste/ethnicity, and poverty. Rather than always seeing marginalization as being on the periphery of countries and at the margins of society, they see it as central to every community and persistent in every area (as suggested by Ferguson, 1990). Marginalized young people's analysis also reflected the fluidity of margins (following Manchala, 2017, see Chapter 2), fitting with the liquid modernity of Bauman (2007). Youth navigated with this fluidity and developed creative solutions to what they see as their certainties of poverty and processes of marginalization faced in their communities, and so take action to find new futures.

The project sought to understand marginalized young people's perceptions of their own status within families and communities. Youth included marginalization issues and criteria as: those involved in hard labour, exploitative work, illegal activities and being in conflict with the law, feelings of alienation and exclusion from families and communities, and experiences of abuse. These additional youth understandings of marginalization can be described as contextual, multi-dimensional, embodied, and emotional, in agreement with Kelly and colleagues (2019: 5). This also fits with Philo et al.'s (2019) 'precarious urbanisms' as young people in the research from Ethiopia and Nepal described their experiences of insecurity and discrimination when they migrated to try to find more positive futures working in the informal sector and often living on the streets (see Chapters 6, 8, 11, 13 on urban sites and 17 on street-connection).

Youth suggested marginalization is very highly gendered, in agreement with government definitions, and linked to caste/ethnicity and also location, but youth added further aspects of their marginalization. They felt their experiences are linked to their developing and shifting identities and individual situations as they grow up. Youth in the research lead highly gendered lives dictated by conventions and social norms that some want and feel need to change, while youth also contribute to positive change in their communities and nationally. The research looked at intergenerational cultural and poverty transmissions. Gendered discrimination is widespread but not simple. In both Ethiopia and Nepal there are gender preferences in families to send boys to school, or restrictions on young women's mobility that include travel for further education. There are differential gendered employment opportunities as young women have more limited exposure to the external world beyond household chores and reproductive work to support families, alongside fewer opportunities and more discrimination in the workplace. Young men who feel marginalized drop out of school and feel they face discrimination to gain formal qualifications and employment. Youth who are genderfluid, interviewed in Nepal, felt intense discrimination within families and communities. (There was no opportunity to explore views of genderfluid youth in Ethiopia, due to illegality.)

In both countries, but particularly in Ethiopia, youth living with disability included themselves as marginalized alongside those who are disabled through living with family and/or caring for family with disabilities (Chapter 18). This aspect of the project was continued with interest from policy-makers, particularly in the National Youth Seminar in Ethiopia (Chapter 15), funded by the ESRC's Impact initiative. Marginalization for young people went beyond their own physical and mental impairments. Youth interviewed who were carers and living with disability in their families felt they had fewer opportunities to pursue new futures and were even more stuck with certainties of poverty and feelings of marginalization. They say more inclusive approaches are needed, such as in education, as has been suggested for sub-Saharan Africa (Carew et al., 2019).

Young people who migrate to cities and become street-connected, experience marginalization related to how they are treated by others in the local community. They feel worse when people call them names, such as '*Khate*' in Nepal, a derogatory term experienced by street-connected youth in Kathmandu. Widespread discriminatory social labelling of street-connected youth as 'thieves' and 'drug dealers' distressed hard-working young people in Addis Ketema in Ethiopia. Far from marginalized youth setting out to seek extremist peer groups that can destabilize communities (one of the outcomes interrogated), most of those interviewed in detailed case studies sought positive relationships with peers. For example, when they migrated internally or internationally, on their return they wanted to belong and maintain a sense of respect within their communities of origin. They admitted having to lie to family if they had had to resort to exploitative labour such as commercial sex work, or any kind of illegal activities. When they were not listened to or supported in trying to set up enterprises in the informal sector, they tended to stay street-connected without adequate access to their rights. Many had stories of authorities presuming they were guilty of crimes when they were not, or of being abused by police. While some had positive stories of interventions by government shelters or NGOs, most felt they were not listened to and preferred the freedom of the street despite its insecurity. They suggested that rather than banning youth from working in the low-paid, informal sector on the streets, and making migration for many marginalized youth illegal, authorities need to work with youth to support them in their strategies before they resort to any illegal activities. Many street-connected youth use drugs to cope with difficult living situations but recognize that they could benefit from support.

Across research sites, youth lack access to services and feel that being marginalized involves being treated with disrespect by service providers. Genderfluid youth said doctors sometimes 'freeze' when they see them (as discussed Chapter 14). Lack of identification documents or legal paperwork for rural and street-connected youth was raised in both countries as an indicator that they are not recognized or treated as citizens. Many young people described experiences of intersecting aspects of marginalization, including not being recognized, accepted or valued because of their sexuality, gender, and other issues of difference, but also not having an ID card and so being unable to gain access to services and employment opportunities. This further accentuated feelings of marginalization and vulnerability. The research aimed to surface voices of the most-marginalized and, while recognizing their creativity and agency, to also acknowledge their vulnerability and feelings of marginalization (following work in Ghana by Mizen and Ofosu-Kusi, 2013).

Youth on aspiration, education, employment, and migration

Aspiration was an unspoken core of the research. The research looked at insecurity and uncertainty in marginalized young people's lives, but at the heart of this is what young people are aspiring to do with their lives in the context in which they are living, as illustrated in case studies used in this book. Their living circumstances and context includes elements of the change-scape, involving peer and intergenerational relationships and negotiations within cultural, economic, political, and environmental contexts (Johnson and West, 2018, 2021a). The change-scape approach fits with Ansell (2017), in that young lives are complex: recognition of power and processes in social, political, economic, and cultural contexts is important in understanding their realities. Young lives are also relational, and the temporality of experiences as they grow up is important, especially when gaining an insight into their aspirations and futures. Youth are actors in their own development and can influence the contexts they inhabit. The research confirmed that, rather than making assumptions about education and/or work being desirable or harmful, children's and young people's perspectives on their lives including what they feel about their work is critical in order to support them in accessing rights (following Bourdillon et al., 2011). The way in which expectations and relationships in households and communities shape young people's decisions to stay or migrate are important to understand if youth are to be supported in their aspirations (Huijsmans, 2016).

Marginalized young people, particularly in the most fragile environments of drought-affected Hetosa in Ethiopia (Chapter 7), and earthquake-affected Sindhupalchowk in Nepal (Chapter 12), see migrants as role models. In Hetosa, with a lack of alternatives for the future, they seek to leave traditional livelihoods as they can no longer meet adult expectations, and feel they need to escape from the certainties of poverty. In the Himalayan regions, with the support of civil society, youth-led organizations have taken a lead in reconstruction and although many youth do still migrate, some find local work opportunities to rebuild, and many others wish to return to their communities (as described in Chapter 12). In both countries, marginalized rural youth felt parental pressure to migrate in order to fulfil what was perceived as success, whether that was to earn money, send remittances, return as successful migrants, or to gain skills and education (more often expected in Nepal). In some situations, especially in rural sites in Ethiopia (Chapters 5 and 7), there is not an open welcome for returning youth who are not seen as 'successful' migrants. Young men were expected to support their families and felt heavy pressure to do so. Young women felt they have to hide sources of income that they are ashamed of and pretend they found decent work in towns and cities to which they migrated in-country, or to hide the extent of exploitation they had endured overseas. This was particularly the case for women who travelled to Middle Eastern countries from Hetosa, and for young women and young men who migrated to India from the Terai in Nepal.

Most youth interviewed who regarded themselves as marginalized had dropped out of school or failed their national exams. Marginalized children and young people found conventional formal education did not meet their requirements, particularly in rapidly changing fragile political and environmental contexts. Instead, they wanted more vocational training, support for small businesses in the informal sector and advice for safer and more productive employment and education through migration. They wanted an end to policies making the most-marginalized 'illegal' when they live or work as street-connected, or become migrants, and wanted instead policies, advice, and support to make them feel safe and valued both in new destinations and in communities of origin. Youth can provide learning for adults in how they creatively and positively face uncertainty and what support they require to find new and alternative pathways out of poverty for themselves and their families and communities.

In both Ethiopia and Nepal, it is wrong to assume that aspiration for the most-marginalized is linked to supposedly established pathways through formal education to employment, and seeking to implement rights to education by a formal conventional curriculum. It was found more productive to embed a conceptualization of aspiration within young people's complex experiences including failure of the education system to actually meet the needs of many marginalized youth and their competing pressures for work (also noted in Ethiopia by Boyden et al., 2019). Young people's expressions of their aspirations were key to articulating understanding of their circumstances, environments, constraints, and strategies for responding to uncertainties and fragilities in their lives (as also noted in Huijsmans et al., 2020).

Once youth have migrated from land-scarce or landless situations, such as from Fogera (Chapter 5), and end up in small towns such as Woreta (Chapter 6), services are straining to support those that lack skills or education and seek alternative livelihoods in the informal sector. As findings from Woreta show, many Ethiopian marginalized youth, migrating in search of work, end up in street situations and feel discriminated against, often exploited or not protected at work. Some end up relying on substances with many young men chewing *khat*. In comparison, in Kapilvastu, Nepal (Chapters 10 and 11), youth move from rural to urban areas, and from both to India in search of alternative futures, while migrants from India often move into the area and take employment in local factories.

Young people's varied aspirations are indicated in particular research locations, depending on their own, their family's and adult expectations of their lives. It is particularly shown in both countries by internal and international migration. Decisions made by Ethiopian youth to migrate internationally stem not only from their own hopes and family expectations but perceptions of hopelessness in youth futures locally. This applies particularly to street-connected youth who rejected formal education as a solution and feel unsupported in their endeavours in the informal sector. In Nepal, mobility stems from precarious living in remote mountainous locations, but is also saturated with hope and positive aspirations to gain a better education and skills. These aspirations were explored in detail in Parts Two and Three, looking at particular themes in each research location in both countries.

Migration is increasing from fragile environments in both countries. In Nepal, youth choose migration as a strategy to gain skills in order to come back and help their communities. In the earthquake-affected Himalayas (Chapter 12), a young woman who lived in a temporary shelter since the 2015 earthquake now sees a future as a community worker. She previously faced discrimination as she was female and Dalit. She now feels that she and other youth have aspirations that they can meet within their own communities because opportunities with reconstruction have arisen. Along with many friends, she dropped out of school, but has now returned to study to become a community worker. In Ethiopia many see uncertainty as a way to break their cycle of poverty and help support families. In the drought-prone research site (Hetosa, Chapter 7), a young woman reflected on choosing positive uncertainty. She described how she felt that migration, despite being fraught with uncertainties, was her only option to escape early marriage and have a chance to find a new future. If she stayed while others went she felt that she would have failed.

Across the research sites in both countries many most-marginalized youth dropped out of school, failed exams, see their pathway is early marriage and unemployment, and want to escape to find new and more hopeful futures. They want to embrace uncertainty in a positive way when their alternative is the certainty of poverty. Many marginalized youth discussed with research teams in detailed case study interviews their wishes to migrate, but ultimately to come back home with seed-money to set up small businesses and be accepted back into their communities. These and other stories in Parts Two and Three show similarities across contexts. Chapters 16 and 17 discuss how many marginalized youth see their futures in migration and how many become street-connected and engaged in the informal sector, seeking support but often not being listened to.

In insecure situations and contexts, young people take the initiative and turn uncertainty into positive strategies by building their skills and capacities, for example in cooking, tailoring, carpentry, and building houses, often to get work in the informal sector. Youth from both countries suggested they need support in training and in building their small enterprises in the informal economy, rather than going back into formal education that previously did not work for them, or meeting conventional expectations of finding formal employment.

Youth on positive uncertainty

Youth interviewed in YOUR World Research expressed uncertainty as negative and positive. Positive uncertainty is a term coined by national teams during the 2016–2019 research process (Johnson et al., 2019b). Many marginalized youth suggested their certainty was poverty and the uncertainty of migration, learning new skills, and becoming involved in informal employment is more positive than following conventionally expected paths in which they see no future. Youth are, in effect, experts in uncertainty as they constantly face uncertainty in their transitions growing up and in ongoing development of their identities and relationships. Marginalized youth seek new futures with creativity and embrace uncertainty. Research has shown that youth are creative and show agency in the face of uncertainty (for example Katz, 2004 in Sudan and the US; Calkins, 2016 in Sudan). The finding that youth embrace uncertainty is reinforced in research in other street-connected and fragile environments where young people's certainties are poverty, marginalization, and sometimes harmful social norms (for example, Di Nunzio's (2019) work with young men in Addis Ababa).

The idea of positive uncertainty may be contrasted with popular attitudes towards uncertainty as being negative. Instead, in some circumstances, young people perceive the uncertainty that they know and even plan they will face, for example in terms of action, movement and outcome, as having positive potential, for themselves or their families, in terms of material or developmental perspectives. The most-marginalized in the research also described their *certainty of hopelessness* if they followed expected transitions to adulthood. This included more traditional trajectories where they were expected to find success in education and formal employment, and to provide for families in the face of environmental fragility, conflict in communities and/or abuse within families, and being subjected to aspects of social norms they identified as harmful to youth such as early marriage. It also included their perceptions of a *certainty of poverty, exclusion, and exploitation* when they find themselves living and working in street situations where services do not reach them or where they are made to feel like they are problems in the informal urban settings in which they find themselves.

Particularly notable across all sites, youth developed creative strategies to navigate uncertainty, find pathways out of poverty and deal with experiences of discrimination and marginalization. In an initial co-construction phase with youth in urban and rural locations in both countries, research teams took note of theory and were open to how young people may regard experiences of uncertainty as positive as well as negative. The youth-centred basis of the research was initially informed by Bauman's (2001) work in relation to uncertainty, insecurity, and community. Although focused on letting young people's perceptions and constructions emerge in order to understand their strategies for dealing with life, circumstances, and environments, in approaching their aspirations, Bauman's ideas enabled an understanding of uncertainty as not only negative, but also positive. In other strands of analysis, Bauman's ideas of youth breaking traditional social bonds to form new bonds with peers was noted, but it was found that in the longer-term youth wanted to feel accepted back into their families, and only wanted to change certain aspects of tradition and social norms they felt were harmful. In interviews across research sites many marginalized youth who had migrated and became street-connected, felt dislocated from families and communities of origin and/or discriminated against in destinations. The increasing aspirations and pressures to migrate to urban areas and internationally, and the feelings of disconnection and 'being a stranger in all places' in home and destination communities were also found in research with young people migrating for family reasons, education, and work by Young Lives in Ethiopia (Birhanu et al., 2021).

During the course of YOUR World Research, ideas of positive uncertainty were co-constructed and developed with young people. This included understanding that temporality of uncertainty results in different youth strategies. For example, in short-term variations, such as when a house burns down or there is an environmental shock such as flooding, drought or earthquake, young people tended to consult with family, relatives, and friends. In the longer term, variations included the consequences of increasing environmental fragility, or for example, lengthy reconstruction from earthquake damage (for example in Sindhupalchowk, Chapter 12 and Kathmandu, Chapter 13, Nepal), or resulting from conflict between religious and ethnic/caste groups (for example in Kapilvastu, Chapters 10 and 11, Nepal). In such longer-term variations, youth find solutions in building new skills and entering the informal sector, or in migrating to find new futures. Although youth do embrace this uncertainty positively and often feel excited in what they may find and gain through migration (especially when their alternative certainty is poverty), it was found that they eventually also want to feel that they belong. As they feel they are entering, or should be entering adult status, they want to have a vision of how they can have a more stable income in order to gain that status, to survive and to support families, including parents, extended families, and their own children. This is problematic especially for transnational families and in fragmented families that have begun to be more prevalent in some fragile rural origin sites of migration.

Throughout this book, youth case studies have been selected from across sites to show different dimensions of uncertainty in their lives. This stratification of uncertainty was developed using theories taken into the research (see Chapter 2) and co-construction with youth in early phases. These domains of uncertainty formulated with youth were the basis of detailed case-study interviews. They include: transitions experienced as they grow up, in terms of developing identities, and adult expectations that they follow certain social norms, traditions, and religious practices; changing youth relationships and feelings about themselves and others; places and spaces youth inhabit and their constantly changing contexts; and youth mobility and migration as strategies in seeking education, employment, and new futures (see Figure 3.1 in Chapter 3 for stratifications of uncertainty).

Youth as experts on uncertainty in their lives need to be included in solutions intended for them, and beyond this they can also help adults understand how to better navigate uncertainty. Wenger-Trainer and Wenger-Trainer (2020) encourage thinking about how learning, including on uncertainty, can be encouraged in social learning spaces. This is particularly relevant to the social pedagogical approach in co-constructing concepts of uncertainty and marginalization in YOUR World Research, and in findings which suggest support for youth to build confidence with peers and to interact in dialogue with decision-makers to contribute their expertise and innovation in dealing with uncertainty. This is also relevant in supporting most-marginalized youth who have not had the opportunity or been successful in formal learning spaces or in more conventional versions of education.

Policy and practice

In both countries, researchers from the UK had longstanding trusted partnerships with academics and nationally registered non-governmental organizations that were thought to be important in such rapidly changing environments, for research that relied on access and follow-up support to some of the most-marginalized youth. These partnerships also proved to be central to achieving impact at site and national levels (Johnson et al., 2019a).

Listening and responding to marginalized youth requires moving away from notions that adults know what children and youth need and want. All adults were once children, but they were young at a different time and in a different context. Youth are experts in their own lives and their developing and shifting identities. They experience many unique processes of marginalization and intersecting aspects of exclusion and inclusion.

Intergenerational and peer relationships and power dynamics are important to making policy and practice sustainable, but understanding this complexity takes time. Detailed qualitative data will continue to help to explain youth realities and their innovative strategies to address structural inequalities and individual processes of marginalization. If adults can support youth agency and creativity, then young people's expertise and strategies can help to develop youth policy and more youth-friendly practices.

Past and current mistakes where youth are suspected of anti-social behaviour and are criminalized need to be avoided in organizations and authorities, as young people are often working hard, trying to survive and support their families. There are social norms and traditional practices with embedded gendered and generational discrimination. To break intergenerational transmission of poverty it is necessary to convince adults in communities and families that youth-centred research and new ways to listen to young people are needed.

Using the concept of youth living rights (Hanson and Nieuwenhuys, 2013), with their agency embedded in family and community power dynamics and relational agency, requires unblocking negative cultural assumptions about young people. Youth can teach us how to negotiate and reverse processes of marginalization and deal with uncertainty positively. If more qualitative research is commissioned to understand complex young lives, and people in positions of power listen to and support their strategies, then youth may be able to translate more of their rights into realities, and also contribute to, and motivate transformational societal change.

Spaces for youth to interact with each other such as youth clubs or societies can build confidence that can in turn gradually influence adults (Johnson, 2010). Young people interviewed in this research wanted to be involved and contribute to policy-making and societal transformation. They wanted to be able to fulfil expectations to support families, but also follow their own aspirations that may depart from traditional practices. Far from trying to reject social bonds with families and communities, youth sometimes had to temporarily break them in order to deal with insecurity and to embrace positive uncertainty. They then wanted to find a sense of belonging in destination communities or new working or street situations, and also back in communities of origin with families and peers. Providing a space for youth to interact with each other and with adults in communities can be productive (also found in Ethiopia by Tefera et al., 2021).

Policy-makers striving for more inclusive policy-making locally, nationally, and internationally have the will and the mechanisms to develop youth policies, especially with new government processes in place in Ethiopia and Nepal. In this project, when engaging with YOUR World Research, government officials recognized they have often not reached most-marginalized youth, but are now developing youth policies that include processes of listening to youth (Johnson et al., 2020b).

Learning from most-marginalized youth

This concluding chapter has looked at the analysis carried out in the comparative research to provide learning on key strands of: listening to marginalized youth; aspiration, education, and employment; youth negotiating social norms and finding new futures; positive uncertainty and youth creativity; migration and street-connection; and core messages that arose for research feeding into policy and practice. The book has shown why we listen to marginalized youth about the complexities of their lives, decisions, and their creativity in navigating uncertainty in transitions growing up and in uncertain contexts.

Particularly in fragile and conflict-affected locations, we need to understand how fast changing political, economic, and environmental contexts influence young lives. In Ethiopia and Nepal the most-marginalized young people were keen to meet adult expectations, negotiating intergenerational relationships and social norms, but may have to break conventional family, community, and social bonds temporarily, often finding support with peers, and take action that can creatively help them navigate uncertainty.

References

Abdu, B. (2019) 'Ethiopia launches "Home-Grown Economic Reform"' *The Reporter*, 31 August 2019 <https://www.thereporterethiopia.com/article/private-engagement> [accessed 24 November 2021].

Abebaw, M.G. (2012) 'Trafficked to the gulf states: the experiences of Ethiopian returnee women', *Journal of Community Practice* 20(1–2): 112–33 <http://doi.org/10.1080/10705422.2012.649203>.

Abebe, T. (2013) 'Interdependent rights and agency: the role of children in collective livelihood strategies in rural Ethiopia', in K. Hanson and O. Nieuwenhuys (eds), *Reconceptualizing Children's Rights in International Development: Living Rights, Social Justice and Translations*, pp. 71–92, Cambridge University Press, New York.

Abualghaib, O., Groce, N., Simeu, N., Carew, M. and Mont, D. (2019) 'Making visible the invisible: why disability-disaggregated data is vital to "leave no-one behind"', *Sustainability* 11(11): 3091 <https://doi.org/10.3390/su11113091>.

Adugna, F. (2018) 'Landlessness, land access modalities, and poverty in rural Oromia National Regional State, Ethiopia', *Ethiopian Journal of Development Research* 40(1): 33–66.

Alderson, P. (2005) 'Designing ethical research with children', in A. Farrell (ed.), *Ethical Research with Children*, pp. 27–36, Open University Press, Buckingham.

Ansell, N. (2017) *Children, Youth and Development*, 2nd edn, Routledge, London.

Appadurai, A. (1998) 'Dead certainty: ethnic violence in the era of globalization', *Development and Change* 29: 905–25 <https://doi.org/10.1111/1467-7660.00103>.

Appadurai, A. (2004) 'The capacity to aspire', in V. Rao and M. Walton (eds), *Culture and Public Action*, Stanford University Press, Palo Alto, CA.

Asman, S. (2016) *Bombay going: Migration, return and anti-trafficking in the lives of Nepali migrant sex workers*, PhD dissertation in Social Anthropology, School of Global Studies, University of Gothenburg, Sweden.

Asnake, K. and Zerihun, M. (2015) *Ethiopian Labor Migration to the Gulf and South Africa*, Forum for Social Studies, Addis Ababa.

Asnakech, A. (2014) *Migration and Household Income Diversification: the Case of Hetosa District, In Oromia Region*, MSc thesis, Addis Ababa University, Ethiopia.

Atnafu, A. (2006) *Aspects of Ethiopian return migration*, Master's thesis, Department of Regional and Local Development Studies., School of Graduate Studies, Addis Ababa University, Ethiopia.

Atnafu, A., Oucho, L. and Zeitlyn, B. (2014) *Poverty, Youth and Rural-Urban Migration in Ethiopia*, Migrating out of Poverty, Working Paper, University of Sussex, Brighton.

Banks, L.M. (2019) *Investigating disability-inclusion in social protection programmes in low- and middle-income countries, with case studies from Vietnam and Nepal*, PhD thesis, London School of Hygiene and Tropical Medicine <https://doi.org/10.17037/PUBS.04655981>.

Banks, L.M., Kuper, H., and Polack, S. (2017) 'Poverty and disability in low- and middle-income countries: a systematic review', *PloS One* 12(12): e0189996 <https://doi.org/10.1371/journal.pone.0189996>.

Barnes, J. (2016) 'Uncertainty in the signal: modelling Egypt's water futures', *JRAI (NS) Special Issue Environmental Futures* 22(S1): 46–66 <https://doi.org/10.1111/1467-9655.12393>.

Bauman, Z. (2001) *Community: Seeking Safety in an Insecure World*, Polity Press, Cambridge.

Bauman, Z. (2004) *Wasted Lives: Modernity and its Outcasts*, Polity Press, Cambridge.

Bauman, Z. (2007) *Liquid Times: Living in an Age of Uncertainty*, Polity Press, Cambridge.

Bauman, Z. (2011) *Collateral Damage: Social Inequalities in a Global Age*, Polity Press, Cambridge.

Beazley, H. and Ennew, J. (2006) 'Participatory methods and approaches: tackling the two tyrannies', in V. Desai and R.B. Potter (eds), *Doing Development Research*, pp. 189–99, Sage, London.

Bevan, P. and Pankhurst, A. (2006) 'Power, poverty & wealth in Ethiopia: lessons from four rural case studies', in G. Alemu and G. Yoseph (eds), *Proceedings of the Fourth International Conference on the Ethiopian Economy*, Ethiopian Economics Association, Addis Ababa.

Bezu, S. and Holden, S. (2014) 'Are rural youth in Ethiopia abandoning agriculture?' *World Development* 64: 259–72 <http://dx.doi.org/10.1016/.worldwidev.2014,06.013>.

Bhandari, P. (2008) The recurrence of violence (a case of Kapilvastu violence), MA thesis, Central Department of Conflict Peace and Development Studies, Tribhuvan University, Kathmandu.

Birhanu, A.M., Bisetegn, T.A., and Woldeyohannes, S.M. (2014) 'High prevalence of substance use and associated factors among high school adolescents in Woreta Town, Northwest Ethiopia: multi-domain factor analysis', *BMC Public Health* 14: 1186 <https://doi.org/10.1186/1471-2458-14-1186>.

Birhanu, K., Pankhurst, A., Heissler, K. and Choi, J. (2021) *'A Stranger in All Places': Patterns and Experiences of Children and Young People Moving from their Home Communities in Ethiopia*, Young Lives Working Paper 169, Young Lives, Oxford.

Boholm, A. (2003) 'The cultural nature of risk: can there be an anthropology of uncertainty?' *Ethnos* 68(2): 159–78 <https://doi.org/10.1080/0014184032000097722>.

Bourdillon, M., Levison, D., Myers, W. and White, B. (2011) *Rights and Wrongs of Children's Work*, Rutgers University Press, London.
Boyden, J. and Ennew, J. (1997) *Children in Focus: A Manual for Participatory Research with Children*, Save the Children, Stockholm.
Boyden, J., Dawes, A., Dornan, P. and Tredoux, C. (2019) *Tracing the Consequences of Poverty: Evidence from the Young Lives Study in Ethiopia, India, Peru and Vietnam*, Policy Press, Bristol.
Braun, V., and Clarke, V. (2006) 'Using thematic analysis in psychology', *Qualitative Research in Psychology* 3: 77–101 <http://dx.doi.org/10.1191/1478088706qp063oa>.
British Council and Association of Youth Organizations Nepal (BC/AYON) (2011) *The Youth Survey*, BC/AYON, Kathmandu.
Calkins, S. (2016) *Who Knows Tomorrow? Uncertainty in North-eastern Sudan*, Berghan, Oxford.
Carew, M.T., Deluca, M.Y., Groce, N., and Kett, M. (2019) 'The impact of an inclusive education intervention on teacher preparedness to educate children with disabilities within the Lakes Region of Kenya', *International Journal of Inclusive Education* 23(3): 229–44 <https://doi.org/10.1080/13603116.2018.1430181>.
Castle, E. with de Groot, A. and Hastsma, M. (2012) *Poverty and Child Labour in Kathmandu*, Mandala, Kathmandu.
Central Bureau of Statistics (CBS) Nepal (2012) *National Population and Housing Census 2011(National Report)*, Government of Nepal, Kathmandu.
CBS Nepal (2014a) *Social Demography, National Population and Housing Census 2011, Volume 2*, Government of Nepal, Kathmandu.
CBS Nepal (2014b) *Social Characteristics, National Population and Housing Census 2011, Volume 5*, Government of Nepal, Kathmandu.
Chambers, R. (1998) 'Foreword', in V. Johnson, E. Ivan-Smith, G. Gordon, P. Pridmore and P. Scott (eds), *Stepping Forward: Children and Young People's Participation in the Development Process*, Intermediate Technology, London.
Chambers, R. (2012) *Provocations for Development*, Practical Action Publishing, Rugby.
Chhetri, G. (2017) 'Perceptions about the "third gender" in Nepal', *Dhaulagiri Journal of Sociology and Anthropology* 11: 96–114 <http://dx.doi.org/11.3126/dsaj.v11i0.18824>.
Christiansen, C., Utas, M., and Vigh, H.E. (eds) (2006) *Navigating Youth, Generating Adulthood: Social Becoming in an African Context*, Nordiska Afrikainstitutet, Uppsala, Sweden.
Connolly, M., and Ennew, J. (eds) (1996) 'Introduction: children out of place', *Childhood (Special Issue on Working and Street Children)* 3(2).
Cooper, E. and Pattern, D. (eds) (2015) *Ethnographies of Uncertainty in Africa*, Palgrave Macmillan, London.
Crivello, G. and Boyden, J. (2011) *Situating Risk in Young People's Social and Moral Relationships: Young Lives Research in Peru*, Working Paper 66, Young Lives, Oxford.

CWIN (2019) *Findings from a Brief Qualitative Research Study on the First Phase of Implementation of Street Children Rescue Working Guidelines 2015–18*, Policy Paper series, no. 2, CWIN Nepal, Kathmandu.

Daiute, C. (2010) 'General introduction', in C. Daiute, Z. Beykont, C. Higson-Smith, and L. Nucci (eds), *International Perspectives on Youth Conflict and Development*, Oxford University, Oxford.

Di Nunzio, M. (2019) *The Act of Living: Street Life, Marginality and Development in Urban Ethiopia*, Cornell University, New York.

Eide, A.H., Neupane, S., and Hem, K-G. (2016) *Living Conditions among People with Disability in Nepal*, SINTEF and Norwegian Federation of Organizations of Disabled People, Trondheim.

Emebet, K. (2002) *Ethiopia: An Assessment of the International Labour Migration Situation: The Case of Female Labour Migrants*, International Labour Office, Geneva.

Ennew, J. (1994) *Street and Working Children: A Guide to Planning*, Save the Children UK, London.

Ennew, J. (1995) 'Outside childhood: street children's rights' in B. Franklin (ed.), *The Handbook of Children's Rights: Comparative Policy and Practice*, pp. 201–14, Routledge, London.

Federal Democratic Republic of Ethiopia, Population Census Commission (FDRE-PCC) (2008) *Summary and Statistical Report of the 2007 Population and Housing Census*, FDRE-PCC, Addis Ababa, Ethiopia.

Feleke, T. (2006) 'Migration and rural livelihood in Ethiopia: case studies of five rural sites in Amhara, Oromia and SNNP regions', paper presented to the *4th International Conference on Ethiopian Economy, Addis Ababa*.

Ferguson, R. (1990) 'Introduction: invisible centre', in R. Ferguson, M. Gever, T.T. Minh-ha, and C. West (eds), *Out There: Marginalization and Contemporary Cultures*, pp. 9–14, The New Museum of Contemporary Art and Massachusetts Institute of Technology, New York.

Freire, P. (1970) *Pedagogy of the Oppressed*, Penguin, London.

Gellner, D.N. (1989) 'Introduction', in D.N. Gellner and D. Quigley (eds), *Contested Hierarchies: A Collaborative Ethnography of Caste among the Newars of the Kathmandu Valley, Nepal*, pp. 1–37, Oxford University Press, New Delhi.

Georgalakis, G. and Rose, P. (eds) (2019) *Exploring Research-Policy Partnerships in International Development, ESRC's Impact Initiative*, IDS Bulletin Special Issue, IDS, Brighton.

Getu, M., Emirie, G., and Habtamu, K. (2018) 'Prevalence and drivers of early marriage in Alefa, Diksis and Gorche Districts of Amhara, Oromia and Southern Nations, Nationalities and Peoples Regions of Ethiopia', research report (unpublished).

Ghimire, D. (2018) *Reflections on Nepalese Society: An Archive of Sociological Essays*, Shangri-La Books, Kathmandu.

Groce, N. (2004) 'Adolescents and youth with disability: issues and challenges', *Asia Pacific Disability Rehabilitation Journal* 15(2): 13–33.

Groce, N. (2013) *The Disability and Development Gap*, Leonard Cheshire Disability and Inclusive Development Centre, London.
Groce, N. (2018) 'Global disability: an emerging issue', *The Lancet* 6: e724–5 <https://doi.org/10.1016/S2214-109X(18)30265-1>.
Groce, N. and Kett, M. (2014) *Youth with Disabilities*, Leonard Cheshire Disability and Inclusive Development Centre, London.
Hanson, K. and Nieuwenhuys, O. (eds) (2013) *Reconceptualizing Children's Rights in International Development: Living Rights, Social Justice, Translations*, Cambridge University Press, New York.
Heinonen, P. (2013) *Youth Gangs and Street Children: Culture, Nurture and Masculinity in Ethiopia*, Berghahn Books, Oxford.
Hofer, A. (1979) *The Caste Hierarchy and the State in Nepal: A Study of the Muluki Ain of 1854*, (2nd edn, 2004), Himal Books, Lalitpur, Nepal.
Huijsmans, R. (2012) 'Beyond compartmentalization: a relational approach towards agency and vulnerability of young migrants', Special issue: Independent Child Migration: Insights into Agency, Vulnerability, and Structure, *New Directions for Child and Adolescent Development* 136: 29–45 <https://doi.org/10.1002/cad.20009>.
Huijsmans, R. (2016) 'Children and young people in migration: a relational approach', in C. Ni Laoire, A. White, and T. Skelton (eds), *Movement, Mobilities, and Journeys*, Geographies of Children and Young People Series, vol. 6, Springer, Singapore.
Huijsmans, R., Ansel, N. and Froerer, P. (2020) 'Development, young people and the social production of aspiration', *The European Journal of Development Research* 33. Epub ahead of print 19 November 2020 <https://doi.org/10.1057/s41287-020-00337-1>.
International Dalit Solidarity Network (IDSN) (2021) 'Nepal' [website] <https://idsn.org/countries/nepal/> [accessed 8 November 2021].
Johnson, V. (2010) 'Are children's perspectives valued in changing contexts? Revisiting a rights-based evaluation children in Nepal', *Journal for International Development* 22(8): 1076–89 <https://doi.org/10.1002/jid.1747>.
Johnson, V. (2011) 'Conditions for change for children and young people's participation in evaluation: "change-scape"', *Child Indicators Research* 4(4): 577–96 <https://doi.org/10.1007/s12187-010-9099-6>.
Johnson, V. (2015) 'Valuing children's knowledge: the politics of listening?' in Eyben, R., Guijt, I., Roche, C., and Shutt, C. (eds), *The Politics of Evidence in International Development: Playing the Game to Change the Rules?* pp. 155–72, Practical Action, Rugby.
Johnson, V. (2017) 'Moving beyond voice in children and young people's participation', *Action Research* 15(1): 104–24 <https://doi.org/10.1177/1476750317698025>.
Johnson, V. and Nurick, R. (2003) 'Developing coding systems to analyse difference', *PLA Notes* 47: 19–24.
Johnson, V. and West, A. (2018) *Children's Participation in Global Contexts: Going Beyond Voice*, Routledge, Abingdon.

Johnson, V. and West, A. (2021a) 'Youth perspectives on uncertainty in Addis Ababa and Kathmandu', in J. Horton, H. Pimlott-Wilson, and S.M. Hall (eds), *Growing Up and Getting By: International Perspectives on Childhood and Youth in Hard Times*, pp. 157–74, Policy Press, Bristol.

Johnson, V. and West, A. (2021b) 'Approaches and creative research methods with children and youth', in D. Burns, J. Howard, and S.M. Ospina (eds), *Handbook of Participatory Research and Inquiry*, pp. 296–310, Sage, London.

Johnson, V., Hill, J., and Ivan-Smith, E. (1995) *Listening to Smaller Voices: Children in an Environment of Change*, ActionAid, London.

Johnson, V., Ivan-Smith, E., Gordon, G., Pridmore, P., and Scott, P. (eds) (1998) *Stepping Forward: Children and Young People's Participation in the Development Process*, IT Publications, London.

Johnson, V., Hart, R. and Colwell, J. (eds) (2014) *Steps to Engaging Young Children in Research: The Guide and The Toolkit*, Bernard van Leer Foundation, the Hague.

Johnson, V., Admassu, A., Church, A., Healey, J. and Mathema, S. (2019a) 'Layered and linking research partnerships: learning from YOUR World Research in Ethiopia and Nepal', in G. Georgalakis and P. Rose (eds), *Exploring Research-Policy Partnerships in International Development, ESRC's Impact Initiative*, IDS Bulletin Special Issue, Brighton.

Johnson, V., West, A., Getu, M., Tuladhar, S., Getachew, M., Shrestha, S., Ahmed, A., Neupane, S., Church, A., and Gosmann, S. (2019b) *YOUR World Research: International Report on Findings and Impact: Comparative Qualitative and Participatory Research from Eight Sites in Ethiopia and Nepal* [online], Goldsmiths, London and University of Brighton <https://www.gold.ac.uk/media/documents-by-section/departments/anthropology/YOUR-World-Research-International-Report.pdf> [accessed 8 November 2021].

Johnson, V., Lewin, T. and Cannon, C. (2020a) *Learning from a Living Archive: Rejuvenating Child and Youth Rights and Participation*, IDS Rejuvenate Working Paper No 1, Rejuvenate, Institute of Development Studies, Brighton.

Johnson, V., Shephard, K., and West, A. (2020b) *Impact Lessons: Engaging marginalized Communities in National Policy Formation, Working Paper: Expert Analysis from the Impact Initiative*, IDS and The Impact Initiative, Brighton.

Johnson, V., Getu, M., Getachew, M., Ahmed, A. and West, A. (2021) 'Trapped bodies, moving minds: case study research on uncertainty, place and migration with marginalized youth in Ethiopia', *Children and Society* 35(6): 944–59 <https://doi.org/10.1111/chso.12476>.

Karna, S., Limbu, S.T., and Jha, K. (2018) '2017 local elections in Madhes: discussions from the margins', *Studies in Nepali History and Society* 23(2): 277–308

Kassa, T. (2018) 'The lived experiences of street children in Addis Ababa: challenges and coping strategies', *Ethiopian Journal of Development Research* 40(1): eISSN: 0378-0813.

Kassa, T.A., Luck, T., Bekele, A., and Riedel-Heller, S.G. (2016) 'Sexual and reproductive health of young people with disability in Ethiopia: a study on knowledge, attitude and practice: a cross-sectional study', *Globalization and Health* 12: 5 <http://doi.org/10.1186/s12992-016-0142-3>.

Katz, C. (2004) *Growing up Global: Economic Restructuring and Children's Everyday Lives*, University of Minnesota Press, Minneapolis, MN.

Kelly, P., Campbell, P. and Howie, L. (2019) *Rethinking Young People's Marginalization: Beyond neo-liberal futures?* Routledge, London.

Kwong, J. (2011) 'Education and identity: the marginalization of migrant youths in Beijing', *Journal of Youth Studies* 14(8): 871–83 <https://doi.org/10.1080/13676261.2011.607435>.

Langevang, T. (2008) '"We are managing!" Uncertain paths to respectable adulthoods in Accra, Ghana', *Geoforum* 39: 2039–47 <https://doi.org/10.1016/j.geoforum.2008.09.003>.

Louw, J., Donald, D. and Dawes, A. (2000) 'Intervening in adversity: towards a theory of practice', in D. Donald, A. Dawes and J. Louw (eds), *Addressing Childhood Adversity*, pp. 244–60, David Philip Publishers, Cape Town.

Mains, D. (2013) *Hope is Cut: Youth, Unemployment and the Future of Urban Ethiopia*, Temple University Press, Philadelphia.

Manchala, D. (2017) 'Moving in the Spirit: called to transforming discipleship. Reflections from the vantage points of the marginalized people', *International Review of Mission* 106(2): 201–15 <https://doi.org/10.1111/irom.12180>.

Martikke, S., Church, A. and Hart, A. (2018) 'A radical take on co-production? Community partner leadership in research', in S. Banks, A. Hart, K. Pahl, and P. Ward (eds), *Co-producing Research: A Community Development Approach*, pp. 49–68, Policy Press, Bristol.

Mayall, B. (2002) 'Conversations with children: working with general issues', in P. Christensen and A. James (eds), *Research With Children: Perspectives and Practices*, Routledge, London.

Mead, M. (1970) *Culture and Commitment: A Study of the Generation Gap*, The Bodley Head/ The American Museum of Natural History, London (originally 1969).

Mega Nepal (2017) *National and District Profile of Nepal 2016/17*, Mega Publication & Research Centre, Nepal.

Ministry of Labour, Employment and Social Security (MoLESS) (2020) *Nepal Labour Migration Report*, MoLESS, Government of Nepal, Kathmandu.

Ministry of Youth and Sports (MoYS) (2010) *National Youth Policy 2010*, MoYS, Kathmandu.

MoYS (2015) *National Youth Policy 2072 (2015)*, MoYS, Kathmandu.

Ministry of Youth and Sports (MYS) (2005) *National Youth Implementation Manual*, Federal Democratic Republic of Ethiopia MYS, Addis Ababa.

MYS (2006a) *Administrative Manual for Basic and Small Range Skill Trainings for the Youth*, Federal Democratic Republic of Ethiopia MYS, Addis Ababa.

MYS (2006b) *Development Package for Urban Youth*, Federal Democratic Republic of Ethiopia MYS, Addis Ababa.

MYS (2006c) *Development Package for Rural Youth*, Federal Democratic Republic of Ethiopia MYS, Addis Ababa.

MYS (2006d) and (2008) *Services Delivery and Management of Youth Centres*, Federal Democratic Republic of Ethiopia MYS, Addis Ababa.

MYS (2008) *Development Package for Rural Youth*, Federal Democratic Republic of Ethiopia MYS, Addis Ababa.

MYS (2010) *A Standard for Youth Voluntary Service*, Federal Democratic Republic of Ethiopia MYS, Addis Ababa.

MYS (2011) *Life Skills Training Manual for Young Persons in Ethiopia*, unpublished final draft report, Addis Ababa.

Ministry of Youth, Sports and Culture (MYSC) (2004) *National Youth Policy*, Federal Democratic Republic of Ethiopia MYSC, Addis Ababa <http://www.youthpolicy.org/national/Ethiopia_2004_National_Youth_Policy.pdf> [accessed 8 November 2021].

Mizen, P. (2004) *The Changing State of Youth*, Palgrave Macmillan, New York.

Mizen, P. and Ofosu-kusi, Y. (2013) 'Agency as vulnerability: accounting for children's movement to the streets of Accra', *The Sociological Review* 61(2): 363–82 <https://doi.org/10.1111/1467-954X.12021>.

Moncrieffe, J. (2009) 'Introduction: intergenerational transmissions: cultivating children's agency?' *IDS Bulletin* 40(1): 1–8 <https://doi.org/10.1111/j.1759-5436.2009.00001.x>.

Nidaw, B., Schippers, A., Van Engen, M., and Klink, J. (2018) 'The experiences of children with disabilities and primary caregivers on the social inclusion of children with disabilities in Ethiopia', *International Journal of Child, Youth and Family Studies* 9(4): 146–67 <https://doi.org/10.18357/ijcyfs94201818645>.

Office of Statistics (OS) and DCC Kapilvastu (2017) *Rural Municipality and Municipality Profile Kapilvastu- 2073 (BS)*, Office of Statistics and Office of District Coordination Committee, Kapilvastu.

Office of the Municipal Executive (OME) Nepal (Bagmati Province) (2021) 'Kathmandu Metropolitan City' [online] <https://kathmandu.gov.np/introduction/?lang=en> [accessed 26 November 2021].

Office of the United Nations High Commissioner for Human Rights (OHCHR) (2017) *Rights of Children in Street Situations: General Comment No 21 on Children in Street Situations*, OHCHR and Consortium for Street Children, London.

Oliver, M. (1990) *The Politics of Disablement*, Macmillan, London.

Oliver, M. (2013) 'The social model of disability: thirty years on', *Disability & Society* 28: 7 <https://doi.org/10.1080/09687599.2013.818773>.

Om Gurung (2009) 'Social inclusion: policies and practices in Nepal', *Occasional Papers in Sociology and Anthropology* 11: 1–15 (Tribhuvan University) <https://doi.org/10.3126/opsa.v11i0.3027>.

Oromia Bureau of Finance and Economic Development (BOFED) (2011) *The National Regional Government of Oromiya: Physical and Socio-Economic Profile of Oromiya*, BOFED, Oromia, Ethiopia.

Oromia BOFED (2013) *The National Regional Government of Oromiya: Physical and Socio-Economic Profile of Oromiya: second edition*, BOFED, Oromia, Ethiopia.

Oromia BOFED (2014) *The National Regional Government of Oromiya: Physical and Socio-Economic Profile of Oromiya: third edition*, BOFED, Oromia, Ethiopia.

Oswell, D. (2013) *The Agency of Children: From Family to Global Human Rights*, Cambridge University Press, Cambridge.

Pankhurst, A. (2015) 'Children combining school and work in Ethiopian communities', in A. Pankhurst, M. Bourdillon, and G. Crivello (eds), *Children's Work and Labour in East Africa: Social Context and Implications for Policy*, pp 111–31, Organization for Social Science Research in Eastern and Southern Africa, Addis Ababa, Ethiopia.

Pankhurst, A. (2017) 'Youth transitions to adulthood and the role of interventions', in A. Pankhurst (ed.), *Change and Transformation in 20 Rural Communities in Ethiopia: Selected Aspects and Implications for Policy*, WIDE, Addis Ababa.

Pankhurst, A. and Dom, P. (2018) 'Twenty rural communities in Ethiopia and how they changed: introducing the WIDE research and the selected policy-relevant topics' [online] <https://ethiopiawide.net/wp-content/uploads/Changing-rural-communities.pdf> [accessed March 2021].

Pankhurst, R. (1998) *The Ethiopians: A History*, Blackwell, Oxford.

Park, A. (2015) *An Inclusive Approach to Surveys of Sexual and Gender Minorities (Kathmandu meeting report)*, UNDP/Williams Institute, Bangkok.

Percy-Smith, B. and Thomas, N. (eds) (2010) *A Handbook of Children and Young People's Participation: Perspectives from Theory and Practice*, Routledge, Oxford.

Philo, C., Parr, H., and Soderstrom, O. (2019) '"On edge?" Studies in precarious urbanisms', *Geoforum* 101: 150–5 <https://doi.org/10.1016/j.geoforum.2019.04.020>.

Population Census Commission (PCC), Federal Democratic Republic of Ethiopia (2008) *Summary and Statistical Report of the 2007 Population and Housing Census*, PCC/UNFPA, Addis Ababa.

Pradhan, P. (2003) *Housing the Urban Poor*, Lumanti Support Group for Shelter, Kathmandu.

Punch, S. (2002) 'Research with children: the same or different from research with adults?' *Childhood* 9(3): 321–41 <https://doi.org/10.1177/0907568202009003005>.

Punch, S. and Sugden, F. (2013) 'Work, education and out-migration among children and youth in upland Asia: changing patterns of labour and ecological knowledge in an era of globalization', *Local Environment* 18(3): 255–70 <https://doi.org/10.1080/13549839.2012.716410>.

Punch, S., Vanderbeck, R. and Skelton, T. (2018) 'Introduction, family, intergenerationality and peer group relations', in T. Skelton (ed.), *Geographies of Children and Young People vol. 5*, pp. 978–81, Springer, Singapore.

Reddy, G. (2005) *With Respect to Sex: Negotiating Hijra Identity in South Asia*, University of Chicago, Chicago.

Roelen, K., Barnett, I., Johnson, V., Lewin, T., Thorsen, D. and Ton, G. (2020) *Understanding Children's Harmful Work: A Review of the Methodological Landscape*, Working Paper 3, Action on Children's Harmful Work in African Agriculture, IDS, Brighton.

Ryckmans, J. (2012) *The Street Children of Nepal: Anthroposociological Study of Social, Cultural and Communicational Practices*, CPCS International, Kathmandu.

Samudayik Sarathi (SS) Nepal (2014) *Slums in Kathmandu Valley: A Comprehensive Survey of 55 Slum Settlements*, SS Nepal, Kathmandu.

Scoones, I. (2019) *What is Uncertainty and Why Does it Matter?* Working Paper 105, STEPS Centre, Brighton.

Sharma, P.R. (2004) *The State and Society in Nepal: Historical Foundations and Contemporary Trends*, Himal Books, Kathmandu.

Sharma, S., Pandey, S., Pathak, D., and Sijapati-Basnett, B. (2014) *State of Migration in Nepal research paper VI*, Centre for the Study of Labour and Mobility, Kathmandu.

Shrestha, C.B. (2004) *Nepal: Coping with Maoist insurgency*, Chetana Lokshum, Kathmandu.

Smith, A. and Pitts, M. (2007) 'Researching the margins: an introduction', in: M. Pitts and A. Smith (eds), *Researching the Margins: Strategies for Ethical and Rigorous Research with marginalized Communities*, pp. 3–41, Palgrave Macmillan, Basingstoke.

Snellinger, A.T. (2018) *Making New Nepal: From Student Activism to Mainstream Politics*, University of Washington Press, Seattle, WA.

Stake, R.E. (1995) *The Art of Case Study Research*, Sage, London.

Stammers, N. (2013) 'Conclusion: child rights and social movements: reflections from a cognate field', in K. Hanson and O. Nieuwenhuys (eds), *Reconceptualizing Children's Rights in International Development: Living Rights, Social Justice and Translations*, pp. 275–92, Cambridge University Press, New York.

Taddei, R. (2012) 'The politics of uncertainty and the fate of forecasters', *Ethics, Policy & Environment* 15(2): 252–67 <https://doi.org/10.1080/21550085.2012.685603>.

Tadele, G. and Ayalew, A. (2018) 'Rural youth transitions to farming in Ethiopia: processes and challenges', *Ethiopian Journal of Development Research* 40(1): eISSN: 0378-0813.

Tefera, B., Getu, M., Zeleke, B., and Desie, Y. (2021) 'Perceived contributions of youth centers to the development of young people in Ethiopia', *Ethiopian Journal of the Social Sciences and Humanities* 16(2) <https://doi.org/10.4314/ejossah.v16i2.3>.

Teferra, T. (1999) 'Inclusion of children with disabilities in regular schools: challenges and opportunities', *The Ethiopian Journal of Education* 11(1): 29–64.

Tegegne, A.D. and Penker, M. (2016) 'Determinants of rural out-migration in Ethiopia: who stays and who goes?' *Demographic Research* 35(34): 1011–44 <https://doi.org/10.4054/DemRes.2016.35.34>.

Thapaliya, M.P. (2016) *A Report on Disability in Nepal*, Australian Himalayan Foundation, Sydney.
Thomas de Benitez, S. (2011a) *State of the World's Street Children: Violence*, Consortium for Street Children, London.
Thomas de Benitez, S. (2011b) *State of the World's Street Children: Research*, Consortium for Street Children, London.
Thorsen, D. (2013) 'Weaving in and out of employment and self-employment: young rural migrants in the informal economies of Ouagadougou and Abidjan', *International Development Planning Review* 35(2): 203–18 <http://dx.doi.org/10.3828/idpr.2013.13>.
Tisdall, K., Davis, J., Prout, A., and Hill, M. (2006) *Children, Young People and Social Inclusion: Participation for What?* Policy Press, Bristol.
Tisdall, K.M., Davis, J.M. and Gallagher, M. (2009) *Researching with Children and Young People: Research Design, Methods and Analysis*, Sage, London.
Tucker, M. (1990) 'Foreword' in R. Ferguson, M. Gever, T.T. Minh-ha, and C. West (eds), *Out There: Marginalization and Contemporary Cultures*, pp. 7–8, The New Museum of Contemporary Art and Massachusetts Institute of Technology, New York.
UKCDR (2021) *Guidance on Safeguarding in International Development Research*, Working Paper, UK Collaborative for Development Research, London.
United Nations (UN) (2008) *Convention on the Rights of Persons with Disabilities*, United Nations, New York.
United Nations Development Program (UNDP) (1999) *Human Development Report 1999*, UNDP, New York.
UNDP (2013) *Human Development Report 2013 – The Rise of the South: Human Progress in a Diverse World*, UNDP, New York.
UNDP/Williams Institute (2014) *Surveying Nepal's Sexual and Gender Minorities: An Inclusive Approach*, UNDP/Williams Institute, Bangkok.
United Nations Population Fund (UNFPA) (2020) 'World Populations Dashboard Ethiopia: Overview' [online] <https://www.unfpa.org/data/world-population/ET> [accessed 10 March 2021].
UN-Habitat (2006) *Cities, Slums and the Millennium Development Goals, 13–16 December 2006, Asia-Pacific Ministerial Conference on Housing and Human Settlements*, UN-Habitat, Nairobi.
UN-Habitat (2007) *Twenty-first Session of Governing Council, 16–20 April 2007: Slum Dwellers to Double by 2030*, UN-Habitat, Nairobi.
UNICEF (2014) *Socio-Educational Issues of Urban Public Schools and the Slums: A Case Study*, UNICEF, Kathmandu.
UNICEF (2018) *Country Programme Action Plan 2018–22*, UNICEF and Government of Nepal, Kathmandu.
UNICEF, MOLSA and Development Pathways (2019) *Situation and Access to Services of People with Disabilities and Homeless People in Two Sub-cities of Addis Ababa*, UNICEF Ethiopia and the Ministry of Labour and Social Affairs, Addis Ababa.

Van Blerk, L. (2008) 'Poverty, migration and sex work: youth transitions in Ethiopia', *Area* 40(2): 245–53 <https://doi.org/10.1111/j.1475-4762.2008.00799.x>.

Wallace, C. and Cross, M. (1990) *Youth in Transition: the Sociology of Youth and Youth Policy*, Falmer Press, Basingstoke.

Walters, T. and Jepson, A.S. (2019) 'Introduction: understanding the nexus of marginalisation and events', in T. Walters and A.S. Jepson (eds), *Marginalization and Events*, pp. 1–16, Routledge, Abingdon.

Wells, K. (2014) 'Children, youth and subjectivity', *Children's Geographies* 12(3): 263–67 <https://doi.org/10.1080/14733285.2014.927053>.

Wells, K. (2017) *Childhood Studies: Making Young Subjects*, Polity, Cambridge.

Wenger-Trainer, E. and Wenger-Trainer, B. (2020) *Learning to Make a Difference: Value Creation in Social Learning Spaces*, Cambridge University Press, Cambridge.

West, A. (1999) 'Children's own research: street children and care in Britain and Bangladesh', *Childhood* 6(1): 145–53.

West, A. (2003) *At the Margins: Street Children in Asia and the Pacific*, Policy and Social Development Papers No 8, Asian Development Bank, Manila.

Whelpton, J. (2005) *A History of Nepal*, Cambridge University Press, Cambridge.

Wickenden, M. and Elphick, J. (2016) 'Don't forget us, we are here too! Listening to disabled children and their families living in poverty', in S. Grech and K. Soldatic (eds), *Disability in the Global South: International Perspectives on Social Policy, Administration, and Practice*, pp. 133–49, Springer, Cham.

World Bank (2020) 'The World Bank in Nepal: Overview: Context', 8 October 2020 [online] <https://www.worldbank.org/en/country/nepal/overview> [accessed March 2021].

Wright, G.N. and Phillips, L.D. (1979) 'Cross-cultural differences in the assessment and communication of uncertainty', *Current Anthropology* 20(4): 845–6.

Young, H. (2016) 'Trans-rights: meet the face of Nepal's progressive "third gender" movement', *The Guardian*, 12 February <https://www.theguardian.com/global-development-professionals-network/2016/feb/12/trans-rights-meet-the-face-of-nepals-progressive-third-gender-movement> [accessed January 2022].

Index

ActionAid Nepal 6, 197
Addis Ababa University 6
Addis Ketema, Ethiopia 51–2, 95–6
  identity, youth marginalization and street-connected 96–8
  informal sector work, services, and authorities 104–7
  informal sector work and education 102–4
  movement and migration to street 99–102
  peer support 107
  substance abuse 107–9
  uncertainty 109
  vulnerability and diversity 98–9
adult status 55–6, 65–7, 81–2, 86, 92, 165, 202, 250
  transitions, Fogera, Ethiopia, 60–2
  see also marriage
adults, interviews with 36–8
agency see youth agency
agriculture and land, Fogera, Ethiopia 57–8
alcohol/drunkenness 61–2, 76, 145, 149, 156, 180 see also substance abuse
Appadurai, A. 23
aspiration see youth aspirations

Bauman, Z. 2, 19, 22, 23, 243, 249–50
Braun, V. and Clarke, V. 38
bride-price 83, 84
British Council with Association of Youth Organizations Nepal (BC and AYON) 198

case studies 29, 32
  co-construction 35–6

caste discrimination, Nepal
  Dalits 115, 131–2, 146, 147, 155, 156, 163, 172
  and ethnic discrimination 131–3
  and gender discrimination 155–6, 163, 171–2
Central Child Welfare Board (CCWB): 'Street Children's Rescue, Protection and Management Guidelines', Nepal 218–19
CERID, Nepal 6
CHADET, Ethiopia 6, 197
Chambers, R. 4
change-scape approach 4–5, 242–3
ChildHope, UK 6
citizenship cards see genderfluid youth
co-construction
  research methods 31, 35–6
  of uncertainty 19–20
coding for individuals 35
communication technology (mobile phones/social media), Nepal 141, 147, 150
comparative research 4–5
  cross-county policy and impacts 197–200
  see also case studies
conflict, Nepal 116, 120, 130–1, 133, 145
conflict-affected contexts 24
consent, ethics, and safeguarding 33–4
consumption, urban Nepal 147–8, 150
creativity
  positive uncertainty and 19–20, 249–51
  youth-centred research 32–3

criminalization
  strategies to avoid 200, 211
  street situations 76, 77, 97, 220, 221
cross-county comparison: policy themes and impacts 197–200
cultural practices *see* intergenerational cultural transmissions

Dalits, Nepal 115, 131–2, 146, 147, 155, 156, 163, 172
decision-making, Nepal 149–50
disabilities 227–8
  Ethiopia 54, 57, 98, 102, 232–4
  Nepal 229–31
  policy and practice messages 234–6
  summary and conclusion 236–7
discrimination *see* Kathmandu, Nepal; *specific types*
domestic violence 62, 149, 156, 180, 216
drought-prone area *see* Hetosa, Ethiopia
drugs *see* substance abuse

early marriage
  Ethiopia 59, 60–1, 83, 84
  Nepal 163, 171, 180–1
early working age, Nepal 137–9
earthquake, Nepal 153, 155, 159, 164, 202
  injuries and disabilities 229
education
  disabilities, Ethiopia 232
  rural Ethiopia 58–60, 84–6
  rural Nepal 156–9
education and employment
  cross-county comparison 198–200
  Ethiopia 52–3, 73–4, 84–6, 102–4
  Nepal 124–5, 137–9, 146–7, 169, 175–8, 187–8
  youth aspirations 246–8
education and training, relevant 200
employment *see* education and employment; informal work sector, Ethiopia; migration

environmental fragility *see* earthquake, Nepal; Hetosa, Ethiopia; Kathmandu, Nepal; Sindhupalchowk, Nepal
ethics, consent, and safeguarding 33–4
Ethiopia 28–9, 43–4, 46–7
  definition of youth 46–7
  disabilities 54, 57, 98, 102, 232–4
  genderfluid youth 125
  impact of youth, government and non-government actions 197
  migration (internal and international) 206–10
  national and local partners 6
  national youth seminars/declarations/recommendations 195–6, 222, 234
  politics/government 45–6
  population diversity 44–5
  research locations 48–52
  research themes 52–4
  street situations 219–22
  youth policy and marginalization 46–8
  see also Addis Ketema; Fogera; Hetosa; Woreta
ethnic discrimination, Nepal 131–3

family absence/breakdown 72, 73, 100, 101, 156, 163
family relationships, Nepal 123–4, 128–9, 148–50
  see also genderfluid youth; Kathmandu, Nepal; Sindhupalchowk, Nepal
Ferguson, R. 15
flooding *see* Kathmandu, Nepal
Fogera, Ethiopia 48–9, 55–6
  adult status, transitions to 60–2
  agriculture and land 57–8
  education and school 58–60
  informal sector work 58
  living situation of marginalized youth 56–7

migration 62–4
return 64–5
uncertainties 65–7

gender discrimination, Nepal 133–5
  menstruation 155–6, 163
  migration 139
  mobility 135–7, 150
gendered mobility 57, 135–7, 150
genderfluid youth
  citizenship cards 189
  education 187
  health services 189–90
  living situation 185–7
  public services 189
  self-knowing and identities 184–5
  uncertainty 190
  violence and support 190
  work 187–8
  see also Kathmandu, Nepal
government and non-government (NGO) interventions
  impact 197
  partnerships 194–5, 197
  street situations 105–6, 108–9, 220–1, 216, 218–19
Gulf states *see* Middle Eastern/Gulf States

health services
  disabilities 230–1
  see also genderfluid youth
Hetosa, Ethiopia 49–50, 81–2
  adult status transitions and marriage 82–4
  education and work 84–6
  informal work sector and mobility 86
  migration, internal and international 86–90
  return 90–1
  uncertainties 91–2
HIV/AIDs
  Ethiopia 71
  Nepal 188

identity 16, 28, 35–6, 69, 95–7, 109, 113–5, 118, 128, 131, 170–2, 181–200, 233
identity cards 189, 200, 222
illegal squatters *see* Kathmandu, Nepal
illegal/irregular migration and work 63, 88–9, 104
  return 90
impact *see* policy themes impact; research impact
India 129–30, 138, 139, 159, 161, 202, 203–4
informal work sector, Ethiopia 52–3, 58, 73–4, 75–6, 86, 102–7
institutional care *see* rehabilitation and vocational training
intergenerational
  cultural transmissions 146–8, 163–4, 243
  power dynamics 2–3, 17–8, 20–3, 29, 32, 146, 243, 251
  relationships *see* family relationships, Nepal; Sindhupalchowk, Nepal and stakeholder analysis 32
international migration *see* India; Middle East/Gulf States; migration (internal and international)
international and national research teams 5–6

Johnson, V. 4, 22, 38
  et al. 4–5, 23, 39, 242, 251
  and West, A. 194

Kapilvastu (rural and urban), Nepal 119–21, 123–4
Kapilvastu (rural), Nepal 127–8
  discrimination and inequalities 130–1
  early working age 137–9
  ethnic/caste discrimination 131–3
  gender discrimination 133–5

gender and migration 139
gendered mobility 135–7
lived experiences of marginalized youth 128–30
uncertainty 140–1
Kapilvastu (urban), Nepal 143–4
family expectations, support, and work 148–50
living situation and marginalization 145–6
migration 144–5
social change 146–8
uncertainty 150–2
Kathmandu, Nepal 6–7, 122–5, 167–90
discrimination 171
early marriage 180
environmental vulnerability 167
family poverty, support, and education 171–9
flooding 169–70, 173, 174
genderfluid 118, 183–90
illegal squatters 169
living spaces 169
marginalization 118, 168
migration to 145–50, 158–61, 168, 179, 205–6
see also genderfluid youth; slum dwellers

landlessness
rural Ethiopia 57–8, 61
rural Nepal 128, 129
landslide threat, Nepal 154–5
languages
Arabic 89–90
Ethiopia 44
Nepal 132–3
LGBTQI *see* genderfluid youth; Kathmandu, Nepal
liquid modernity 19, 22
listening to marginalized youth 4–5, 241–52
living rights, concept of 20–1, 242–3, 251–2

Manchala, D. 15
marginalization
concept and definitions 15–17
learning from most-marginalized youth 252
selection of youth participants 34–5
youth analysis of 143–6
youth definitions of 16–17, 117–18
see also Addis Ketema, Ethiopia; Ethiopia; Fogera, Ethiopia; Kathmandu, Nepal; Kapilvastu (rural); Kapilvastu (urban); listening to marginalized youth; Nepal; Sindhupalchowk, Nepal; slum dwellers; Woreta, Ethiopia; youth definitions of marginalization
marriage
and adult status transitions, Ethiopia 82–4
Nepal 141, 150, 163
vs migration, Ethiopia 209
see also early marriage
menstruation, Nepal 155–6, 163
methodology 1, 7–8, 13, 16, 22, 27–39, 195
Middle Eastern/Gulf States
and Ethiopia 62, 63, 64, 65, 73, 84, 87, 88, 207, 209, 210
and Nepal 159, 163, 188, 204
'Migrating out of Poverty Consortium' 23–4
migration (internal and international) 201–2, 246–8
cross-country comparison 198
Ethiopia 206–10
Nepal 202–6
policy and practice messages 210–11
summary and conclusion 211–12
see also India; Middle Eastern/Gulf States; *specific research locations*
migration return *see* return
mobility, gendered 57, 135–7, 150

Nepal 28–9, 113–14
  changing definitions of marginalization 16, 117–18
  definition of youth 14–15, 117
  disability 229–31
  impact of youth, government and non-government actions 197
  migration (internal and international) 202–6
  national and local partners 6
  national youth seminar and declaration 196
  politics/government 114, 116
  population diversity 114–15
  research locations 118–23
  research themes 123–5
  street situations 216–19
  youth policy and marginalization 117–18
  see also genderfluid youth; Kapilvastu (rural and urban); Kathmandu, Nepal; Sindhupalchowk; slum dwellers
non-government organizations (NGOs) *see* government and non-government (NGO) interventions

OHCHR 24–5, 215

Pankhurst, A. 43–4
parents/guardians *see* Sindhupalchowk, Nepal; *entries beginning* family
participation 31–3, 47, 146, 195–6, 225, 234–6
partnerships
  and personnel 5–7
  research and action 194–5, 197
peer support 77, 87, 98, 100, 107, 190, 233, 242–3
police/militia 76, 99, 104–5, 217, 221
policy and practice messages 251–2
  disabilities 234–6
  migration (internal and international) 210–11
  street situations 223–4
policy themes 193–4
  cross-county comparison 197–200
  impact 193–7
  national youth seminars and declarations/recommendations 195–6, 222, 234
  research uptake 194–5
  summary and conclusion 200
Provincial and National Youth Seminars 194
public services
  Ethiopia 220, 232
  Nepal 146, 171, 189

qualitative research 29

re-migration triggers 91
reference groups 7
rehabilitation and vocational training
  Ethiopia 105–6, 108–9, 220–1
  Nepal 216, 218–19
religions, Ethiopia 45, 48, 49, 70
religions, Nepal 115, 128
  conflicts 131, 145
  discrimination 132
  shamanic practices 163–4, 230–1
remittances 90–1, 209
research impact 2, 6–9, 38–9
research methodology *see* methodology
research participation *see* participation
research study 1–2
  case studies *see* case studies
  change-scape approach 4–5, 242–3
  locations 7, 27, 29, 31, 35, 43, 48, 96, 118, 195, 247
  methodology *see* methodology
  objectives 5
  personnel and partners 5–7

youth perspectives on uncertainty 2–3
see also youth-centred research method and approach
research uptake 193–200
return
  Ethiopia 55–6, 62, 64–7, 82, 87–93, 96
  Nepal 140, 152, 165
  Ethiopia and Nepal 3, 201–2, 205–6, 212, 223, 245–6
rights *see* living rights; UN Convention on the Rights of the Child
rural areas *see* Fogera, Ethiopia; Hetosa, Ethiopia; Kapilvastu (rural), Nepal

safeguarding, ethics and consent 33–4
sampling criteria 34–5
Save the Children: 'Youth Survey', Nepal 198
savings and credit associations 104
sex workers
  Ethiopia 71, 96–7, 99, 101, 103, 220
  see also genderfluid youth
sexual abuse/violence
  Ethiopia 72, 74, 98, 101, 107
  Nepal 133, 155, 173, 190
  street situations 217
shamanic practices, Nepal 163–4, 230–1
Sindhupalchowk, Nepal 121–2, 124, 153–4
  changing family relationships 162–3
  education 156–9
  marginalization and family life 154–5
  social change 163–4
  uncertainties 164–5
  work, migration and changing family dynamics 159–62
skills training and study, Nepal 149, 176–7

slum dwellers 122–3, 124, 167–8
  early marriage 180–1
  education and work 175–8
  in-migration and living space 168–70
  marginalization 170–3
  poverty and family support 173–5
  uncertainties 181–2
  unemployment: drugs and out-migration 178–80
  see also Kathmandu, Nepal
social norms 3–4, 8, 19–23, 32, 34, 38, 143, 241–4, 249–52
stakeholders
  analysis 32
  piloting and interviews 37–8
'street children and youth', UN definition of 215
Street-connections and situations 24–5, 52, 95, 213–14
  dimensions, characteristics and backgrounds 214–15
  Ethiopia 219–22
    see also Addis Ketema; Woreta
  Nepal 216–19
  policy and practice message 223–4
  summary and conclusion 224–5
structural inequalities 2, 22
substance abuse
  Ethiopia 53–4, 61–2, 77–8, 107–9, 221
  Nepal 172–3, 178–9, 217–18
  see also alcohol/drunkenness
support
  peer 77, 87, 98, 100, 107, 190, 233, 242–3
  shelter and 76–7

technology *see* communication technology (mobile phones/social media), Nepal
third gender *see* genderfluid youth; translation of concepts and terms 17
Tucker, M. 15

UN Committee on the Rights of the Child 24–5
UN Convention on the Rights of the Child 21
UN definitions
  'street children and youth' 215
  youth 4
uncertainty
  concept of 17–18
  dimensions and stratification 29–30
  importance of addressing 1–3
  positive 19–20, 249–51
  see also Addis Ketema, Ethiopia; co-construction; creativity; Fogera, Ethiopia; genderfluid youth; Hetosa, Ethiopia; Kathmandu, Nepal; Kapilvastu (rural); Kapilvastu (urban); research study; Sindhupalchowk, Nepal; slum dwellers; Your Uncertainty Rights (YOUR) World Research; youth-centred research method and approach; Woreta, Ethiopia
unemployment
  urban Ethiopia 75
  urban Nepal 147, 178–80
urban settings *see* Addis Ketema, Ethiopia; genderfluid youth; Kathmandu, Nepal; Kapilvastu (urban), Nepal; slum dwellers; street situations; Woreta, Ethiopia

violence
  abuse and exploitation 75–6, 89
  by teachers 175
  domestic 62, 149, 156, 180, 216
  genderfluid youth 184, 186, 190
  police/militia 76, 99, 104–5, 217, 221
  see also sexual abuse/violence
vocational training *see* rehabilitation and vocational training

Wenger-Trainer, E. and Wenger-Trainer, B. 2–3
West, A. 22
women/girls *see* domestic violence; early marriage; marriage; sex workers; sexual abuse/violence; *entries beginning* gender
Woreta, Ethiopia 48–9, 69–70
  education 73–4
  employment 75–6
  in-migration and background 71–3
  marginalized youth and street situations 70–1
  shelter and support 76–7
  substance abuse 77–8
  uncertainties 78–80
work *see* education and employment; migration

Young, H. 184, 190
Young Lives, Ethiopia 198
Your Uncertainty Rights (YOUR) World Research *see* research study; youth-centred research method and approach
youth, concept and definitions of 14–15
youth agency 4–5, 20–1, 23–4, 83, 133, 201, 224, 241–3, 249, 251–252
youth aspirations 23–4, 246–8
  migration 60, 64, 72–3, 87–8, 104, 145, 148, 150, 246–8
youth clubs, Nepal 146
youth culture and fashions, Nepal 147–8
youth declarations/recommendations 195–6, 222, 234
youth definitions of marginalization 16–17, 117–18
youth participation 34, 195 *see also* participation
youth responsibilities *see* Sindhupalchowk, Nepal

youth-centred research method and
approach 27–8
  analysis 38
  building mechanisms to gain
impact 38–9
  countries and locations 28–9
  creative methods 32–3
  ethics, consent, and safeguarding
33–4
  interviews with adults 36–8
  key approaches 31–2
  overall approach 29
  uncertainty dimensions and
stratification 29–30
youth-centredness 21–2
youth policy 4, 14, 43, 46–7,
53, 113, 117–8, 194–7, 200,
224, 251

www.ingramcontent.com/pod-product-compliance
Lightning Source LLC
Chambersburg PA
CBHW070914030426
42336CB00014BA/2407